THE SOUTHERNER
AS AMERICAN

THE SOUTHERNER
AS AMERICAN

Edited by CHARLES GRIER SELLERS, JR.

JOHN HOPE FRANKLIN

THOMAS P. GOVAN

CHARLES GRIER SELLERS, JR.

DAVID DONALD

GRADY MCWHINEY

GEORGE B. TINDALL

L. D. REDDICK

DEWEY W. GRANTHAM, JR.

C. HUGH HOLMAN

Chapel Hill

THE UNIVERSITY OF NORTH CAROLINA PRESS

917.5
S4675
89618

PRINTED BY THE SEEMAN PRINTERY, DURHAM, N. C.

INTRODUCTION

WHAT DOES IT MEAN to be a Southerner? The segregation crisis has once again posed this question unavoidably for Americans reared below the Potomac and the Ohio; and never since the secession crisis of a hundred years ago has so much depended on their answer. Will history repeat itself? Will the Sumter centennial find Southerners* once again defining their Southernism in desperate, unreasoning revolt against the larger society of which they have always been a part, against social values which they have always shared? Will the Appomattox centennial find them once again overborne by superior force, once again returning sorely to the larger society, their regional heritage further eroded by the vicissitudes of their struggle for a cause which they themselves could not believe altogether just?

The outcome will depend heavily on the South's image of itself—on Southerners' understanding of their Southernism—and for this image the region's historians bear a heavy responsibility. This book is written because of a growing conviction among historians that southern historical writing has been subject to serious distortion. The authors believe that the traditional emphasis

* We follow the common usage of the word "Southerner" as meaning "white Southerner" only as a kind of shorthand admission that the Negro Southerner has been denied full participation in the society of which he is a part.

on the South's differentness and on the conflict between Southernism and Americanism is wrong historically. This distorted historical image, we believe, makes it harder for the South to understand both its Southernism and its Americanism, and hence to escape the defensiveness, prejudice, and belligerence of its regional self-preoccupation, while enriching the national life with many valuable elements of its distinctive regional heritage. Thus we write of *The Southerner As American* from the standpoint of the Southerner as American. Though all of us are Southerners, born, reared, and largely trained in the South, we regard it as more an advantage to our present purpose than otherwise that some of us are now living north of Mason and Dixon's line.

All of us do not agree with everything that is said in all the essays, but we do share a common approach to southern history. We all agree that the most important fact about the Southerner is that he has been throughout his history also an American. The conflicts that have been so much a part of the southern experience have occurred, we insist, between Southerners and within Southerners, as much as between North and South.

Viewed in this light, southern history is essentially tragic. First there was the tragedy of the Old South, the tragedy of a people who believed themselves compelled to defend a "peculiar institution" that was at war with their own deepest values, and who as a consequence drove themselves down the suicidal road to Appomattox. Yet the Old South's tragedy was compounded when the New South failed to understand or even to remember it. Bitter with defeat and humiliation in the postwar years, Southerners sought emotional balm in the sentimental myth of the Lost Cause, a pseudo-tragedy which gave the South a false history, a false image of itself, and a mythical social ideal that Southerners had not really accepted even in the heyday of secession. The Confederate myth, as a perceptive young North Carolinian, Walter

Hines Page, complained, chained southern loyalties "not to living ideas, but to . . . distorted traditions."

This was the tragedy of the New South. By taking refuge in pseudo-tragedy, said Page, Southerners forgot that the Civil War "was not merely a fierce war—it was a fierce civil war." By forgetting the tragedy of the Old South, they cut themselves off from the very elements in their historical tradition that might have helped them to resolve their inner conflicts and escape their tragic dilemma. This was the ground of Page's bitter charge that the ex-Confederates "unwittingly did us a greater hurt than the war itself." "We did not become ourselves till they were buried," he wrote in 1909, "if we indeed are become ourselves yet."*

Fifty years later, as the South is once again challenged to make itself whole, Southerners may well still wonder whether "we indeed are become ourselves yet." Though the self-defeating attitudes bound up with the myth of the Lost Cause have gradually loosened their grip on the southern mind, Page himself was eloquently symbolic of how completely they have destroyed any alternative southern tradition. His whole life was a quest for a tradition by which he could remain a Southerner outside the constrictions of the Confederate myth, but the only tradition he could find was that of northern business society. Eventually winning spectacular success as a New York publisher and adopting the views of the industrialists and financiers with whom he associated, Page became the leading national spokesman for the movement to make the South over in the northern image, through industrialization, education, and public health.

Page's personal dilemma was the dilemma of the modern South. As its Atlantas and Birminghams and Houstons expand and multiply, is the South fated simply to reproduce in a sunnier latitude the urban mass society of the Northeast, while manifesting

* Nicholas Worth (pseud. for W. H. Page), *The Southerner* (New York, 1909), 46-47.

its Southernism only by last-ditch resistance along the crumbling segregation line? Are the Southerner's stubborn individualism and his respect for the individuality of others incompatible with "progress" and "the American way of life"? Is his Christianity, with its blend of realism and idealism arising from his experience of the reality of sin and evil, rendered anachronistic by the pragmatic scientism of modernity? Does modern life require that he forget his history and repudiate much of what he is? Must he hail "the vanishing South" while succumbing to an undifferentiated Americanism?

The South's crisis of a century ago raised issues that were strikingly similar, though infinitely more difficult of resolution. In 1854 an Independence Day orator warned students at the Virginia Military Institute of two opposite dangers. One was that the Union would be destroyed, and with it "the brightest hopes that ever dawned upon humanity." On the other hand, if the Union survived, "the peculiar type of Virginia character" might be "blotted out forever" by the tide of industrial and commercial development sweeping down from the North. The orator had "ever felt that I should be a better American as I was a truer Virginian," and he welcomed economic progress under Virginia auspices, but he would consider "prosperity too dearly bought if effected by foreign hands." "Though the State were covered with improvements," he said, "though each half hour were proclaimed by the warning note of the rushing train—though populous cities and fertile fields should give us assurance of a mighty prosperity, I should still mourn the loss of that type of Man and Woman which belong peculiarly to the Southern States."*

Yet this Virginian-as-American failed to perceive a third and greater danger—the danger of making the cause of human slavery the cause of the South. By succumbing to this danger

* B. J. Barbour, *An Address Delivered before the Literary Societies of the Virginia Military Institute, at Lexington, on the 4th of July, 1854* (Richmond, 1854), 19.

the Southerner of 1860 propelled himself into a suicidal assault on his cherished Union, and in the aftermath suffered a steady erosion of his southern character and heritage.

Must Southerners of the 1960's repeat, on a meaner scale and under less extenuating circumstances, the mistakes of a century before? Or can they rediscover their forbears and discern the tragic dimension of their history? Only thus can they escape the meretricious and recover the viable in their tradition. Only thus can they become themselves.

The editor and authors wish to express their indebtedness to Professor Robert A. Lively of Princeton University, who contributed more than any of us to the dialogue from which this book emerged, who suggested its title, and who shared in the early stages of editorial work.

We are also grateful to Professor William H. Masterson, editor of the *Journal of Southern History,* for permission to reprint from its pages the essay by David Donald and portions of the essay by Thomas P. Govan.

CHARLES GRIER SELLERS, JR.

The University of California, Berkeley
  February, 1960

CONTENTS

CONTENTS

THE SOUTHERNER
AS AMERICAN

CHAPTER ONE

"AS FOR OUR HISTORY..."

By John Hope Franklin

"Our poetry is our lives," boasted William Lowndes Yancey on the eve of the Civil War; "our fiction will come when truth has ceased to satisfy us; and as for our history, we have made about all that has glorified the United States." Yancey's historical illusions were well calculated for his campaign to "fire the Southern heart," for the sectional crisis was creating in the South of the 1850's a historical consciousness that would long remain both acute and polemical.   Inventing and glorifying a fictitious historical South, a pliant southern Clio furnished one of the weapons that enabled Yancey's forces of sectional chauvinism to "precipitate the cotton states into a revolution."[1]   The myth did not die with the crisis that produced it, for the succeeding experiences of defeat and humiliation made it even more a psychological necessity to Southerners.   For a hundred years southern historians found the dream so warm, the truth so cold, that they were slow to construct for the South an image of itself that was true to the reality of its past or relevant to its changing circumstances.

Before the 1850's the South had been too much a "bundle of contrasting and conflicting interests, classes, and values"[2] to see itself as an entity, historical or contemporary; and its people had shown little interest in history of any kind.   During the colonial period the writing of history, along with other literary activities, had been discouraged by the preoccupation with survival, the lack of leisure, the absence of a large literate population, and the Southerner's apparent preference for action over contemplation. But the South had shared in the burst of national pride that accompanied the American Revolution and mounted steadily during the early decades of the nineteenth century; and a few Southerners had expressed their American nationalism in historical writings. David Ramsay's influential *History of the American Revolution,* published in 1789, was the most notable early product of this impulse; while as late as 1841 a Virginian, George Tucker, could write an impressive *History of the United States* that showed little sectional bias.

By and large, however, Southerners left historical writing to Americans in other sections, and what histories they did produce were for the most part histories of individual states. These state histories[3] revealed almost no consciousness of the South as a distinctive section. Rather, each claimed for its state a larger contribution to the nation's liberal Revolutionary tradition. Reading them along with their northern counterparts, one is struck by "how much good will was shown." Localistic only in their spirit of competition with other states, the southern state historians were essentially nationalistic in that they competed for national honors; and they uniformly recognized that the honors were to be awarded according to a standard that "had been fixed by the national ideal."[4] Indeed, some Southerners conceded the claims to primacy staked out by the more active New England historians. "The Yankee is the man, who first hung out the banner of liberty . . . and determined to be free," wrote William Gilmore Simms in 1830; while as late as 1854 the eminent Virginia historian, Hugh Blair Grigsby, contrasted his state's beginnings at Jamestown unfavorably with the "grand and noble achievement" of the Pilgrims.[5]

Yet by the 1840's the South was beginning to view its past in a less national spirit. The southern states were asserting their historical claims more stridently, and some Southerners were rejecting altogether the liberal national tradition as the theme of their history. Virginians, for example, began to argue that royalist refugees from Cromwellian England had given their commonwealth its distinctive tone. This cavalier thesis was propagated by politicians, literary men, and publicists, against the opposition of Virginia's abler historians, for it arose not from new historical knowledge, but from the exigencies of the mounting sectional controversy.[6]

During these years the pressures of sectional conflict were causing Southerners to minimize the physiographic variations within their section, the differences in the economic and social status of the people, and the several disagreements in political allegiances and philosophies. Committed to perpetuating a system of servitude increasingly condemned by the rest of the western world, southern whites began to think of themselves as having a set of common values, common problems, common dangers, and common aspirations that set them apart from other Americans. Inevitably they came to believe also that they had a common and distinctive history.

The shrewder southern leaders perceived, moreover, that history could be a major weapon in the sectional struggle. By demonstrating their section's glorious past and common dangers and destiny, southern historians could help forge the unity that was indispensable, whether to maintain the South's position within the American Union, or to prepare the way for separate nationhood.[7] Consequently the late 1840's and 1850's witnessed a gradual but decided shift from a history that asserted the various southern states' peculiar contributions to the American tradition, to a history that asserted the South's difference from and superiority to the North.

This shift was facilitated by a growing sectional feeling among northern historians, whose "breach of faith" shocked Southerners out of their historical complacency and inactivity. In their effort to demonstrate the immoralities and deficiencies of the southern way of life, northern writers and speakers began to say that the South's contribution to the growth of the nation had been negligible. In 1847, for example, Lorenzo Sabine of Massachusetts brought out his *American Loyalists,* the first comprehensive treatment of those colonists who supported England during the War for Independence. He argued that Loyalist sentiment was so strong in the South that the section's contribution to the winning of independence was extremely limited and, on the whole, without effect. "South Carolina, with a Northern army to assist her could not, or would not, preserve her own capital," Sabine concluded.[8]

If Sabine had deliberately planned it, he could not have wounded Southerners more deeply or evoked from them a more spirited retaliation. They regarded his book as a part of a dark northern design to impugn their loyalty, their integrity, and their way of life. It could not be ignored any more than the attacks of the abolitionists; and for the next ten years they refuted it in the press, on the platform, on the floor of the Congress, and anywhere they could find an audience.[9] Even more significant than the immediate, vehement reaction to the Sabine thesis was the way in which it convinced a section, daily growing more conscious of its minority status in the Union, that it must write its own history of the Revolution and of everything else.

Three years before the Sabine volume appeared, William Gilmore Simms had argued that South Carolina needed no written history. "It is already deeply engraven on the everlasting monuments of the nation," he said. "It is around us, a living trophy upon all our hills. It is within us, an undying memory in all our hearts. It is a record which no fortune can obliterate—inseparable from all that is great and glorious in the work of the Revolution."[10] Within a year after Sabine's assault Simms had changed his mind about the writing of the history of his state and of the South. He had become convinced that the men of the section would have to assume the task, for their history was being written "by superficial and corrupt historians, who are quite numerous in our country and who abuse the confidence of the reader."[11] One of the South's leading firebrands, Lawrence M. Keitt, agreed and added that South Carolina should "gather together the Records of her History, and put them beyond the reach of flame and casualty . . . ."[12] In the late fifties William Porcher Miles rejoiced to see in the South a "disposition, at last, beginning to manifest itself, to recall and perpetuate . . . the glorious memories" of the past.[13]

The argument over the South's role in the struggle for independence did not result in a victory for the South, but it did teach Southerners the importance of writing their history in order, from their point of view, to keep it straight. The numerous historical societies that had come into existence in several southern states in the 1830's and 1840's as scarcely more than social organizations now began to enlarge their activities. Anniversaries of battles and other historic events became the occasions for reviewing the South's peculiar contributions to the history of the nation.[14] Virginia paid homage to her George Washington, "who had led an earlier crusade for independence; Maryland recalled her heroes in Randall's stirring stanzas; Carolina cherished the cult of Calhoun; Louisiana pointed to her proud Creole heritage."[15] By 1860 a student of southern history could declare in all earnestness: "The Southern States were settled and governed, in a great measure . . . by and under the direction of persons belonging to the blood and race of the reigning family, and belong to that stock recognized as CAVALIERS. . . . The Southern people come from that race . . . to whom law and order, obedience and

command, are convertible terms, and who do command, the world
over. . . ."[16]

The student of history in the ante-bellum South was, therefore, more concerned with supporting the position his section was
taking than he was with the precise accuracy of the facts.   In
fanning the flames of southern nationalism the historian—whether
he was an accomplished man of letters like William Gilmore Simms
or a shrewd lawyer-planter-amateur historian like David F. Jami-
son—contributed much to the feeling of homogeneity and unity.
Although this meant ignoring the religious, ethnic, and cultural
differences among the peoples of the South or creating myths about
them, it was a task that had to be performed.   With few exceptions
southern historians performed it zealously and faithfully.[17]

The South's historians served the cause of southern nationalism
with more lasting effect than did its armies.   Having failed to
establish a separate nation and having gone down to defeat on
the field of battle, Southerners in the period after the Civil War
turned their attention to their own past with a concentration so
great that the cult of history became a permanent and important
ingredient of the southern culture.   Through monuments, patriotic societies, songs, verse, memorial celebrations, and informal
reminiscing, they kept before southern youth the glorious yester-
year when the South stood on the threshold of greatness.   Especially
did they seek to explain and justify their past actions to their contemporaries and to posterity through historical writings.   Southerners must win with the pen what they had failed to win with the
sword.

In the second issue of his *Southern Review* Alfred Taylor
Bledsoe showed his profound respect for history in general and the
history of his beloved South in particular.   He especially ap-
preciated its importance in binding a people together; and he made
it clear that it must not be neglected in the South.   In part, he

said: "The world is too apt to forget its heroes whose efforts have not been crowned with visible success, and its martyrs whose sufferings have been borne in obscurity. 'They failed,' is too often the verdict that discrowns them of their well-worn laurels. . . . Must it be so with these. . . . If we could forget the blackened ruins of Vicksburg, Fredericksburg or Columbia, the track of desolation, the rapine and the carnage, still, of the deeds of our heroic brothers, of the lessons and legacy of their life and death, there can be no forgetfulness."[18]

Thus the writing of history became an act of sectional allegiance and devotion. Many of the leaders of the secession movement and officials of the Confederacy published their memoirs or histories of the southern cause, relying confidently on the observation of Benjamin H. Hill that the greatest resource the South had was history—"impartial, and unpassioned, un-office-seeking history."[19] Several of them organized, in 1869, the Southern Historical Society, which collected and preserved the records of the Confederacy and published articles in the *Southern Magazine* and later in its own publication, the *Southern Historical Society Papers*. In other publications such as *The Land We Love, Field and Fireside,* and the *Southern Review,* Southerners depicted the sunnier aspects of ante-bellum life, the righteousness of the South's position in secession and war, and the horrors of Reconstruction. So well tailored was this cult of the Lost Cause to the emotional needs of the rank and file of southern whites that the section's Bourbon politicians took it up and made it the panoply under which they promoted their incongruous but eminently practical program of economic and political reconciliation with the North.

Yet some of the most ardent devotees of the Lost Cause remained dissatisfied with the work of the post-Civil War generation of southern historians. Too many historical societies and magazines had begun with a burst of enthusiasm, only to die within a few months or years. Too many of the memoirs and sketches that told the South's story were undeniably mediocre. "There is no true history of the South," Thomas Nelson Page complained in 1892. "In a few years there will be no South to demand a history." This was all the more regrettable from Page's point of view, for no civilization as unique had existed "since the dawn of history, as potent in its influence, and yet no chronicle of it has been made by any but the hand of hostility."[20]

While Page complained primarily of the quantity of southern historical writing, a few Southerners began to complain of its quality, and to realize that southern history could receive no intellectual recognition as long as it remained merely reminiscent, uncritical, and self-pitying. "No man with instincts for accuracy can be satisfied with our statement of our own case," John Spencer Bassett told his students and colleagues at Trinity College in 1897. The Confederate-Brigadier-General school of historians who, having fought bravely with their swords, were now "tempted to make asses of themselves with the pen," had convinced Bassett that southern historians needed other qualifications than their Confederate experience and devotion to the Lost Cause. The student of southern history must, like any scholar, "know how to weigh evidence; he must have the scientific spirit for facts, he must have the clear light of truth." But Bassett saw little prospect of rapid improvement, for any southern historian who departed from the traditional view would be "denounced as a traitor and mercenary defiler of his Birthplace."[21]

Despite Bassett's pessimism, the scholarly ideals he voiced were just about to transform the writing of southern history. Bassett was only one of a number of capable, energetic young Southerners who had begun entering the seminars of Herbert Baxter Adams at the Johns Hopkins University, William Archibald Dunning at Columbia, and the great masters at the European universities, to acquire the skills and techniques of the new scientific history. By the first decade of the twentieth century they were publishing numerous studies on southern history, and a remarkable flowering of southern historiography was under way. Professors at some of the leading southern colleges and universities began to concentrate on the section's history, and some northern universities engaged southern scholars and encouraged them to offer courses and do research on the South's past.[22] Southern states established archives and historical commissions; and state and local historical societies were revitalized. In these years of reviving American nationalism, the history-conscious South was claiming a conspicuous place in the national movement to develop a scientific historiography.

Yet the sincere aspirations to scientific method of this first generation of professional southern historians failed to result in the scientific, or completely unbiased and objective, history at which they aimed. There could be no more eloquent evidence of the continuing power of the South's mythology than the curious mixtures of science, polemics, folklore, and phantasy that these scholars produced under the impression that they were being scientific. Almost invariably they concentrated on two aspects of southern history: the heyday of slavery and the period of the Civil War and Reconstruction. These were the two heroic ages of southern history; one was the age of the apex of a glorious civilization, the other the age of a tragic but glorious defeat.

These histories were dominated by inherited sectional prejudices and assumptions of which the authors seemed largely unaware. One of the most distinguished historians of slavery rhapsodized that the plantation was a "parish, or perhaps a chapel of ease," and that it was "a matrimonial bureau, something of a harem perhaps, a copious nursery, and a divorce court."[23] One of the most influential of the historians of Reconstruction described the first results of the Ku Klux Klan movement as "good" since, as he insisted, it "quieted the Negroes, made life and property safer, gave protection to women, stopped burnings . . . and started the

whites on the way to gain political supremacy."[24]   Readers of these
histories could draw the inference that slavery was a positive good,
since whites were free and Negroes were slaves, and that Reconstruction was an unmitigated evil, since many whites were without
the vote and most Negroes had the vote.

Shot through with an uncritical and unrealistic judgment of
some of the facts and ignoring many other facts, these histories
did not provide the basis for a mature understanding of the South
and its problems.   More seriously, they gave the white South the
intellectual justification for its determination not to yield on many
important points, especially in its treatment of the Negro, that set it
apart from the rest of the nation.   Claiming as they did to be
"scientific" and "impartial," the new southern historians even
helped persuade many non-Southerners that through the years the
South had been treated unjustly, that its own course of action had
been substantially right, and that its racial attitudes should be
condoned if not imitated.

At the same time, however, these pioneer professional historians strengthened the cult of history in the South and established
scientific ideals and methods that paved the way for sounder
historical writing.   Some of them did try to rise above their
prejudices, and an occasional Bassett succeeded.   Most important,
by trying to write history as others were writing it, they sought
to emphasize the fact that they were Americans writing about the
South, just as other Americans were writing about the West or
North.   They differed from their predecessors in their willingness
to concede that the past was really irretrievably gone; and although
they cast longing eyes over their shoulders they were resigned to
the reality of being a part of the United States.   It is not without
significance, therefore, that when they brought out their first great
collaborative history of the section, they gave it the title, *The
South in the Building of the Nation.*[25]

Since Bassett's death more than twenty-five years ago, the standards of scholarly objectivity so warmly avowed but so imperfectly realized by his generation have steadily, if with painful slowness, gained headway among southern historians. The process has been accelerated within the present generation, as the new focus of national attention on the South and its problems has forced the section to re-examine its position within the nation. Perhaps the new introspection has also been stimulated by the indisputable findings of the social sciences that have branded as a hoax some of the long-held southern views regarding race. Court decisions adverse to these southern views have underlined the urgency of this re-examination, and increasing pressures, social and economic, have made it imperative for the South to take another look at itself.

It was inevitable that in any new stock-taking the South would look at its past. For a section where the cult of history is so deeply imbedded and where the past looms so large in the present, no critical evaluation of its position would be complete without a careful examination of its heritage. There could have been no more propitious moment for enlarging the role of history in understanding the South than the recent years. Historical scholarship has reached a maturity and respectability that give its findings greater credence and wider acceptance than at any previous period. The opportunities for research have been greatly broadened by the physical improvement of local and state libraries and archives and the employment of trained personnel.[26] Finally, there has emerged a new generation of scholars who have escaped the most serious traumatic effects of the nineteenth-century experience.

The study of the South's history has been nationalized in much the same way that its other problems have been. Northerners with no particular brief for John Brown are studying the South. Southerners with no defense of slavery or the fire-eaters are among the most zealous students of the new history of the South. Negroes with no feeling of inadequacy are examining various phases of the South's history and are writing about whites as well as about Negroes.

The range of problems being fruitfully explored by these contemporary historians as they seek new insight into the South's past is most impressive. It runs the gamut of the section's experience, from the earliest colonial days to the present, from agriculture to industry, from intricate political and economic problems to complex social and intellectual developments.[27] The new skills and resources of the historical profession are currently being used to study the back country of the colonial South and the South's role in the American Revolution. Historians are re-examining with meticulous care the institution of slavery and the structure of society in the ante-bellum South. They are studying the many ramifications of the Reconstruction, including the Freedmen's Bureau, Negro office-holding, the Ku Klux Klan, and the Union League. They are giving attention to the history of civil rights, disfranchisement, the rise of cities, the growth of industry, and the labor movement. It may be said, in fact, that hardly any significant phase or aspect of the South's history is escaping the scrutiny of today's historians.[28]

As impressive as the range and scope of the historical problems under consideration is the approach of the historians themselves. They appear to possess at least the normal amount of skepticism and disinterestedness, and they seem to lack the excessive preconceptions and presuppositions that have perpetuated so many myths about the South. Most of them do not appear to be studying the South to prove a point or to take sides. They seem to be reasonably free of the acrimony that has beclouded so much of the South's history and rendered it polemical and unscientific. Their approaches are seldom merely iconoclastic, for most of them recognize the distinctiveness and validity of a Southernism that springs from the physiographic, ethnic, and experiential factors peculiar to the region. At least some of them are more interested in understanding the South's past than in merely tolerating it.[29] At least some of them recognize the complete uselessness of either condemning or defending the South. At the same time they seem to appreciate the value of critically examining and analyzing its history with a view to understanding more clearly the relationship between the past and the present as well as between the South and the rest of the country.

One would be contributing a new myth to the South's historiography if he asserted that all historians of the South shared these views and employed these new approaches. There are still some who, with strong commitments to the old order or with vested interests in long-held points of view, have escaped entirely the spirit of the new southern historical scholarship. These, however, seem to be decreasing in numbers and influence. They who once constituted such a confident majority may soon be, as Bassett once was, a voice crying in the wilderness.

The new research in southern history is already yielding much in the way of broad and significant results for the section. Where a healthy skepticism, an indefatigable zeal, and a truly scientific approach are employed, they frequently result in facts and interpretations that demand a revision of some long-held view of southern history. Even as the process is underway one can see some significant revisions taking place. Recent studies of the ante-bellum social structure, for example, have made it clear that the vast majority of southern whites owned no slaves and had no hope of owning slaves.[30] This incontrovertible fact has, of course, only slowly made headway in popular thinking against the more attractive, exotic view, sustained in historical fiction, that slavery provided an idyllic existence for all or most southern whites. But as southern whites come to understand slavery as an institution that materially benefited a very small segment of the southern population, they may be freed from personal involvement in the defense not only of the Old South's defunct "peculiar institution," but also its surviving corollary, the doctrine of white superiority.

Other recent research in southern history has shown that Southerners answered Lincoln's attempted relief of Sumter with gunfire because, among other things, of their long tradition of individualism carried to the point of lawlessness, and because of a continuing fascination with military show. Goaded almost into a persecution complex on the score of their inordinate racism, Southerners could boast only so long of their military prowess— could repress only for a time some further expression of their ardent expansionism—before giving explosive expression to their sensitivity. Southern historians have found it easy to glorify the explosion without reflecting on its cause.

Not long ago a young southern white historian showed conclusively that during the Civil War the loyalty of slaves to their masters was the exception rather than the rule.[31] Even more recently a young Negro historian has described in detail the role of the nearly 200,000 Negroes who fought on the side of the Union in that war.[32] When more white Southerners learn these facts and accept them, they will gain an insight into the views and aspirations of Negroes that should materially lessen the empty assertions that they "understand" Negroes.

In recent years we have learned that corruption during Reconstruction was not only bi-racial but also bi-partisan.[33] Even more recently a southern white historian has adduced convincing evidence that the corruption of the Reconstruction period continued unabated after the southern whites had thrown Negroes and carpetbaggers out and "redeemed" their states.[34] As this view becomes accepted for the cold historical truth that it is, it will perhaps be possible for the South to modify its view of the Reconstruction. As the section comes to realize that some of its own white sons were guilty of the same things it has denounced in others, it may even adopt the view that integrity, like blackguardism, is not the monoply of a particular race or party and that there are more valid standards by which to judge a people than race and party.

No one can say with certainty just what influence historical conceptions have had on the minds of men, nor can one accurately predict the impact of such conceptions on human relations in the future. But historical traditions have controlled the attitudes and conduct of peoples too often to permit a denial that history has been an important instrument in shaping human affairs. History gave to the Prussians a tradition of military prowess that influenced European affairs profoundly for more than a century. It has given to Americans an almost eerie sense of national virtue and destiny, as well as a deep attachment to their historically grounded democratic institutions.

Nowhere in the United States, however, has the cult of history flourished as it has flourished in the South. Nowhere are the consequences of a historical tradition more apparent, for from its history the South derived the image of itself that has in large measure governed its reactions to successive changes and challenges. If the South has often reacted churlishly and shortsightedly, the fault does not lie with history itself, but with a distorted historical tradition of which even the South's historians have been victims, but which only they can correct.

Thus it may be fortunate that the cult of history still flourishes in the South, as can be seen in the generous public support of its historical activities, in the vitality of its historical societies, and in the rich variety of its historical publications. The historians themselves—North and South, Negro and white—are at last shaking off the blinders fashioned by the Yanceys of the 1850's and the events of the 1860's and 1870's. As they do, they are discovering the historical South whose emerging outlines are described in the following pages.

The southern past unearthed by recent scholarship deserves a long hard look from all Southerners, for it reveals a section that has been continuously both southern and American and a people who rushed upon tragedy by making virtues of their vices. Only as the South understands what it has been can it come to know itself well enough to value and preserve the valuable in both its Southernism and its Americanism, while discarding the attitudes and habits so long and so fatefully perpetuated by a false history.

CHAPTER TWO

AMERICANS BELOW THE POTOMAC*

By Thomas P. Govan

THE OLD SOUTH, a part of the United States in which slavery continued for some sixty years after it had been given up in other areas, had a sense of unity within itself and of separation from the rest of the nation sufficiently strong to permit eleven of the states composing it to withdraw from the union and to fight for four years in an unsuccessful effort to maintain a separate existence as the Confederate States of America. To this extent, it was different, because no other area or group at any time in the national history challenged in such a way the continued unity of the American nation. Many historians, however, have not been satisfied with stating this substantial difference which did distinguish the Old South from the other areas of the country. They have insisted that by the time of the Civil War there were two divergent and irreconcilable social and economic systems, "two civilizations, in fact," in the United States.[1]

The North, according to this point of view, was commercial-financial-industrial, the South agrarian, and these differences led to war between the two. One of the clearest statements of this conception is to be found in Morison and Commager's *Growth of the*

* Part of this essay was originally published in *The Journal of Southern History*, XXI (November, 1955), 447-55, under the title, "Was the Old South Different?" and is used with the permission of the editor.

American Republic where they write that the break between Jefferson and Hamilton was not personal but the "political expression of a deep lying antagonism between two great American interests— the planting-slaveholding interest, typified by Virginia; and the mercantile-shipping-financial interest, typified by Massachusetts. . . . American political history until 1865 is largely the story of these rival interests, capitalist and agrarian, Northern and Southern, contending for the control of the government."[2]

This statement seems to mean that the planter with an investment in slaves, tools, and land, who raised staple crops to be sold at a profit in the markets of the United States and Europe, was somehow not a capitalist but an agrarian; that the merchants in the southern ports and interior towns were not engaged in mercantile activity; and that the southern bankers and brokers were not affiliated with the financial interest.   The farmers who engaged in profitable agricultural operations in New York, Pennsylvania, New Jersey, Connecticut, New Hampshire, Vermont, Maine, Ohio, Indiana, Illinois, Michigan, Wisconsin, Iowa, and the territories, by this description were left completely out of account, as were those who engaged in the manufacture of tobacco in Virginia, North Carolina, South Carolina, Georgia, and Alabama; those who mined gold in Virginia, North Carolina, and Georgia; those who established iron foundries and coal mines in Virginia, North and South Carolina, Georgia, Tennessee, and Alabama; and the sugar mills which made every plantation from Baton Rouge to New Orleans an industrial as well as an agricultural enterprise.

What is even stranger about this widely accepted conception is the assertion of a supposed conflict of interest between the merchants, bankers, and shippers engaged in international trade and the producers of the commodities which were the basis of that trade. None of these groups could have prospered, or even existed, without the others.   If there were a division of the American people into two segments with separate and conflicting economic interests, it was not between those who engaged in agriculture on the one side and those engaged in banking, merchandizing, and transportation on the other. Rather, it was between those whose primary concern was the market outside the United States, and those whose principal market was within the country. The growers of wool, sugar, hemp, and foodstuffs for domestic consumption had a different interest from those who grew cotton, rice, and tobacco, while the producers of wheat, whose market was sometimes mainly within the United States and at other times in the West Indies or Europe, wavered between the two.

Merchants, bankers, and shippers were as divided as the farmers since their interest coincided with that of whatever group of producers they served. If their principal activity was providing facilities for internal trade, then their interest led them to support measures which would increase that trade; but, if their facilities were used by the producers of export crops, then their interest was fostered by an increase in international trade. American manufacturers, confronted by competition from older and stronger industries of Great Britain and the continent, needed and desired protection, and they, almost as a unit, threw their influence in favor of measures that would discourage international trade and increase the consumption of domestic goods. This economic group was exceptional in its unity of interest, but until late in the nineteenth century it could not rival the influence or power of the earlier established, larger and wealthier agricultural, mercantile, and financial groups.

Southerners were to be found in each of these groups and shared their point of view and interest. Within the South, as in all the major geographical regions of the United States, there were distinctions in occupation based upon geological formations, climatic conditions, facilities for transportation, and other factors. Manufacturing was but a minor activity in the southern states during most of the period before 1865. The principal deposits of iron ore and coal were deep in the interior mountains, far from any market. Their exploitation had to wait until the railroads penetrated this area. The iron and coal of the northeast, on the other hand, were located in the vicinity of New York and Philadelphia, and were exploited earlier, as were those in the northwest at Pittsburgh, at the head of navigation of the Ohio River, which provided transportation to the great market of the Mississippi Valley. Southerners were not unaware of the importance of this activity, nor hostile to it, and whatever deposits of iron and coal were found in the areas that had transportation facilities—South Carolina, Virginia, or the Cumberland River valley of Tennessee—were developed and used.

In addition, the water power of the southern rivers was more difficult to utilize than that of the smaller rivers of New England, New Jersey, and Pennsylvania; and the fall line was more distant from the principal markets. These handicaps postponed the development of the textile and other industries. But the activities of William Gregg in South Carolina, the building of the power canal at Augusta, Georgia, as well as the mills at Athens, Columbus, and other towns on the fall line, followed very rapidly after the initial development of the textile industry in other regions.

The Old South, consequently, like the Northwest and part of New England, New York, Pennsylvania, and New Jersey, was primarily agricultural, but it was not united by this fact. Each of the major crops required different climatic conditions and different methods of cultivation. Rice, which needed ample water, was confined to the coastal regions. Sugar, essentially a semitropical growth, could be profitably raised only in the lower Southwest; and cotton, a hardier plant, became the basic product of the interior in the lower South. The great limestone areas of the mountain valleys and of the Lexington and Nashville basins, on the other hand, provided a soil that enabled its cultivators to engage in a mixed agriculture that had more in common with the agriculture of the northeastern United States than it did with the industrialized, single-crop agriculture of the cotton, rice, and sugar plantations in other areas of the South.　Tobacco, a plant requiring relatively intense cultivation on small acreage, also had little in common with the other staple crops, and if its cultivation was a bond of unity then it should have united those who grew it in the Connecticut valley with those who grew it in the South.

The people of the United States were not brought together or separated by these similarities and differences in sectional occupation and interest.　The doctrine of sectional economic antagonism, though it had its origin in the early years of the American republic, was not an accurate reflection of economic reality in the United States; and it has been persuasive to twentieth-century historians largely because of their uncritical enthusiasm for that explanation of past events which views them as the determined result of economic forces and conflicts.　This interpretation of the nature of the American economic society was never fully accepted by most Americans, and when Pierce Butler, a delegate from South Carolina to the Constitutional Convention, said that "he considered the interests of the [southern] and Eastern States to be as different as the interests of Russia and Turkey," Gouverneur Morris, a nationalist delegate from Pennsylvania, replied, "Either this distinction is fictitious or real; if fictitious, let it be dismissed and let us proceed with due confidence.　If it be real, instead of blending incompatible things, let us at once take a friendly leave of each other."[3]

The delegates chose to proceed with confidence, and the economic society they created was as united as their national government.　A few political leaders, within the convention and afterwards, continued to use divisive sectional rhetoric when debating economic questions, but a majority of Americans, North and South, were unimpressed.　Merchants, farmers, and bankers, most of the time, believed that their individual, local, and sectional prosperity was dependent upon economic conditions in the rest of the nation, and it was only in moments of financial or political crisis that the doctrine of sectional economic antagonism had any substantial number of adherents.

This doctrine was more influential in the South than in any other area, and the reason for its greater success in this section was closely connected with the career and ambitions of one of the nation's most effective and magnetic leaders, John C. Calhoun. This powerful South Carolinian began as a nationalist, and it would be difficult to find a more explicit rejection of sectionalism than his statement in the Congress following the War of 1812: "Blessed with a form of government at once combining liberality and strength, we may reasonably raise our eyes to a most splendid future, if we only act in a manner worthy of our advantages. If, however, neglecting them, we permit a low, sordid, selfish, and sectional spirit to take possession . . . this happy scene will vanish. We will divide and in its consequences will follow misery and degradation."[4]

He was arguing in this speech for a federally financed system of roads and canals, which was vetoed by the President, but the same spirit was present in his more successful effort to charter the second Bank of the United States and to enact a protective tariff. Calhoun's nationalist measures did not have the effect that he and other sponsors anticipated, and the American economy, instead of being prosperous, was generally depressed between 1818 and 1828. The nation's import and export trade, and all those dependent upon it—farmers, merchants, bankers, and brokers, North, South, and West—suffered particularly; and Calhoun himself admitted in 1828 that "there is almost universal embarrassment among the people of the staple states, which they almost unanimously attribute to the high duties."[5]

The American tariff, despite this almost unanimous belief, had little to do with the low prices and reduced sales of the export crops of the South, the relatively small volume of the import and export trade in the ports, and the financial difficulties of this segment of the national economy. The principal cause of the depressed conditions between 1818 and 1822 was the improper management of the national bank, which forced the United States to liquidate the large private debt accumulated under the inflationary conditions of the War of 1812, through the painful processes of default, bankruptcy, and foreclosure. Virtually no one prospered during these four years, but, in 1822, the economy, aided by a change in management and policy at the Bank of the United States and by easy money and credit in Great Britain, began to recover.

Prices and business activity increased, and, by 1825, all trace of the earlier difficulties was gone. Just at this moment, however, the Bank of England, weakened and frightened by the speculative export of British capital to all areas of the world, contracted credit and precipitated one of the most severe crises in the history of Great Britain. The domestic segment of the American economy, protected and aided by the national bank, did not suffer as severely as it had in the earlier depression, but those engaged in international trade once more encountered major financial difficulties. The British markets for three years could absorb but a small volume of American exports at much reduced prices, and British merchants and manufacturers had little money or credit with which to finance American purchases of their manufactured goods.

These economic depressions were international and national in character, rather than sectional, and the connection between them and the American tariff was slight, if it existed at all. The relation between these depressions and the import and export trade, on the other hand, was direct, immediate, and decisive, and the volume and profits of this trade immediately revived in 1828 when the British pressure was removed. Producers of cotton, tobacco, rice, and other export staples began to make profits, as did the international merchants, bankers, and brokers, but this return of prosperity, instead of reducing the anti-tariff agitation, strengthened it and increased its virulence.

The center of the radical anti-tariff movement between 1828 and 1833 was South Carolina, and Calhoun, who had been the legislative sponsor of the protective system, was eventually compelled to become the most notable advocate of its repeal. He justified this reversal by returning to Butler's argument that the economic interests of the South and North were mutually antagonistic and conflicting, an argument which had been used effectively against him by his political enemies in South Carolina and other southern states, and he thus outwitted his local opponents by adopting their views. The tariff, according to Calhoun, was an instrument for the economic aggrandizement of the North, but his anti-tariff position received effective support from many powerful individuals and groups outside of the South. The builders of railroads and canals (private, public, and mixed) sought lowered tariff rates on iron and other building materials, and the northwestern wheat farmers, whose external market was greatly expanded after 1828, joined the growers of cotton, rice, and tobacco in opposing the protective system.

The northeastern seaports, with a permanent interest in international trade, continued their support of the anti-tariff movement, and the manufacturers, miners, and the growers of a few agricultural products such as wool, sugar, and hemp, were thus left isolated in their need or desire for protection. The repeal of the protective tariff in 1833 was a victory, not for the South or any other section, but for those in all areas of the country whose interests lay in international rather than domestic trade, and, from this period on, the tariff was to be less important as a political issue between the sections than it had previously been made to appear.

The defeat of the protective system had little effect upon economic activity within the country. The years from 1828 to

1837, in contrast to the previous decade, were, on the whole, prosperous, but the fundamental cause of this prosperity was the general financial ease throughout the world, not American economic policy. The one interruption was during 1833-34, when the Bank of the United States, under political and financial attack by President Andrew Jackson and his administration, was forced to contract its loans for self-protection and to precipitate a severe but short domestic panic. The President, who had vetoed the bill rechartering the national institution in 1832, was determined to discredit it by proving it insolvent, but the Bank of the United States, soundly and intelligently managed, survived the attack. Economic activity, all over the country, was slowed down by this conflict, but when it ended, without a victory for either side, prosperity returned and continued for three years.

Calhoun, though Vice President in the first Jackson administration, did not share the President's hostility to the national bank. One of his closest political associates, George McDuffie of South Carolina, was the leading advocate of the recharter of the institution in the House of Representatives, and the Vice President himself, in a private letter in March, 1830, stated: "Every sentiment I ever expressed in relation to the Bank remains unchanged."[6] Robert Y. Hayne, senator from South Carolina, and others of Calhoun's friends and supporters, on the other hand, were opposed to the recharter, and this division within the ranks of his political faction continued after he and they were forced out of the Jackson party early in 1831.

Similar divisions existed in all political factions and parties and in all areas because the issue precipitated by Jackson's attack upon the central financial institution of the country transcended party and sectional loyalties. Calhoun's dismissal from the administration party was not caused by his stand on the bank, the tariff, state rights, or nullification. Its purpose was to eliminate him as a rival to Martin Van Buren for the presidential nomination when Jackson retired, and it was accomplished so skillfully that he and his closest associates were left in a position of almost complete political isolation.

His adoption of the radical anti-tariff position, and his advocacy of nullification as a constitutional bar to unconstitutional action by the federal government, were in part an attempt to recover from this severe blow to his political ambitions. If Southerners could be united by an appeal to state rights and their particular economic interests, Calhoun, as their leader, could initiate the creation of a national coalition independent of those already committed to President Jackson or his opponents. He failed in this effort, but gained sufficient strength to believe that in the congressional session of 1833-34 he could join the opposition party with a good chance to capture its leadership. He cooperated with Henry Clay, Daniel Webster, and the rest of the Whigs in their denunciation of the administration's arbitrary removal of the federal deposits from the national bank, but, at the same time, he began the formulation of an independent financial policy that would, if he failed with the Whigs, open the way, he hoped, for a triumphant return to the party from which he had been expelled.

Calhoun, until this moment, had never expressed the opinion that the Bank of the United States was a dangerous institution, hostile to the interests of the South, or that its currency, bank-notes redeemable in gold or silver, was not adequate and safe. He had never been a critic of the state banks or of the mercantile and credit system which handled the marketing of staple crops. But Jackson and his associates all over the country had proved that arousing the suspicions and fears of farmers about the activities and profits of merchants and bankers was politically effective, and Calhoun adopted these arguments. He also had another reason for changing his mind about banks, credit, and paper money, for, in 1833, he had become the owner of a gold mine in the former Cherokee country of northeastern Georgia, and also an enthusiastic advocate of an exclusively gold currency. He justified his reversal on this issue, as he had justified his reversal in regard to the protective tariff, by sectional arguments, and he cooperated with Jackson, Thomas Hart Benton of Missouri, and others in the administration hostile to banks, in their attacks upon these institutions.*

He supported the specie circular, the distribution bill, and other measures which had as their purpose the increased use of specie, particularly gold, as currency, and when the banks of the country, severely pressed by internal and external demands upon their metallic reserves in May, 1837, suspended specie payments, he joined with those who were calling for the creation of an Independent Treasury—"a system whereby the 'collection, safekeeping, transfer and disbursement of the public money' would be managed by officers of the government without the aid or intervention of any bank or banks."[7]

When Jackson's successor, Van Buren of New York, adopted the same position in the depression summer of 1837, Calhoun returned to the Democratic party but continued his efforts to create a disciplined southern faction to support his presidential ambitions. "We now have a fair opportunity to break the last of our commercial shackles," he told southern Democrats, "I mean the control which the North through the use of government credit acting through the banks have exercised over our industry and commerce. How wonderful that . . . the favorite of New York (the state above all others the most benefitted by the union of bank and state) should be forced by circumstances to give the fatal blow." Francis W. Pickens, a political ally of Calhoun, was equally enthusiastic,

* Calhoun's first indication that he had become an advocate of hard money was in a letter on February 8, 1834, in which he wrote, "There is no alternative but hard money or a United States Bank. The country is not, I think, ripe for the first; and all that can be done is, I apprehend, to raise the value of gold to 16 to 1 so as to make it the metallick currency instead of silver, and fix some amount, 10 or 20$ below which no Bank bill shall be received into the Treasury. These . . . would be taking a great step toward a specie currency."—J. C. Calhoun to James Edward Calhoun, February 8, 1834, Jameson, ed., *Correspondence*, 331-32.

writing, "We now have a great issue made up [and] the war is between capitalists in labour and land. The struggle is for ascendancy
and if the former are sustained in their swindling career they will
control and own the latter. I go for land and Negroes. Break
down the swindling of banks and the capitalists of the South will
control the Confederacy."[8]

The majority of Southerners again refused to follow Calhoun.
Large numbers of Democrats were hostile to banks on the same
anti-business and anti-inflationary grounds that motivated northern
loco-focos, while the Whigs and a group that called themselves
Conservative Democrats blamed the existing economic difficulties
upon "executive misrule in the finances." These southern defenders
of the banking system were convinced that the economic interests of
the "capitalists in labour and land" and those of the "capitalists in
stocks and corporations" were inter-dependent, and that the de-
flationary monetary and credit policies advocated by Van Buren,
Calhoun, and Pickens would be injurious to both and to all other
groups in the nation. They were also suspicious of Calhoun's
political objectives and successfully opposed his attempt to establish
himself as the dominant leader of the South and the Democratic
party.

"Mr. Calhoun is a great man," Senator John P. King of Georgia
wrote, "and in private life a most exemplary one; but he is so
eccentric and changeable that as a guide there is no confidence to
be placed in him. Look back at his opinions of a national bank
. . . his former opinions of the protective system. . . . Then there
is Pickens. . . . I'd as soon depend on Beelzebub to defend me. . . .
Pickens . . . appeals adroitly . . . as does Mr. Calhoun, to the sectional feelings of the South, to sustain that which he fears their
reason would not approve." Senator King denied that the banking
system "centralized commerce at the North." Calhoun had it
exactly reversed. It was commerce that centralized banking in
New York where nine-tenths of the imports into the country

entered because it was "the natural, and, with all its advantages, the cheapest depot for the consumption of nine-tenths of the people of the United States."[9]

What Senator King wanted for the South and the nation was an expansion of credit, not continued deflation, but he and those in other areas of the country who thought as he did were defeated by a combination of political and economic forces in the United States and Great Britain. The advocates of deflation as the proper remedy for a financial crisis were temporarily victorious, and in 1839, after a brief economic recovery, Great Britain, the United States, including the South, and the rest of the world entered into a prolonged depression. Partial prosperity returned to the nation through the stimulus of the Mexican War, but full recovery was delayed until the discovery of gold in California provided the base for expanded economic activity all over the world.

There were but few economic complaints during the 1850's. The principal political debates in this decade were sectional, but not economic, and a majority of Southerners were content with economic conditions as they were. Only a few southern nationalists upheld the doctrine of sectional economic antagonism in newspapers and magazines and at commercial and agricultural conventions, and this propaganda was ignored by most of the planters, merchants, and bankers to whom it was addressed.

The white inhabitants of the South, even in the 1850's, thought of themselves as Americans economically and in most other respects, and identified themselves politically and culturally with all people, except Indians and Negroes, who lived in the United States. State and sectional loyalty was a more important influence in their thought and conduct than it was with others, but this exaggeration of a point of view common to all Americans did not constitute a break in the essential cultural unity of the United States. The nation, from its beginning, was a single national society, an organic part of the unified western culture which had its origin in medieval Europe and which had been transformed by the Renaissance, the Reformation, the commercial, scientific, and industrial revolutions, and political democracy. The spiritual and intellectual fathers of this culture were the Hebraic, Greek, Hellenic, and European thinkers whose teaching and writing shaped and formed the minds of all men in the West including those who lived in the southern United States.

Viewed against this background, the cultural distinctions which separated one group of Americans from another during the ante-bellum period seem minor and inconsequential, and no more important than the cultural distinctions between the inhabitants of the different counties of the small and unified kingdom of England. Deeply rooted and persistent provincial differences in language, customs, religion, and other major aspects of life, such as appear in Germany, Spain, Italy, or France (not to mention India or China), were foreign to the American experience and had no parallels in the slight differences to be found among the people of the ante-bellum period who lived in the various parts of this vast territory.

These distinctions and differences among Americans, as a general rule, coincided more nearly with the natural geographical regions than with state or sectional lines. Those who lived in the coastal plain, the regions behind the first fall line, and the valleys and coves of the mountains could be distinguished from the others by appearance, manner, and language; while those who lived in the Mississippi Valley, west of the Appalachians, were different from those living in the East. Occasional enclaves, such as the Germans in Pennsylvania and the Valley of Virginia or the Creoles and Cajuns of southern Louisiana, further complicated the cultural patterns; but the greatest internal distinction to be found among the people of the United States was that between those who lived in the city and those who lived in the country, which existed in all parts of the nation, including the Old South, until its relatively recent modification by the paved road, electricity, and the consolidated school. In addition there were the distinctions between the sensible and the stupid, the educated and the uneducated, the genteel and the crude, the rich and the poor, the powerful and the weak, which are to be found in all societies at all times and in all places.

These cultural distinctions, as has been said before, were minor, and, like the differences in occupation and economic interest, give little support to those historians who insist that in the United States there were "two civilizations." The South did not secede because of differences in culture, nor even because of the tariff or the Bank of the United States, but rather because of its "peculiar" sectional interest. The one important sectional conflict in the nation's history arose from the fact that Negroes were held as slaves in the southern states until 1865. The defense of slavery against attacks from other areas of the country gradually affected the thinking of most white Southerners and led them to seek independence outside the American Union.

The institution of slavery as an accepted part of society had a long history, and its essential morality was never challenged until the beginning of the modern era. Gradually, however, the idea of the free individual became dominant in the western world, and the founders of the American republic, in their Declaration of Independence, stated that all men are created equal and are endowed by their Creator with the right to life, liberty, and the pursuit of happiness. When this statement was written, chattel slavery existed in all but one of the thirteen colonies. This glaring contradiction to their expressed principles was continued under the new government. The reason for their lack of action was their political wisdom. Politics, they knew, was the art of the possible, for, as they said in the Declaration of Independence, "all experience hath shown, that mankind are more disposed to suffer, while evils are sufferable, than to right themselves by abolishing the forms to which they are accustomed."

Southerners accepted slavery as one of those evils. Thomas Jefferson, a slaveholder, writing of the institution, said, "Indeed I tremble for my country when I reflect that God is just: that his justice cannot sleep for ever";[10] and James Madison, another Virginian, lamented the fact that "we have seen the mere distinction of colour made in the most enlightened period of time, a ground of the most oppressive dominion ever exercised by man over man." They were joined by George Mason, one of the largest slaveowners in the country, who insisted that "slavery discourages arts and manufactures. The poor despise labor when performed by slaves. They prevent the immigration of Whites, who really enrich and strengthen the country. They produce the most pernicious effect on manners. Every master of slaves is born a petty tyrant. They bring the judgment of heaven on a Country. As nations can not be rewarded or punished in the next world they must be in this. By an inevitable chain of causes and effects providence punishes national sins, by national calamities."[11]

The defenders of slavery in the Constitutional Convention justified the institution primarily on economic grounds, and they did not object when Madison said that he "thought it wrong to admit in the Constitution the idea that there could be property in men," or when Hugh Williamson of North Carolina admitted that "both in opinion and practice he was against slavery." The moral argument, according to the South Carolina and Georgia delegates, was unimportant, but they insisted, nevertheless, that "the security the Southern States want is that their Negroes not be taken from them, which some gentlemen within or without doors, have a good mind to do."

Their adoption of this adamant attitude had its effect, and the position accepted by the Convention was that "the morality or wisdom of slavery are considerations belonging to the states themselves." The hope was expressed, however, that "the abolition of slavery seemed to be going on in the United States, and . . . the good sense of the several states would probably by degrees complete it." The general consensus was stated by Oliver Ellsworth of Connecticut, who said, "Let us not intermeddle. As population increases poor laborers will be so plenty as to render slaves useless. Slavery in time will not be a speck in our Country. Provision is already made in Connecticut for abolishing it. And the abolition has already taken place in Massachusetts. As to the danger of insurrections from foreign influence, that will become a motive for the kind treatment of the slaves."[12]

The optimistic belief that slavery, an economic institution, would automatically be ended as it inevitably became unprofitable was apparently confirmed in the first years under the new Constitution. All of the states north of Delaware and Maryland joined Massachusetts and Connecticut in abolishing the institution, and the Congress, by confirming the provisions of the Northwest Ordinance of 1787, permanently prohibited slavery in the territory north of the Ohio and west of the mountains. Most men thought that the other states would follow, if not immediately, at least within a generation, but they were wrong.

One source of their error was the belief that slavery was uneconomic in comparison with free labor, and that since it was unprofitable, it would be abolished. Slavery did not prove to be unprofitable; instead the invention of machines to gin, spin, and weave cotton into cloth opened the way to vast profits from the exploitation of bound labor in the cotton fields; and the opening of new lands throughout the interior South created a market for the food and other produce of slave labor in earlier-settled areas. The owners of slaves were unwilling to give up these profits, but, as an equally important influence on their attitude, they were also afraid to risk the dangers they thought involved in emancipation.

One of their spokesmen in the Convention had said that he "was not apprehensive of insurrections," but shortly thereafter an event occurred outside the United States which was basically to alter the pro-slavery argument. The Negro slaves and free men of color in San Domingo, influenced by the French Revolutionary doctrines of freedom and equality, rose in revolt against the white masters of the island, and the ensuing wars and massacres sent a wave of fear through the slaveholding regions of the United States. Slavery became more than an economic institution. It was, in the opinion of the whites, the sole means through which two such different peoples could live peaceably together, and fear of insurrection became as influential as economic interest in causing a majority of Southerners both to defend the institution and to insist on its permanence.

Opponents of slavery outside the South did not realize that any change had occurred, but Edward Coles of Charlottesville, Virginia, an anti-slavery Southerner in the tradition of Jefferson, Madison, and Mason, was aware by 1815 that any efforts he might make would be futile. "My objections and abhorrence to slavery, on the one hand," he wrote, "and my partiality for my relations and friends and my native state, on the other, still continue to . . . disturb me. . . . Yet my feelings on the subject of slavery are so strong that I feel as if nothing could induce me even to remain among them, except the hope of being in some degree useful in ameliorating their condition. But as I cannot harbor this pleasing hope, notwithstanding the flattering assurances I have received to the contrary from . . . Mr. Jefferson . . . I am preparing to set out for the country northwest of the Ohio in June."[13]

He went to Illinois, free soil by the provisions of the Northwest Ordinance, and became governor of the state. But he was not to escape from slavery so easily, because his first task was to prevent his fellow inhabitants from legalizing the institution by their constitution. He won this fight and kept his area free. Some forty years later (a long time in the life of a man, but short from the point of view of history) another man from Illinois was to lead the final battle in the same campaign. These forty years were the decisive ones in the history of the American republic. Slowly but certainly, one man after another looked at the basic principles of the Declaration and then at slavery and found them incompatible. The slaves themselves, without arms, weak and divided, became restive. In their songs and prayers they expressed their longing for freedom, and, on rare occasions, they spoke through wrath and violence.

The white inhabitants of the South during this same period, because of their fears of the unknown dangers which they thought might result from emancipation and also because of their resentment of outside criticism, became stubborn and blocked all action. They admitted at first that slavery was immoral and in conflict with principles which they not only affirmed but also believed, but gradually many of them began to question the principles themselves. They became afraid of the moral teachings of the Declaration and so involved the freedom of all men with the fate of those held in formal bondage, for as long as there were free men capable of reading and believing these principles the cry against slavery could not be downed.

Tension mounted, tempers grew short, and finally in 1861 war came between the two parts of the country. Here was a problem that could not be handled by ordinary political means, and force, in such instances, is the only arbiter. But even in 1861 the cause of the war could not be avowed. Men, at least white men who shared the common western view of white superiority over all other peoples, would not fight their fellow-countrymen so that Negroes might be free. And Lincoln, who had few illusions about men, with great political skill made certain that the war should be fought for nationalism, the Union; for such a cause, though it lacked moral grandeur, would unite more men than any other.

In the closing months of the war, however, he frankly avowed the more fundamental cause. "One eighth of the whole population," he said, "were colored slaves. . . . These slaves constituted a peculiar and powerful interest. All knew that this interest was, somehow, the cause of the war."[14] The institution ended with the war, and the great majority of southern people, accepting the result of the test by arms and its consequences, re-accepted the responsibilities and privileges of American citizenship and membership in the national society. They abandoned sectional loyalty except in conversation, political speeches (not actions), and on Memorial Day, even though now, for the first time, they had a separate historical experience during the Civil War and Reconstruction to give them a feeling of unity among themselves and of difference from the rest of the nation.

The emancipation of the slaves eliminated the "peculiar institution" which distinguished the South from other areas of the country and eliminated the sole cause for its desire to be separate and independent. Its subsequent concern with the maintenance of white supremacy was not an evidence of its difference from other areas of the country, but of its unhappy identity with most men of European origin when they come into contact with large numbers of people of different origin, whether this be the Spanish with the Indians of Middle and South America, the Dutch in South Africa and the East Indies, the English in all parts of the colonial world, the French in North Africa and Indochina, or white Americans in California, Detroit, or Chicago.*

The South re-accepted membership in the national society with little or no change in basic attitudes and beliefs, because

* The moral and political criticism of white supremacy, which has steadily increased throughout the twentieth century, and the renewal of southern intransigence following the decision of the Supreme Court on segregation in schools, does not invalidate this statement. White and Negro Southerners have been among the leaders in voicing this criticism and defending the decision of the court, and they are effectively participating in the effort to eliminate this "glaring contradiction" to the expressed principles of the American nation.

none was required. Its return to the nation was not an abandonment of its ancient tradition, but a return to it, and the subsequent changes, including industrialization, were a continuation of movements already well developed in the southern states before the outbreak of the war. The new South differed from the old only as the latter part of the nineteenth century differed from the earlier part, and most of the changes were the products of the scientific, industrial, and intellectual revolutions which were shared in common by all men of the western world.

CHAPTER THREE

THE TRAVAIL OF SLAVERY

By CHARLES GRIER SELLERS, JR.

THE AMERICAN EXPERIENCE knows no greater tragedy than the Old South's twistings and turnings on the rack of slavery. Others suffered more from the "peculiar institution," but only the suffering of white Southerners fits the classic formula for tragedy. Like no other Americans before or since, the white men of the ante-bellum South drove toward catastrophe by doing conscious violence to their truest selves. No picture of the Old South as a section confident and united in its dedication to a neo-feudal social order, and no explanation of the Civil War as a conflict between "two civilizations," can encompass the complexity and pathos of the ante-bellum reality. No analysis that misses the inner turmoil of the ante-bellum Southerner can do justice to the central tragedy of the southern experience.*

The key to the tragedy of southern history is the paradox of the slaveholding South's devotion to "liberty." Whenever and wherever Southerners sought to invoke their highest social values—in schoolboy declamations, histories, Fourth of July orations, toasts, or newspaper editorials—"liberty" was the incantation that sprang most frequently and most fervently from their lips and pens. "The

* My interpretation of the Old South draws heavily on the brilliant insights of Wilbur J. Cash in *The Mind of the South* (New York, 1941), and also on Clement Eaton's *Freedom of Thought in the Old South* (Durham, 1940).

love of liberty had taken deep root in the minds of carolinians [sic] long before the revolution," explained South Carolina's historian David Ramsay in 1809. The "similarity of state and condition" produced by the early settlers' struggle to subdue the wilderness had "inculcated the equality of rights" and "taught them the rights of man."[1]

The Revolutionary struggle made this implicit colonial liberalism explicit and tied it to patriotic pride in the new American Union. From this time on, for Southerners as for other Americans, liberty was the end for which the Union existed, while the Union was the instrument by which liberty was to be extended to all mankind. Thus the Fourth of July, the birthday of both liberty and Union, became the occasion for renewing the liberal idealism and the patriotic nationalism which united Americans of all sections at the highest levels of political conviction. "The Declaration of Independence, and the Constitution of the United States—Liberty and Union, now and forever, one and inseparable," ran a Virginian's toast on July 4, 1850. The same sentiment and almost the same phrases might have been heard in any part of the South in any year of the ante-bellum period.[2]

Now "liberty" can mean many things, but the Old South persistently used the word in the universalist sense of the eighteenth-century Enlightenment. At Richmond in 1826 John Tyler eulogized Jefferson as "the devoted friend of man," who "had studied his rights in the great volume of nature, and saw with rapture the era near at hand, when those rights should be proclaimed, and the world aroused from the slumber of centuries." Jefferson's fame would not be confined to Americans, said Tyler, for his Declaration of Independence would be known wherever "man, so long the victim of oppression, awakes from the sleep of ages and bursts his chains." The conservative, slaveholding Tyler would soon be indicted by northern writers as a leader of the "slave power conspiracy" against human freedom;

yet in 1826 he welcomed the day "when the fires of liberty shall be kindled on every hill and shall blaze in every valley," to proclaim that "the mass of mankind have not been born with saddles on their backs, nor a favored few booted and spurred to ride them. . . ."[3]

Although a massive reaction against liberalism is supposed to have seized the southern mind in the following decades, the Nullifiers of the thirties and the radical southern sectionalists of the forties and fifties did not ignore or reject the Revolutionary tradition of liberty so much as they transformed it, substituting for the old emphasis on the natural rights of all men a new emphasis on the rights and autonomy of communities. It was ironic that these slaveholding defenders of liberty against the tyranny of northern domination had to place themselves in the tradition of '76 at all, and the irony was heightened by their failure to escape altogether its universalist implications. Even that fire-eater of fire-eaters, Robert Barnwell Rhett, declaimed on "liberty" so constantly and so indiscriminately that John Quincy Adams could call him "a compound of wild democracy and iron bound slavery."[4]

Indeed the older nationalist-universalist conception of liberty remained very much alive in the South, and Southerners frequently used it to rebuke the radical sectionalists. Denouncing nullification in 1834, a Savannah newspaper vehemently declared that Georgians would never join in this assault on America's Revolutionary heritage. "No!" said the editor, "the light of the 4th of July will stream across their path, to remind them that liberty was not won in a day. . . ." Even a Calhounite could proudly assure an Independence Day audience in Virginia a few years later that American principles were destined "to work an entire revolution in the face of human affairs" and "to elevate the great mass of mankind." In North Carolina in the forties, citizens continued to toast "The Principles of the American Revolution—Destined to revolutionize the civilized world"; and editors rejoiced that the Fourth sent rays of light "far, far into the dark spots of oppressed distant lands." In Charleston itself a leading newspaper proclaimed that Americans were "the peculiar people, chosen of the Lord, to keep the vestal flame of liberty, as a light unto the feet and a lamp unto the path of the benighted nations, who yet slumber or groan under the bondage of tyranny."[5]

Throughout the ante-bellum period the South's invocation of liberty was reinforced by its fervent devotion to the Union. "America shall reach a height beyond the ken of mortals," exclaimed a Charleston orator in the 1820's; and through the following decades Southerners continued to exult with other Americans over their country's unique advantages and brilliant destiny. The Old South's Americanism sometimes had a surprisingly modern ring, as when a conservative Georgia newspaper called on "True Patriots" to join the Whigs in defending the "American Way" against the "Red Republicanism" of the Democratic party. Even that bellwether of radical Southernism, *De Bow's Review,* printed article after article proclaiming the glorious destiny of the United States.[6]

To the very eve of the Civil War the Fourth of July remained a widely observed festival of liberty and union in the South. By 1854, a hard-pressed orator was complaining that there was nothing fresh left to say: "The Stars and Stripes have been so vehemently flourished above admiring crowds of patriotic citizens that there is hardly a rhetorical shred left of them. . . . The very Union would almost be dissolved by eulogizing it at such a melting temperature." The rising tide of sectional antagonism did somewhat dampen Independence Day enthusiasm in the late fifties, but even after the Civil War began, one southern editor saw "no reason why the birth of liberty should be permitted to pass unheeded wherever liberty has votaries. . . . The accursed

Yankees are welcome to the exclusive use of their 'Doodle' but let the South hold on tenaciously to Washington's March and Washington's Principles and on every recurring anniversary of the promulgation of the Declaration, reassert the great principles of Liberty."[7]

What are we to make of these slaveholding champions of liberty? Was the ante-bellum Southerner history's most hypocritical casuist? Or were these passionate apostrophes to the liberty of distant peoples a disguised protest against, or perhaps an escape from, the South's daily betrayal of its liberal self? Southerners were at least subconsciously aware of the "detestable paradox" of "our every-day sentiments of liberty" while holding human beings in slavery, and many Southerners had made it painfully explicit in the early days of the republic.[8]

A Virginian was amazed that "a people who have declared 'That all men are by nature equally free and independent' and have made this declaration the first article in the foundation of their government, should in defiance of so sacred a truth, recognized by themselves in so solemn a manner, and on so important an occasion, tolerate a practice incompatible therewith." Similarly, in neighboring Maryland, a leading politician expressed his astonishment that the people of the Old Free State "do not blush at the very name of Freedom." Was not Maryland, asked William Pinkney, "at once the fair temple of freedom, and the abominable nursery of slaves; the school for patriots, and the foster-mother of petty despots; the asserter of human rights, and the patron of wanton oppression?" "It will not do," he insisted, "thus to talk like philosophers, and act like unrelenting tyrants; to be perpetually sermonizing it with liberty for our text, and actual oppression for our commentary."[9]

Still another leading Marylander pointed out that America's Revolutionary struggle had been "grounded upon the *preserva-*

tion of those rights to which God and nature entitled *us,* not in *particular,* but in common with *all the rest of mankind."* The retention of slavery, declared Luther Martin in 1788, was "a solemn mockery of, and insult to, that God whose protection we had then implored, and could not fail to hold us up to detestation, and render us contemptible to every true friend of liberty in the world." During the Revolution, said Martin, "when our liberties were at stake, we warmly felt for the common rights of men."[10]

Martin did not exaggerate the inclusiveness of the liberal idealism that had accompanied the Revolutionary War in the southern states. Many of the Revolutionary county committees had denounced slavery, and Virginia's Revolutionary convention of 1774 had declared its abolition to be "the greatest object of desire in those colonies where it was unhappily introduced in their infant state." The implications of universalist liberalism for slavery were recognized most clearly, perhaps, by the Georgia county committee which resolved early in 1775 "to show the world that we are not influenced by any contracted motives, but a general philanthropy for all mankind, of whatever climate, language, or complexion," by using its best endeavors to eliminate "the unnatural practice of slavery."[11]

It is well known that the South's great statesmen of the Revolutionary generation almost unanimously condemned slavery as incompatible with the nation's liberal principles. Though these elder statesmen proved incapable of solving the problem, Thomas Jefferson consoled himself with the thought that it could safely be left to the "young men, grown up, and growing up," who "have sucked in the principles of liberty, as it were, with their mother's milk."[12] Such young men did indeed grow up, and they kept most Southerners openly apologetic about slavery for fifty years following the Declaration of Independence.

When, in the mid-thirties, John C. Calhoun declared on the floor of the Senate that slavery was "a good—a great good," one of Jefferson's protégés and former law students was there to denounce "the obsolete and revolting theory of human rights and human society by which, of late, the institution of domestic slavery had been sustained and justified by some of its advocates in a portion of the South." Slavery was "a misfortune and an evil in all circumstances," said Virginia's Senator William C. Rives, and he would never "deny, as has been done by this new school, the natural freedom and equality of man; to contend that slavery is a positive good." He would never "attack the great principles which lie at the foundation of our political system," or "revert to the dogmas of Sir Robert Filmer, exploded a century and a half ago by the immortal works of Sidney and Locke."[13] *

Though open anti-slavery utterances grew infrequent after the 1830's, the generation which was to dominate southern life in the forties and fifties had already come to maturity with values absorbed from the afterglow of Revolutionary liberalism. On the eve of the Civil War *De Bow's Review* was to complain that during these earlier years, "when probably a majority of even our own people regarded the existence of slavery among us as a blot on our fair name . . . our youth [were allowed] to peruse, even in their tender years, works in which slavery was denounced as an unmitigated evil."[14] Some of these youngsters had drawn some vigorous conclusions. "How contradictory" was slavery to every principle of "a republican Government where liberty is the boast and pride of its free citizens," exclaimed the son of a slaveholding family in South Carolina. Similarly a fifteen-year-old Tennessee

---

* Almost as significant as Rives' own position is the fact that he touched Calhoun at a tender point when he associated him with the anti-libertarian Filmer. The South Carolinian "utterly denied that his doctrines had any thing to do with the tenets of Sir Robert Filmer, which he abhorred." "So far from holding with the dogmas of that writer, he had been the known and open advocate of freedom from the beginning," Calhoun was reported as saying. "Nor was there any thing in the doctrines he held in the slightest degree inconsistent with the highest and purest principles of freedom."

boy called slavery "a foul, a deadly blot . . . in a nation boasting of the republicanism of her principles" and owing allegiance to "the sacred rights of man."[15]

A whole generation cannot transform its most fundamental values by a mere effort of will. Though Southerners tended during the latter part of the ante-bellum period to restrict their publicly voiced libertarian hopes to "oppressed distant lands," the old liberal misgivings about slavery did not die. Instead they burrowed beneath the surface of the southern mind, where they kept gnawing away the shaky foundations on which Southerners sought to rebuild their morale and self-confidence as a slaveholding people.

Occasionally the doubts were exposed, as in 1857, when Congressman L. D. Evans of Texas lashed out at the general repudiation of liberalism to which some defenders of slavery had been driven. The doctrine of human inequality and subordination might do for the dark ages of tyranny, he declared, "but emanating from the lips of a Virginia professor, or a statesman of Carolina, it startles the ear, and shocks the moral sense of a republican patriot." But Evans only illustrated the hopelessness of the southern dilemma by his tortured argument for transforming slavery into a kind of serfdom which would somehow preserve the slave's "natural equality," while gradually evolving into a state of "perfect equality."[16]

The same year a Charleston magazine admitted that "We are perpetually aiming to square the maxims of an impracticable philosophy with the practice which nature and circumstances force upon us." Yet on the very eve of war, few Southerners were ready to resolve the dilemma by agreeing with the writer that "the [liberal] philosophy of the North is a dead letter to us."[17]

If the Southerner had been embarrassed by his devotion to liberty and Union alone, he would have had less trouble easing his mind on the subject of slavery. But as a Virginia legislator exclaimed in 1832, "This, sir, is a Christian community." Southerners "read in their Bibles, *'Do unto all men as you would have them do unto you';* and this golden rule and slavery are hard to reconcile."[18]   During those early decades of the nineteenth century, when the South was confessing the evils of slavery, it had been swept by a wave of evangelical orthodoxy.   Though the wave crested about the time some Southerners, including some clergymen, began speaking of slavery as a positive good, it does not follow that the evangelical reaction against the eighteenth century's religious ideas contributed significantly to the reaction against the eighteenth century's liberalism with regard to slavery.

On the contrary, the evangelical denominations had strong anti-slavery tendencies.   Methodists, Quakers, and Baptists nurtured an extensive abolitionist movement in the upper South during the twenties, when the rest of the country was largely indifferent to the slavery question; and the Presbyterians were still denouncing slavery in Kentucky a decade later.   It would be closer to the truth to suggest that as Southerners wrestled with their consciences over slavery, they may have gained a first-hand experience with the concepts of sin and evil that made them peculiarly susceptible to Christian orthodoxy.   At any rate, as late as 1849, a pro-slavery professor at the University of Alabama complained to Calhoun that no one had yet published a satisfactory defense of slavery in the light of New Testament teachings.   The "many religious people at the South who have strong misgivings on this head," he warned, constituted a greater threat to the peculiar institution than the northern abolitionists.[19]

Even the irreligious found it hard to resist the claims of simple humanity or to deny that slaves, as one Southerner put it, "have hearts and feelings like other men."   And those who were proof against the appeals to Revolutionary liberalism, Christianity, and humanity, still faced the arguments of Southerners in each succeeding generation that slavery was disastrous to the whites. Jefferson's famous lament that the slaveholder's child, "nursed, educated, and daily exercised in tyranny . . . must be a prodigy who can retain his manners and morals undepraved," was frequently echoed. George Mason's lament that slavery discouraged manufactures, caused the poor to despise labor, and prevented economic development, found many seconders in Virginia's slavery debate of 1831-32 and received elaborate statistical support from Hinton Rowan Helper in the fifties. The seldom mentioned but apparently widespread practice of miscegenation was an especially heavy cross for the women of the South. "Under slavery we live surrounded by prostitutes," wrote one woman bitterly. ". . . . Any lady is ready to tell you who is the father of all the mulatto children in everybody's household but her own. . . . My disgust sometimes is boiling over."[20]

It is essential to understand that the public declarations of Southerners never revealed the full impact of all these anti-slavery influences on the southern mind. Fear of provoking slave insurrections had restrained free discussion of slavery even in the Revolutionary South, and an uneasy society exerted steadily mounting pressure against anti-slavery utterances thereafter. Only when Nat Turner's bloody uprising of 1831 shocked Southerners into open debate over the peculiar institution did the curtain of restraint part sufficiently to reveal the intensity of their misgivings. Thomas Ritchie's influential Richmond *Enquirer* caught the mood of that historic moment when it quoted a South Carolinian as exclaiming, "We may shut our eyes and avert our faces, if we please, but there it is, the dark and growing evil at our doors; and meet the question we must, at no distant day. . . . What is to be done? Oh! my God, I do not know, but something must be done."[21]

Many were ready to say what had to be done, especially a brilliant galaxy of the liberty-loving young Virginians on whom the dying Jefferson had pinned his hopes. "I will not rest until slavery is abolished in Virginia," vowed Governor John Floyd; and during the winter of 1831-32 a deeply earnest Virginia legislature was wrapped in the Old South's only free and full debate over slavery. Not a voice was raised to justify human servitude in the abstract, while a score of Virginians attacked the peculiar institution with arguments made deadly by the South's endemic liberalism and Christianity. Two years later a Tennessee constitutional convention showed a tender conscience on slavery by admitting that "to prove it to be an evil is an easy task." Yet in both states proposals for gradual emancipation were defeated.[22]

The outcome was no surprise to the editor of the Nashville *Republican*. Few would question the moral evil of slavery, he had written back in 1825, "but then the assent to a proposition is not always followed by acting in uniformity to its spirit." Too many Southerners believed, perhaps from "the exercise of an interested casuistry," that nature had ordained the Negro to slavery by giving him a peculiar capacity for labor under the southern sun. Furthermore, southern white men would have to "be convinced that to labor personally is a more agreeable, and desirable occupation, than to command, & superintend the labor of others." Consequently, "as long as slavery is conceived to advance the pecuniary interests of individuals, they will be slow to relish, and reluctant to encourage, any plan for its abolition. They will quiet their consciences with the reflection that it was entailed upon us— that it has grown up with the institutions of the country—and that the establishment of a new order of things would be attended with great difficulty, and might be perilous."[23]

Thus when Nat Turner frightened Southerners into facing squarely the tragic ambiguity of their society, they found the price for resolving it too high. The individual planter's economic stake in slavery was a stubborn and perhaps insurmountable obstacle to change; and even Jefferson's nerve had failed at the task of reconstituting the South's social system to assimilate a host of Negro freedmen.

The whole South sensed that a fateful choice had been made. Slowly and reluctantly Southerners faced the fact that, if slavery were to be retained, things could not go on as before. The slaves were restive, a powerful anti-slavery sentiment was sweeping the western world, and southern minds were not yet nerved for a severe struggle in defense of the peculiar institution to which they were now committed. The South could no longer ease its conscience with hopes for the eventual disappearance of slavery, or tolerate such hopes in any of its people. "It is not enough for them to believe that slavery has been entailed upon us by our forefathers," proclaimed Calhoun's national newspaper organ. "We must satisfy the consciences, we must allay the fears of our own people. We must satisfy them that slavery is of itself right—that it is not a sin against God—that it is not an evil, moral or political. . . . In this way, and this way only, can we prepare our own people to defend their institutions."[24] So southern leaders of the Calhoun school began trying to convince themselves and others that slavery was a "positive good," while southern legislatures abridged freedom of speech and press, made manumission difficult or impossible, and imposed tighter restrictions on both slaves and free Negroes. The Great Reaction was under way.

Yet the Great Reaction, for all its formidable façade and terrible consequences, was a fraud. Slavery simply could not be blended with liberalism and Christianity, while liberalism and Christianity were too deeply rooted in the southern mind to be torn up overnight. Forced to smother and distort their most fundamental convictions by the decision to maintain slavery, and goaded by criticism based on these same convictions, Southerners of the generation before the Civil War suffered the most painful loss of social morale and identity that any large group of Americans has ever experienced.

The surface unanimity enforced on the South in the forties and fifties by the Great Reaction concealed a persistent hostility to slavery. It is true that large numbers of the most deeply committed anti-slavery men left the South. They were usually men of strong religious conviction, such as Levi Coffin, the North Carolina Quaker who moved to Indiana to become the chief traffic manager of the Underground Railroad, or Will Breckinridge, the Kentucky Presbyterian who declared, "I care little where I go—so that I may only get where every man I see is as free as myself." In fact the national banner of political anti-slavery was carried in the forties by a former Alabama slaveholder, James G. Birney, who had rejected slavery for the same reasons that bothered many other Southerners—because it was "inconsistent with the Great Truth that all men are created equal, . . . as well as the great rule of benevolence delivered to us by the Savior Himself that in all things whatsoever ye would that men should do unto you do ye even so to them."[25]

Many zealous anti-slavery men remained in the South, however, to raise their voices wherever the Great Reaction relaxed its grip. If this almost never happened in the lower South, a dissenter in western Virginia could exult in 1848 that "anti-slavery papers and anti-slavery orators are scattering far and wide the seeds of freedom, and an immense number of persons are uttering vaticinations in contemplation of a day of emancipation"; while the reckless courage of Cassius Clay and his allies kept the anti-slavery cause alive in Kentucky. "The contention of planter politicians that the South had achieved social and political unity," concludes the ablest student of the peculiar institution, "appears, then, to have been the sheerest of wishful thinking."[26]

Far more significant than outright anti-slavery opinion was the persistent disquietude over slavery among the many white

Southerners who found the new pro-slavery dogmas hard to swallow. The official southern view held that slaveholders "never inquire into the propriety of the matter, . . . they see their neighbors buying slaves, and they buy them . . . leaving to others to discuss the right and justice of the thing." In moments of unusual candor, however, the pro-slavery propagandists admitted the prevalence of misgivings. Calhoun's chief editorial spokesman thought, the principal danger of northern abolitionism was its influence upon "the consciences and fears of the slave-holders themselves." Through "the insinuation of their dangerous heresies into our schools, our pulpits, and our domestic circles," Duff Green warned, the abolitionists might succeed in "alarming the consciences of the weak and feeble, and diffusing among our own people a morbid sensitivity on the question of slavery."[27]

Slavery's apologists were particularly irritated by the numerous instances "in which the superstitious weakness of dying men . . . induces them, in their last moments, to emancipate their slaves." Every manumission was an assault on the peculiar institution and a testimony to the tenacity with which older values resisted the pro-slavery dogmas. "Let our women and old men, and persons of weak and infirm minds, be disabused of the false . . . notion that slavery is sinful, and that they will peril their souls if they do not disinherit their offspring by emancipating their slaves!" complained a Charleston editor in the fifties. It was high time masters "put aside all care or thought what Northern people say about them."[28]

Yet the manumissions went on, despite mounting legal obstacles. The census reported more than 3,000 for 1860, or one manumission for every 1,309 slaves, which was double the number reported ten years before. If this figure seems small, it should be remembered that these manumissions were accomplished against "almost insuperable obstacles"—not only southern laws prohibiting manumission or making it extremely difficult, but also northern laws barring freed Negroes.   The evidence indicates that there would have been many more manumissions if the laws had been more lenient, and if masters had not feared that the freed Negroes would be victimized.[29]

The explanations advanced by men freeing their slaves illustrate the disturbing influence of liberalism and Christianity in the minds of many slaveholders.   A Virginia will affirmed the testator's belief "that slavery in all its forms . . . is inconsistent with republican principles, that it is a violation of our bill of rights, which declares, *that all men are by nature equally free;* and above all, that it is repugnant to the spirit of the gospel, which enjoins universal love and benevolence."   A North Carolinian listed four reasons for freeing his slaves: (1) "Agreeably to the rights of man, every human being, be his colour what it may, is entitled to freedom"; (2) "My conscience, the great criterion, condemns me for keeping them in slavery"; (3) "The golden rule directs us to do unto every human creature, as we would wish to be done unto"; and (4) "I wish to die with a clear conscience, that I may not be ashamed to appear before my master in a future World."   In Tennessee, one man freed his slave woman because he wanted her to "Enjoy Liberty the birthright of all Mankind."   Another not only believed "it to be the duty of a Christian to deal with his fellow man in a state of bondage with humanity and kindness," but also feared that his own "happiness *hereafter*" depended on the disposition he made of his slaves.   Still another, after ordering two slaves freed, hoped that "no one will offer to undo what my conscience tole me was my duty," and that "my children will consider it so and folow the futsteps of their father and keep now [no] slaves longer than they pay for their raising and expenses."[30]

But conscience was a problem for many more Southerners than those who actually freed their slaves, as the pro-slavery philosophers were compelled to recognize.   "I am perfectly aware that slavery is repugnant to the *natural* emotions of men," confessed

William J. Grayson on the eve of the Civil War. James H. Hammond was one of many who sought to quiet the troublesome southern conscience by picturing slavery as an eleemosynary institution, maintained at considerable cost by generous slaveholders. Southerners must content themselves, said Hammond, with "the consoling reflection, that what is lost to us is gained to humanity." Grayson, on the other hand, despaired of quieting conscience and concluded grimly that conscience itself must be discredited. "I take the stand on the position that our natural feelings are unsafe guides for us to follow in the social relations."[31]

But a host of Southerners, perhaps including Grayson and Hammond, could neither satisfy nor ignore their consciences. One troubled master confided to his wife, "I sometimes think my feelings unfit me for a slaveholder." A North Carolina planter told his son that he could not discipline his slaves properly, believing that slavery was a violation of "the natural rights of a being who is as much entitled to the enjoyment of liberty as myself." In the rich Mississippi Delta country, where many of the largest slaveholders remained loyal to the Union in 1861, one man had long sought "some means . . . to rid us of slavery, because I never had any great fondness for the institution although I had been the owner of slaves from my youth up." Another Mississippi slaveholder was "always an abolitionist at heart," but "did not know how to set them free without wretchedness to them, and utter ruin to myself." Still another "owned slaves & concluded if I was merciful & humane to them I might just as well own them as other Persons . . . [but] I had an instinctive horror of the institution." How many masters held such opinions privately can never be known, but observers at the close of the Civil War noted a surprisingly general feeling of relief over the destruction of slavery. An upcountry South Carolinian certainly spoke for many Southerners when he said, "I am glad the thing is done away with; it was more plague than pleasure, more loss than profit."[32]

The nub of the Southerner's ambivalent attitude toward slavery was his inability to regard the slave consistently as either person or property. Slaves "were a species of property that differed from all others," James K. Polk declared as a freshman congressman, "they were rational; they were human beings."[33] The slave's indeterminate status was writ large in the ambiguity of the whole structure of southern society. A sociologist has analyzed the institutional features of slavery as lying along a "rationality-traditionalism range," whose polar points were mutually contradictory. At one pole lay the economic view. Since slavery was a labor system employed in a highly competitive market economy, a minimum of rational efficiency was necessarily prescribed for economic survival. This called for a "sheerly economic" view of slavery, one which regarded the slave as property, which gave the master unlimited control over the slave's person, which evaluated the treatment of slaves wholly in terms of economic efficiency, which structured the slave's situation so that his self-interest in escaping the lash became his sole motivation to obedience, which sanctioned the domestic slave trade and demanded resumption of the foreign slave trade as essential mechanisms for supplying and redistributing labor, and which dismissed moral considerations as both destructive of the labor supply and irrelevant. Though the plantation system tended during the latter part of the slavery period to approach the ideal type of a purely commercial economic organization, especially with the geographical shift to the new lands of the Southwest, few if any Southerners ever fully accepted this "sheerly economic" view of slavery.

At the other pole lay a "traditional" or "familial" view, which regarded the slave more as person than property and idealized "the patriarchial organization of plantation life and the maintenance of the family estate and family slaves at all costs." Both the "sheerly economic" and the "familial" views of slavery were sanctioned by southern society; economics and logic drove Southerners toward the former, while sentiment, liberalism, and Christianity dragged them in the other direction.[34]

This fundamental ambivalence was most clearly apparent in the law of slavery. Early colonial law had justified the enslavement of Negroes on the ground that they were heathens, so that the conversion of slaves to Christianity raised a serious problem. Though the Negro was continued in bondage, the older conviction that conversion and slave status were incompatible died hard, as was demonstrated by the successive enactments required to establish the new legal definition of slavery on the basis of the Negro's race rather than his heathenism. Even then problems remained. Not all Negroes were slaves, and the South could never bring itself to reduce free Negroes to bondage. Moreover the slave's admission to the privilege of salvation inevitably identified him as a person. But slavery could not be viewed as a legal relationship between legal persons; in strict logic it had to be a chattel arrangement that left the slave no legal personality.

Was the slave a person or merely property in the eyes of the law? This question southern legislatures and courts never settled. He could not legally marry, own property, sue or be sued, testify, or make contracts; yet he was legally responsible for crimes he committed, and others were responsible for crimes committed against him. The ambiguity was most striking in the case of a slave guilty of murder; as a person he was responsible and could be executed; but he was also property, and if the state took his life, his owner had to be compensated. "The slave is put on trial as a *human being*," declared a harrassed court in one such case. "Is it not inconsistent, in the progress of the trial, to treat him as property, like . . . a horse, in the value of which the owner has a pecuniary interest which makes him incompetent as a witness?"[35]

The Southerner's resistance to the legal logic of making slavery a simple property arrangement is amply illustrated in court decisions. "A slave is not in the condition of a horse," said a Ten-

nessee judge. "He has mental capacities, and an immortal principle in his nature." The laws did not "extinguish his high-born
nature nor deprive him of many rights which are inherent in
men." Similarly a Mississippi court declared that it would be "a
stigma upon the character of the State" if a slave could be murdered "without subjecting the offender to the highest penalty
known to the criminal jurisprudence of the country. Has the
slave no rights, because he is deprived of his freedom? He is
still a human being, and possesses all those rights of which he is not
deprived by the positive provision of the law."[36]

The anguish induced by the legal logic of slavery was expressed most clearly in a North Carolina decision. Recognizing
the objectives of slavery to be "the profit of the master, his security and the public safety," and recognizing the slave to be
"doomed in his own person, and his posterity, to live without
knowledge, and without the capacity to make any thing his own,
and to toil that another may reap the fruits," the court concluded
that, "Such services can only be expected from one . . . who sur-
renders his will in implicit obedience to that of another. . . . The
power of the master must be absolute." The judge felt "as deeply
as any man can" the harshness of this proposition. "As a principle of moral rights, every person in his retirement must repudiate
it. . . . It constitutes the curse of slavery to both the bond and
the free portions of our population. But it is inherent in the relation of masters and slaves."[37]

The slave's indeterminate status was not just a legal problem,
but a daily personal problem for every master. "It is difficult to
handle simply as property, a creature possessing human passions
and human feelings," observed Frederick Law Olmsted, "while, on
the other hand, the absolute necessity of dealing with property as a
thing, greatly embarrasses a man in any attempt to treat it as a
person." Absentee owners and the masters of large, commercially
rationalized plantations might regard their field hands as economic

units, but few of them could avoid personalizing their relationships with house servants in a way that undercut the sheerly economic conception of the peculiar institution. The majority of slave-holders, moreover, were farmers who lived and worked closely with their slaves, and such masters, according to D. R. Hundley, "seem to exercise but few of the rights of ownership over their human chattels, making so little distinction between master and man, that their Negroes [are] . . . in all things treated more like equals than slaves."[38]

The personalized master-slave relationship was a direct threat to the peculiar institution, for slavery's stability as an economic institution depended upon the Negro's acceptance of the caste line between himself and the white man. Sociologists tell us that such caste systems as India's were stabilized by the fact that "those goals and value-attitudes which were legitimate for the dominant caste had no implications concerning their legitimacy for the sub-ordinate caste." In the South, however, where the values of the dominant caste produced personalized master-slave relationships, and where Negroes could view manumission as the crucial prod-uct of personalization, members of the subordinate caste learned to regard the value system and goals of the dominant caste as at least partly valid for themselves. The presence of free Negroes in southern society meant that the caste line did not coincide com-pletely with the color line, and the overlap made liberty a legiti-mate goal even for the slave. Thus the slave's passion for freedom, manifested in countless escapes and insurrection plots, was not "lit up in his soul by the hand of Deity," as a Virginia legislator thought, but was implanted by the white man's own inability to draw the caste line rigidly.[39]

Though Southerners could guard against the dangers of per-sonalization in the abstract, as when legislatures prohibited manu-mission, the individual master, face to face with his human prop-erty, found it harder to behave in accordance with the sheerly economic view of slavery. Economic efficiency demanded "the painful exercise of undue and tyrannical authority," observed a North Carolina planter; and the famous ex-slave Frederick Douglass testified that kind treatment increased rather than diminished the slave's desire for freedom. Consequently humanity and the profit motive were forever struggling against each other in the the master's mind. While the profit motive frequently won out, humanity had its victories too. "I would be content with much less . . . cotton if less cruelty was exercised," said a disturbed planter in Mississippi. "I fear I am near an abolition[i]st." Most often, perhaps, the master's humanitarian and economic impulses fought to a draw, leaving him continually troubled and frustrated in the management of his slaves. Slaveholding, concluded one master, subjected "the man of care and feeling to more dilemmas than any other vocation he could follow."[40]

Certainly southern opinion condemned thoroughgoing economic rationality in the treatment of slaves. This was most apparent in the low social status accorded to slave traders and overseers, when by normal southern canons of prestige their intimate relation with the peculiar institution and their control over large numbers of slaves should have given them a relatively high rank. Both groups were absolutely essential to the slavery system, and both bore a purely economic relation to it. The overseer, who was judged primarily by the profits he wrung out of slave labor, typified the sheerly exploitative aspects of slavery; while the slave trader, who presided over the forcible disruption of families and the distribution of slaves as marketable commodities, was the most conspicuous affront to the familial conception of the peculiar institution. These men certainly developed a cynical attitude toward the human property they controlled, but they did not uniformly exhibit the dishonesty, greed, vulgarity, and general immorality that southern opinion ascribed to them. By thus stereotyping these exemplars of the sheerly economic aspects of slavery, southern society created scapegoats on whom it could discharge the guilt feelings arising from the necessity of treating human beings as property.[41]

These guilt feelings seem to have increased during the final years of the ante-bellum period, as slavery approximated the sheerly economic pattern on more and more plantations. Never had Southerners regaled themselves and others so insistently with the myth of the happy slave. A European traveler met few slaveholders who could "openly and honestly look the thing in the face. They wind and turn about in all sorts of ways, and make use of every argument . . . to convince me that the slaves are the happiest people in the world, and do not wish to be placed in any other condition." At the same time there developed a strong movement to extend and implement the paternalistic-personalistic pattern. Some states amended their slave codes to prescribe minimum standards of treatment, and there was agitation for more fundamental reforms—legalization of slave marriages, protection against disruption of slave families, and encouragement of Negro education.[42]

Especially significant was the crusade for religious instruction of slaves. "We feel that the souls of our slaves are a solemn trust, and we shall strive to present them faultless and complete before the presence of God," declared that high priest of southern Presbyterianism, Dr. James Henley Thornwell. The argument for religious instruction was also a justification for slavery, and the only one that effected any kind of real accommodation between the peculiar institution and the white Southerner's innate disposition to regard the slave as a human being. It was precisely for this reason that the religious interpretation of slavery quieted more southern qualms than any other facet of the pro-slavery argument. "However the world may judge us in connection with our institution of slavery," said Georgia's Bishop Stephen Elliott, "we conscientiously believe it to be a great missionary institution—one

arranged by God, as he arranges all the moral and religious influences of the world so that the good may be brought out of the
seeming evil, and a blessing wrung out of every form of the
curse."

Yet the religious argument was ultimately subversive of slavery.
By giving the slave's status as person precedence over his status as
property, and by taking as its mission the elevation of the slave
as a human being, the movement for religious instruction necessarily called into question the inherent beneficence and permanence
of the institution.   Dr. Thornwell resolutely argued that slavery
could end only in heaven, because only there could the sin that
produced it end; meanwhile the Christian's duty was to mitigate its
evils.   Bishop Elliott, on the other hand, believed that by giving
the slaves religious instruction "we are elevating them in every
generation" here on earth, and he spoke for many another southern churchman when he conceded that this implied ultimately
some change in the slaves' worldly status. Thus, by the close of
the slavery era, the religious defense of the institution was bringing
the South back toward its old colonial doubts about the validity
of continued bondage for converted men and women.[43]

Nowhere, in fact, was the South's painful inner conflict over
slavery more evident than in the elaborate body of theory by
which it tried to prove (mainly to itself) the beneficence of its
peculiar social system.   "It has not been more than . . . thirty
years since the abolition of slavery was seriously debated in the
legislature of Virginia," observed the *Southern Literary Messenger* on the eve of the Civil War.   "Now, on the contrary . . . the
whole Southern mind with an unparalleled unanimity regards the
institution of slavery as righteous and just, ordained of God, and
to be perpetuated by Man."   Yet the stridency with which southern
unanimity was ceaselessly proclaimed stands in suggestive contrast
to the private views of many Southerners.   "To expect men to

agree that Slavery is a blessing, social, moral, and political," wrote a North Carolina Congressman to his wife, "when many of those who have all their lives been accustomed to it . . . believe exactly the reverse, is absurd." Even the fire-eaters confessed privately that outside South Carolina most slaveholders were "mere negro-drivers believing themselves wrong and only holding on to their negroes as something to make money out of." South Carolinians themselves had "retrograded," wrote Robert W. Barnwell in 1844, "and must soon fall into the same category."[44]

Close examination of the superficially impressive pro-slavery philosophy reveals, as Louis Hartz has brilliantly demonstrated, a "mass of agonies and contradictions in the dream world of southern thought." The peculiar institution could be squared theoretically with either the slave's humanity or democratic liberalism for whites, but not with both. Thus the necessity for justifying slavery, coupled with the white South's inability to escape its inherited liberalism or to deny the common humanity it shared with its Negro slaves, inspired "a mixture of pain and wild hyperbole."[45]

Recognizing that the religious argument by itself was a threat to the peculiar institution, one school of pro-slavery philosophers sought to preserve both slavery and the slave's humanity by sacrificing democratic liberalism and falling back to a neo-feudal insistence on the necessity of subordination and inequality in society. "Subordination rules supreme in heaven and must rule supreme on earth," asserted Bishop Elliott, and he did not attempt to disguise the repudiation of democratic liberalism that followed from this principle. Carried away by Revolutionary fervor, Southerners along with other Americans had "declared war against all authority and against all form"; they had pronounced all men equal and man capable of self-government. "Two greater falsehoods could not have been announced," Elliott insisted, "because the one struck at the whole constitution of civil society as it had ever existed, and because the other denied the fall and corruption of man."[46]

George Fitzhugh, the most logical and impressive of the pro-slavery philosophers and the leading exponent of southern neo-feudalism, would have preserved the humanity of the Negroes but denied freedom to the white masses by making both subject to the same serf-like subordination. Only thus could men be saved from the frightful corruption and turbulence of "free society." But southern planters were too much bourgeois capitalists and southern farmers were too much Jacksonian democrats to entertain the neo-feudalists' vituperation at "free society." "Soon counties, neighborhoods, or even individuals will be setting up castles," commented a sarcastic Alabamian.[47] Fitzhugh and his fellow intellectuals might talk all they pleased about reducing the masses, white and black, to serfdom, but practical politicians and publicists knew better than to fly so directly in the face of the South's liberal bias.

At the hands of men like James H. Hammond, therefore, neofeudalism became a racial "mud-still" theory, which divided society along the color line, relegating Negroes to bondage and reserving democratic liberalism for white men only. In the late forties a school of southern ethnologists arose to declare the Negro a distinct and permanently inferior species; and by 1854 Mississippi's Senator Albert G. Brown could invite Northerners to his state "to see the specimen of that equality spoken of by Jefferson in the Declaration of Independence." Nowhere else in the Union, said Brown, was there such an exemplification of Jefferson's beautiful sentiment. "In the South all men are equal. I mean of course, white men; negroes are not men, within the meaning of the Declaration."[48]

The racist argument was attacked with surprising vehemence by both religionists and feudalists. At least one Southerner went far beyond most northern abolitionists in asserting that "the Afri can is endowed with faculties as lofty, with perceptions as quick, with sensibilities as acute, and with natures as susceptible of improvement, as we are, who boast a fairer skin." Indeed, said this Virginian, if Negroes were "operated upon by the same ennobling impulses, stimulated by the same generous motives, and favored by the same adventitious circumstances, they would, as a mass, reach as high an elevation in the scale of moral refinement, and attain as great distinction on the broad theatre of intellectual achievement, as ourselves."[49]

While few Southerners would go as far as this, the religionists did maintain stoutly "that the African race is capable of considerable advance." Religious instruction of slaves would have been pointless without some such assumption, but the churchmen objected more fundamentally to the racist argument because it robbed the slave of his essential humanity. The feudalists, too, rejected the idea of racial inferiority, with Fitzhugh arguing that "it encourages and incites brutal masters to treat negroes, not as weak, ignorant and dependent brethren, but as wicked beasts, without the pale of humanity." The Negro was essential to the web of reciprocal duties and affections between superiors and subordinates that was supposed to knit the idyllic neo-feudal world together. "The Southerner is the negro's friend, his only friend," said Fitzhugh. "Let no intermeddling abolitionist, no refined philosophy dissolve this friendship."[50]

The debate between the religionists and feudalists, on the one hand, and the racists, on the other, defined the Old South's central dilemma. The first two championed personalism and the familial view of the peculiar institution. The religionists were willing to question the beneficence and permanence of slavery in order to assert the slave's humanity; and the feudalists were willing to surrender democratic liberalism in order to retain a personalized system of servitude. The racists, on the other hand, denied the slave's full human status in order to reconcile slavery with democratic liberalism for whites. The South's ingrained liberalism and Christianity, in short, were continually thwarting the logic-impelled effort to develop a fully rationalized, sheerly economic conception of slavery, warranted by the racist argument.

It was this inner conflict which produced the South's belligerent dogmatism in the recurrent crises of the fifties. The whole massive pro-slavery polemic had the unreal ring of logic pushed far beyond conviction. "I assure you, Sir," Fitzhugh confessed in a private letter, "I see great evils in Slavery, but in a controversial work I ought not to admit them."[51] If the South's best minds resolutely quashed their doubts, it is small wonder that crisis-tossed editors and politicians took refuge in positive and extreme positions.

The final open collision between the two contradictory tendencies in the South's thinking about slavery came on the very eve of the Civil War, when some Southerners relentlessly pursued the logic of slavery's beneficence to the conclusion that the foreign slave trade should be reopened. "I would sweep from the statute-book every interference with slavery," shouted a fire-eating South Carolina congressman. "I would repeal the law declaring the slave trade piracy; I would withdraw our slave squadron from the coast of Africa; and I would leave slavery unintervened against, wherever the power of the country stretches."[52]

Despite the lip service paid to the "positive good" doctrine, majority southern opinion was deeply shocked by its logical extension to sanction the foreign slave trade. Few Southerners were willing "to roll back the tide of civilization and christianity of the nineteenth century, and restore the barbarism of the dark ages," declared a Georgia newspaper, and churchmen denounced the proposal with special vehemence. Even one of its original advocates turned against it when he witnessed the suffering of the Negroes aboard a captured slave ship. This "practical, fair evidence of its effects has cured me forever," confessed D. H. Hamilton. "I wish that everyone in South Carolina, who is in favor of re-opening of the Slave-trade, could have seen what I have been compelled to witness. . . . It seems to me that I can never forget it."[53] This was the agony of the pro-slavery South under the shadow of Civil War.

How, then, did the fundamentally liberal, Christian, American South ever become an "aggressive slavocracy"?* How did it bring itself to flaunt an aristocratic social philosophy? To break up the American Union? To wage war for the purpose of holding four million human beings in a bondage that violated their humanity? The answer is that Southerners did not and could not rationally and deliberately choose slavery and its fruits over the values it warred against. Rather it was the very conflict of values, rendered intolerable by constant criticism premised on values Southerners shared, which drove them to seek a violent resolution.

Social psychologists observe that such value conflicts—especially when they give rise to the kind of institutional instability revealed by the ambiguities of southern slavery—make a society "suggestible," or ready to follow the advocates of irrational and aggressive action.† Thus it was fateful that the Old South de-

* The viewpoint of the present essay is not to be confused with the interpretation of the Civil War in terms of a "slave power conspiracy." Chauncey S. Boucher has demonstrated convincingly that the South was incapable of the kind of concerted action necessary for conspiracy. "*In Re* That Aggressive Slavocracy," *Mississippi Valley Historical Review,* VIII (June-September, 1921), 13-79. He is less persuasive, however, in demonstrating the equal inappropriateness of the designation "aggressive slavocracy." Boucher does admit (p. 30) that many Southerners "took a stand which may perhaps best be termed 'aggressively defensive.'" This is not too far from the attitude of the present essay, especially in view of Boucher's tantalizing suggestion (p. 70) that when Southerners talked of slavery as a divinely ordained institution, they were in the position of "saying a thing and being conscious while saying it that the thing is not true . . . but a position forced upon them by necessity of circumstances for their own immediate protection."

† Hadley Cantril, *The Psychology of Social Movements* (New York, 1941), 61-64. The social sciences have much to contribute to southern historical scholarship; in fact, the essential key to understanding the Old South seems to lie in the area of social psychology. Though Harry Elmer Barnes asserted as much nearly forty years ago, scholarly efforts in this direction have hardly moved

veloped an unusually able minority of fire-eating sectionalists, who labored zealously, from the 1830's on, to unite the South behind radical measures in defense of slavery. Though a majority of Southerners remained profoundly distrustful of these extremists throughout the ante-bellum period, their unceasing agitation steadily aggravated the South's tensions and heightened its underlying suggestibility. By egging the South on to ever more extreme demands, the Calhouns, Rhetts, and Yanceys provoked violent northern reactions, which could then be used to whip the South's passions still higher. At length, in 1860, capitalizing on intrigues for the Democratic presidential nomination, the fire-eaters managed to split the Democratic party, thus insuring the election of a Republican President and paving the way for secession.

---

beyond the naive enthusiasm of Barnes' suggestion that "southern chivalry" was "a collective compensation for sexual looseness, racial intermixture, and the maltreatment of the Negro."—"Psychology and History: Some Reasons for Predicting Their More Active Cooperation in the Future," *American Journal of Psychology*, XXX (October, 1919), 374. A psychologist has interpreted southern behavior in terms of defense mechanism, rationalization, and projection.— D. A. Hartman, "The Psychological Point of View in History: Some Phases of the Slavery Struggle," *Journal of Abnormal Psychology and Social Psychology*, XVII (October-December, 1922), 261-73. A psychoanalyst has traced the white South's treatment of the Negro to the general insecurities of Western man uprooted by industrialism, and to an unconscious sexual fascination with the Negro as "a symbol which gives a secret gratification to those who are inhibited and crippled in their instinctual satisfaction."—Helen V. McLean, "Psychodynamic Factors in Racial Relations," *Annals of the American Academy of Political and Social Science*, CCLIV (March, 1946), 159-66. And a sociologist has sought to explain the South in terms of a concept of "social neurosis."—Read Bain, "Man Is the Measure," *Sociometry: A Journal of Inter-Personal Relations*, VI (November, 1943), 460-64.

These efforts, while suggestive, seem hardly more systematic and considerably less cautious than the historian's unsophisticated, commonsense way of trying to assess psychological factors. Yet Hadley Cantril's *Psychology of Social Movements* has demonstrated that the infant discipline of social psychology can, even in its present primitive state, furnish the historian with extremely useful concepts. Historians of the Old South have special reason for pressing their problems on their brethren in social psychology, while the social psychologists may find in historical data a challenging area for developing and testing hypotheses. Especially rewarding to both historians and social scientists would be a collaborative study of ante-bellum southern radicalism and its peculiar locus, South Carolina.

Inflammatory agitation and revolutionary tactics succeeded only because Southerners had finally passed the point of rational self-control. The almost pathological violence of their reactions to northern criticism indicated that their misgivings about their moral position on slavery had become literally intolerable under the mounting abolitionist attack. "The South has been moved to resistance chiefly . . . by the popular dogma in the free states that slavery is a crime in the sight of GOD," said a New Orleans editor in the secession crisis. "The South, in the eyes of the North, is degraded and unworthy, because of the institution of servitude."[54]

Superimposed on this fundamental moral anxiety was another potent emotion, fear. John Brown's raid in October, 1859, created the most intense terror of slave insurrection that the South had ever experienced; and in this atmosphere of dread the final crisis of 1860-61 occurred. The press warned that the South was "slumbering over a volcano, whose smoldering fires, may at any quiet starry midnight, blacken the social sky with the smoke of desolation and death." Southerners believed their land to be overrun by abolitionist emissaries, who were "tampering with our slaves, and furnishing them with arms and poisons to accomplish their hellish designs." Lynch law was proclaimed, and vigilance committees sprang up to deal with anyone suspected of abolitionist sentiments. A Mississippian reported the hanging of twenty-three such suspects in three weeks, while the British consul at Charleston described the situation as "a reign of terror."[55]

Under these circumstances a large part of the southern white population approached the crisis of the Union in a state of near-hysteria. One man thought that "the minds of the people are aroused to a pitch of excitement probably unparalleled in the history of our country." "The desire of some for change," reported a despairing Virginian, "the greed of many for excitement, and the longing of more for anarchy and confusion, seems to have unthroned the reason of men, and left them at the mercy of passion and madness."[56]

Just as important as the hysteria which affected some Southerners was the paralysis of will, the despair, the sense of helplessness, which the excitement created in their more conservative fellows. Denying that the southern people really wanted to dissolve the Union, a Georgia editor saw them as being "dragged on, blindfolded, to the consummation of the horrid act." A "moral pestilence" had "swept over the South," said a prominent North Carolinian, "dethroning reason, & paralyzing the efforts of the best Union men of the country." But even some who decried the hysteria felt that "no community can exist & prosper when this sense of insecurity prevails," and concluded that almost any alternative was preferable to the strain of these recurrent crises. It was this conviction, more than anything else, which caused moderate men to give way to the bold and confident radicals.[57]

From the circumstances of the secession elections—the small turnouts, the revolutionary tactics of the fire-eaters, the disproportionate weighting of the results in favor of plantation areas, the coercive conditions under which the upper South voted, and the hysteria that prevailed everywhere—it can hardly be said that a majority of the South's white people deliberately chose to dissolve the Union in 1861. A member of South Carolina's secession convention frankly admitted that "the common people" did not understand what was at stake. "But whoever waited for the common people when a great movement was to be made?" he asked. "We must make the move and force them to follow. That is the way of all revolutions and all great achievements."[58]

The leaders made the move, and the people followed, but with what underlying misgivings the sequel only too plainly demonstrated. The first flush of enthusiasm was rapidly supplanted by an apathy and a growing disaffection which historians have identified as major factors in the Confederacy's failure. During the dark winter of 1864-65, North Carolina's Governor Zebulon Vance commented on the supineness with which the southern population received the invading Sherman. It was evidence, said Vance, of what he had "always believed, that *the great popular heart* is not now, and never has been in this war! It was a revolution of the *Politicians,* not the *People.*"[59]

And when the cause was lost, Southerners abandoned it with an alacrity which underscored the reluctance of their original commitment. It was left for a leading ex-fire-eater to explain why they returned to the Union of their fathers with so little hesitation. Standing before the Joint Congressional Committee on Reconstruction in 1866, James D. B. De Bow attested in all sincerity the South's willingness to fight once again for the flag of the Union. "The southern people," he said, "are Americans, republicans."[60]

Yet it is idle to wonder whether secession represented the deliberate choice of a majority of white Southerners, or to speculate about the outcome of a hypothetical referendum, free from ambiguity, coercion, and hysteria. Decisions like the one that faced the South in 1860-61 are never reached in any such ideal way. And even had the South decided for the Union, its and the nation's problem would have remained unsolved, and a violent resolution would only have been postponed. Slavery was doomed by the march of history and by the nature of Southerners themselves, but so deeply had it involved them in its contradictions that they could neither deal with it rationally nor longer endure the tensions and anxieties it generated. Under these circumstances the Civil War or something very like it was unavoidable. It was also salutary, for only the transaction at Appomattox could have freed the South's people—both Negro and white—to move again toward the realization of their essential natures as Southerners, liberals, Christians, and Americans.

CHAPTER FOUR

THE SOUTHERNER AS A FIGHTING MAN*

By David Donald

THE CONFEDERATE SOLDIER was, in most important respects, not materially different from one of Xenophon's hoplites or Caesar's legionnaires. He enlisted for a variety of reasons; he was brave or he was cowardly; he fought till the end of the war, he deserted, or he was killed, wounded, or captured. If it is hard to generalize about him, it is even more difficult to think of him as unique. His story is that of all soldiers in all wars.

In basic attitudes he was very much like World War II GI's. A recent study of *The American Soldier* would puzzle him by its sociological lingo, but, if translated into layman's language, it would not surprise him by its conclusions. Like his GI descendants, the Confederate soldier agreed that the infantry was the most dangerous and difficult branch of service, and he preferred his own equivalent of the air force—the cavalry. Depending upon what the psychologists call his "personal esprit," his "personal commitment," and his "satisfaction with status and job," he would have expressed varying opinions when asked how well the Confederate army was run. He did not have any very clear idea as to what caused the Civil War, but, if questioned, he would

* This essay was originally published in *The Journal of Southern History*, XXV (May, 1959), 178-93, under the title, "The Confederate as a Fighting Man," and is used with the permission of the editor.

very probably have responded as did ninety-one per cent of World War II soldiers who felt, "Whatever our wishes in the matter, we have to fight now if we are to survive."[1]

Johnny Reb was even more similar to Billy Yank, his opponent in the Union forces. In two fascinating and learned studies of the everyday life of Civil War soldiers Bell I. Wiley has amply proved that "the similarities of Billy Yank and Johnny Reb far outweighed their differences. They were both American, by birth or by adoption, and they both had the weaknesses and the virtues of the people of their nation and time."*

Yet contemporaries with opportunities to observe soldiers in both the opposing armies found the southern fighting man subtly and indefinably different. He looked "the genuine rebel." That astute British diarist, Colonel Fremantle, found that "in spite of his bare feet, his ragged clothes, his old rug, and tooth-brush stuck like a rose in his buttonhole," the Confederate warrior had "a sort of devil-may-care, reckless, self-confident look, which is decidedly taking."[2]

Most impartial observers found a want of discipline among Confederate troops, a peculiar indifference to "their obligations as soldiers."[3] At the outset of the war, one participant later wrote, "The Southern army . . . was simply a vast mob of rather ill-armed young gentlemen from the country."[4] Six months before Appomattox the inspector-general of the Army of Northern Virginia concluded that things had not greatly changed: ". . . the source of almost every evil existing in the army is due to the difficulty of having orders promptly and properly executed. There is not that spirit of respect for and obedience to general orders which should pervade a military organization. . . ."[5]

* Bell Irvin Wiley, *The Life of Billy Yank: The Common Soldier of the Union* (Inidianapolis, 1952), 361. My indebtedness in these pages to Professor Wiley's massive researches is very great. His studies provide a vivid and detailed portrait of the southern soldier.

The Southerners' want of military discipline is not surprising. Confederate soldiers were mostly recruited from the independent small farmers who composed the vast majority of the ante-bellum southern population.[6] They came from a society that was not merely rural but, in many areas, still frontier; and isolation of settlements, absence of established traditions, and opportunities for rapid social mobility encouraged a distinctive southern type of self-reliance.[7] In the years before the Civil War political democracy triumphed in the South, and demagogues repeatedly capitalized upon Southerners' resentments against the planter aristocrats. Even slavery was defended in terms of equalitarian ideals. "With us," said Calhoun, "the two great divisions of society are not the rich and poor, but white and black; and all the former, the poor as well as the rich, belong to the upper classes, and are respected and treated as equals. . . ."[8]

Southerners were citizens before they were soldiers, and they did not take kindly to military discipline. At the outbreak of the war they rushed to enlist, fearing the fighting would be over before they could get to the front. Instead of "fun and frolic,"[9] they soon learned that being a soldier meant drill, spit-and-polish, military discipline, and more drill. An Alabama enlisted man became disillusioned: "A soldier is worse than any negro on Chatahooche [sic] river. He has no privileges whatever. He is under worse task-masters than any negro. He is not treated with any respect whatever. His officers may insult him and he has no right to open his mouth and dare not to do it."[10]

Such a reaction was, of course, perfectly normal; it has happened in all American wars. Fifty-one per cent of our soldiers in World War II felt that discipline was "too strict about petty things" and seventy-one per cent thought they had "Too much 'chicken' to put up with."[11] But the distinctive thing about the Confederate army is that southern soldiers never truly accepted the idea that discipline is necessary to the effective functioning of a fighting force. They were "not used to control of any sort, and were not disposed to obey anybody except for good and sufficient reason given. While actually on drill they obeyed the word of command, not so much by reason of its being proper to obey a command, as because obedience was in that case necessary to the successful issue of a pretty performance in which they were interested. Off drill they did as they pleased, holding themselves gentlemen, and as such bound to consult only their own wills."[12]

They found routine training assignments tedious, and they shirked them. A Mississippi sergeant reported that his men objected to being put on details "because they said they did not enlist to do guard duty but to fight the Yankies."[13] When they did serve, they behaved with characteristic independence. Colonel Fremantle at first thought Confederate sentries "quite as strict as, and ten times more polite than, regular soldiers" when they challenged him as he entered Longstreet's camp. But when he complimented the Confederate commander, Longstreet "replied, laughing, that a sentry, after refusing you leave to enter a camp, might very likely, if properly asked, show you another way in, by which you might avoid meeting a sentry at all."[14]

On the march southern troops were seldom orderly. Even Stonewall Jackson had trouble with stragglers,[15] and Lee's men moved "at a slow dragging pace" and were "evidently not good marchers naturally." In spite of repeated orders from headquarters, Confederates could never see the need for carrying heavy packs, and they were "constantly in the habit of throwing away their knapsacks and blankets on a long march." Particularly in the early years of the war, southern soldiers found victory nearly as demoralizing as defeat, and after a battle "many would coolly walk off home, under the impression that they had performed their share."[16]

Toward their officers, and particularly toward their immediate superiors, they exhibited a typical democratic disrespect for authority. The whole highly stratified system of military organization, "in which hierarchies of deference were formally and minutely established by official regulation,"[17] was a denial of the principle of equality. Confederates disliked "the restrictions placed on the privates," when the officers were permitted to "go to town at option, stay as long as they please, and get gloriously drunk in and out of camp when it suits them to do so." Like one peevish Texan, they felt that officers "are living better and wear better clothes than they did before the war." Officers had, another private echoed hungrily, "bacon to eat, Sugar to put in their coffee and all luxuries of this kind," while the common soldier had "the hardships to undergo." Another Texan wrote home: ". . . I will stay and tuffit out with Col Young and then he can go to Hell . . . he has acted the dam dog and I cant tell him so if I do they will put me in the Guard House . . . but I can tell him what I think of him when this war ends . . . I will come [home] when my time is out or die I wont be run over no longer not to please no officers they have acted the rascal with me."[18] Clearly most Confederates would have agreed with the American soldier in World War II who grumbled: "Too many officers have that superior feeling toward their men. Treat them as if they were way below them. . . . What's the matter with us enlisted men, are we dogs?"[19]

Such resentments against a caste system are normal among democratic citizen-soldiers. But where American troops in World Wars I and II had to vent their aggressions in grumbling and goldbricking, Confederates more often took direct action against their superiors. Confederate court martial records are full of such cases as that of Private George Bedell of Georgia, who called his commanding officer "a damned son of a bitch, a damned tyrant, a damned puppy, a damned rascal." If an officer persisted in acting like a martinet, his men might ride him on a rail until he promised "better behavior,"[20] or they might petition for his resignation.[21]

In fact, to an extent almost unparalleled in any other major war, the Confederate common soldier was the master of his officers. Southern armies were organized upon the principle that the men might voluntarily choose their commanders. The system grew up without much planning. The peacetime militia, a quasi-social, quasi-political organization, had always elected officers, and the Confederate army was constituted on the same basis. When volunteers enlisted, they chose from among themselves noncommissioned officers, lieutenants, and captains; in general the man who organized and helped outfit a company was elected its captain. "The theory was," as George Cary Eggleston noted, "that the officers were the creatures of the men, chosen by election to represent their constituency in the performance of certain duties, and that only during good behavior."[22]   Only the high-ranking field officers were appointed by Richmond.

A wartime emergency compelled the Confederate government to continue the inefficient elective system. At first Southerners had thought the war would be short, and most original Confederate volunteers enrolled for only twelve months' service. In December, 1861, the Confederate Congress abruptly awoke to the fact that these troops, the mainstay of the southern army, would be mustered out in the spring. To oppose McClellan's magnificently equipped northern troops, the South would have only a skeleton army. Hurriedly the southern Congress passed a law to encourage re-enlistment by granting furloughs and bounties to veterans who promised once more to volunteer. As a special inducement the measure provided that all troops who re-enlisted should have the power to reorganize themselves into companies and elect new company officers; these companies, in turn, should "have the power to organize themselves into battalions or regiments and to elect their field officers." The law, as General Upton tersely remarked, should have borne the title, "An act to disorganize and dissolve the . . . Army."[23]

In the spring of 1862, while McClellan's army pushed up the Peninsula and Halleck's troops moved on Corinth, southern forces were "in the agony of reorganization."[24] In some few cases, company officers managed the elections with a high hand. A North Carolina officer, for example, had his men fall in with arms, read the official order for the election of a second lieutenant, and said: "Men, there are but two candidates for the office, and there is but one of them worth a damn. I nominate him. All who are in favor of electing Sergeant Blank, come to a shoulder. Company, Shoulder arms. . . . Sergeant, take charge of the company and dismiss them."[25]

But in most companies there was an orgy of electioneering. Candidates were "interested and busy." "I could start out here and now," a Georgia private reported, "and eat myself dead on 'election cake,' be hugged into a perfect 'sqush' by most particular eternal, disinterested, affectionate friends. A man is perfectly bewildered by the intensity of the affection that is lavished upon him. I never dreamed before that I was half as popular, fine looking, and talented as I found out I am during the past few days."[26] The demoralization did not end with the voting. After a typical election, a Mississippi volunteer recorded, "The new Lt. Col. celebrated his election by 'treating' the men of each company to a gallon or two of whiskey, consequently there is considerable noise in the air."[27]

The painful process of reorganization had a disastrous effect on military efficiency. The Confederate common soldier sharply reacted against discipline and order. The "men have defeated almost every good officer," T. R. R. Cobb lamented, "and elected privates and corporals to their places."[28] General E. P. Alexander agreed that "the whole effect was very prejudicial to the discipline of the army."[29] General Beauregard in the West and General

Joseph E. Johnston in the East united in reporting that their troops were "demoralized" by the elections.[30]

Though professional military men unanimously disapproved of the elective system, subsequent Confederate legislation retained it without material alteration. Until almost the end of the war Confederate companies were repeatedly disorganized by these political campaigns for military office. In September, 1862, a Mississippi company saw "Great electioneering" with "Party lines . . . sharply drawn, two tickets . . . in the field, and the adherents of each . . . manfully working for success."[31] The following April the proud First Virginia Infantry was almost wrecked when recently-added conscripts threatened to elect one of themselves lieutenant. That calamity was averted only when the colonel "told the Company in case any *raw recruit was elected* that he would instantly have him *examined* before the board," which weeded out incompetent officers.[32] As late as January, 1864, Texas troops prepared to choose new commanders. "There is great wire-pulling among the officers just at this time," one Confederate wrote his wife. "Some that I know of will not *reign* again unless I am much mistaken."[33]

Time after time Confederate military authorities demanded that the election of officers be stopped. "This system has almost utterly destroyed the efficiency of non-commissioned officers, whose services in the work of discipline are incalculably important," the assistant adjutant-general reported in November, 1863, "while it perpetuates day after day all the derelictions of duty winked at by successful aspirants." Secretary of War James A. Seddon agreed: ". . . the policy of elections . . . may be well questioned, since inseparable from it [arise] an undue regard to popularity, especially among the non-commissioned officers, and a spirit of electioneering subversive of subordination and discipline."[34]

Though militarily indefensible, the system was politically necessary, and it was retained until the closing months of the war.

Confederate soldiers, liberty-loving citizens from a democratic society, cherished the right to elect their officers, and the politicians defended them. Soldiers "are not automatons," a Confederate congressman insisted, "dancing to the turning of some official organ grinder. The best *mind* and the best *blood* in the country are in the army, and much of both are found in the ranks. They have not lost the identity of the citizen in the soldier."[35]   Even President Jefferson Davis justified the system: "The citizens of the several States volunteered to defend their homes and inherited rights . . . the troops were drawn from the pursuits of civil life. Who so capable to judge of fitness to command a company, a battalion or a regiment as the men composing it?"[36]

The election of officers unquestionably contributed to the chronic lack of discipline in Confederate forces, but it was also a reflection of the fact that southern soldiers were unwilling to obey orders which struck them as onerous or commanders who seemed to them unreasonable. Like a tedious refrain, the theme of poor discipline runs through the official reports of all Confederate commanders. Even the Army of Northern Virginia, for all its intense devotion to Lee, was poorly controlled. When Lee took command in 1862, his troops were described as "an 'Armed mob' . . . magnificent material, of *undisciplined individuality,* and, as such, correspondingly unreliable and disorganized."[37]   Three more years of fighting saw some improvement; yet in November, 1864, Lee sorrowfully announced: "The great want in our army is firm discipline."[38]

Few southern soldiers showed deference to the officers whom they themselves had elected, but some felt that there was another sort of rank which should be maintained and respected, namely, that of social position. "The man of good family felt himself superior, as in most cases he unquestionably was, to his fellow-soldier of less excellent birth; and this distinction was sufficient, during the early years of the war, to override everything like military rank."[39]

These upper-class Southerners belonged to that small group of planter, merchant, and professional families who still dominated the social and economic, if no longer the political, life of the region. Membership in this southern aristocracy depended not merely upon wealth but upon family, education, good breeding, and intelligence. Nineteenth-century equalitarian currents had eroded the political power once held by the southern gentry, but they had left the plantation ideal untouched as the goal of social aspiration.[40]

The members of this upper class were dedicated Southerners, but they saw no reason why war should seriously alter their pattern of life. Some brought along slaves to serve as their personal attendants while in the army. Such was Tom, who cared for Richard Taylor, son of a former President of the United States, throughout the war. A "mirror of truth and honesty," Tom "could light a fire in a minute under the most unfavorable conditions and with the most unpromising material, made the best coffee to be tasted outside of a creole kitchen, was a 'dab' at camp stews and roasts, groomed . . . horses . . ., washed . . . linen, and was never behind time."[41]

George Cary Eggleston has left a classic, if exaggerated, account of the life these young aristocrats under arms led during the opening months of the war: ". . . it was a very common thing indeed for men who grew tired of camp fare to take their meals at the hotel, and one or two of them rented cottages and brought their families there, excusing themselves from attendance upon unreasonably early roll-calls, by pleading the distance from their cottages to the parade-ground. Whenever a detail was made for the purpose of cleaning the camp-ground, the men detailed regarded themselves as responsible for the proper performance of the task by their servants, and uncomplainingly took upon themselves the duty of sitting on the fence and superintending the work. The two or three men of the overseer class who were to be found in nearly every company turned in some nimble quarters by standing other men's turns of guard-duty at twenty-five cents an hour; and one young gentleman of my own company, finding himself assigned to a picket rope post, where his only duty was to guard the horses and prevent them . . . from becoming entangled in each other's heels and halters, coolly called his servant and turned the matter over to him, with a rather informal but decidedly pointed injunction not to let those horses get themselves into trouble if he valued his hide."[42]

Such young bloods might not be numerous, but they contributed to the want of discipline in the Confederate forces. They resented having to take orders. When one well-to-do private could not take "a dozen face and a smaller number of foot or bath towels" on a campaign with him, he "actually wrote and sent into the captain an elegant note resigning his position."[43] "It is," wrote another of these snobs, "galling for a gentleman to be absolutely and entirely subject to the orders of men who in private life were so far his inferiors, & who when they met him felt rather like taking off their hats to him than giving him law and gospel."[44] When the gentleman-soldier found army regulations unduly restrictive, he was likely to defy them, and if he had good family connections, he was fairly certain not to suffer for his insubordination. A Mississippi judge complained that it was "but a mockery of form" to "convict a soldier of any offense, who has social position, friends, and influence."[45]

These southern aristocrats were, of course, at a great disadvantage in competing in company elections. A planter's son had to be facile in concealing his social superiority and skilful in the arts of mass persuasion if he hoped to rise from the ranks through popular choice. All the class tensions and prejudices felt against him in civilian life carried over into military service, and the poorer soldiers were suspicious of "the genteel men," who "think all you are fit for is to stop bullets for them, your betters, who call you poor white trash."[46] A high Confederate administrator concisely summarized the social consequences of having elected officers: ". . . in our armies . . . to be an officer is not necessarily to be a gentleman. . . ."[47]

If he was handicapped at the lower levels of advancement in the Confederate army, the southern aristocrat found that the upper command posts were reserved almost exclusively for men of his class. Far more than the Confederate civilian administration, which had few claims to social distinction and included among the cabinet officers a one-time plantation overseer, the son of a keeper of a dried-fish shop, and a penniless German orphan immigrant,[48] the southern army leadership was recruited from the most exclusive elements of ante-bellum society.

A list of southern generals reads like a roster of the South's best and oldest families. During the four years of war, one hundred and three men were given commissions as generals, lieutenant-generals, and major-generals in the Confederate army.[49] Senators, congressmen, governors, state legislators, and wealthy planters clustered thickly upon their family trees.[50] The fathers of these ranking Confederate officers included one president of the United States, two senators, two congressmen, three governors, one French nobleman, ten officers at the regular United States army, eleven physicians, and six lawyers. Their remote relatives were even more distinguished. One was a grandnephew of Patrick Henry, another of James Robertson, and yet another of Andrew Jackson. There were nephews of Matthew F. Maury, the oceanographer; A. B. Longstreet, the author and college president; and A. P. Butler, the South Carolina senator. These generals had the kind of education only wealth and breeding could procure. Most, naturally, had been to the United States Military

Academy, but others were graduates of Virginia Military Institute, South Carolina College, Harvard, Yale, Princeton, and assorted smaller southern schools.

It was natural that the Confederacy should turn to this trained leadership when hostilities broke out. But it is significant that as the war wore on and deaths and resignations made new promotions possible, the South continued to recruit its military leaders from the same small aristocratic social stratum. Southerners appointed to high military rank in 1864 were, to be sure, much younger than the commanders chosen in 1861, and a significantly smaller proportion of them had been trained at West Point.* But in family background, wealth, and social position there was no real change. At the end of the war as at its beginning the Confederacy recruited its military chiefs from its finest families.

Though the southern armies in the West were mostly raised from the rough, semi-frontier Gulf states, their commanders also came from the upper-class planter aristocracy. In the West as in the East, field officers were drawn almost exclusively from wealthy families, usually associated with planting, which had a long tradition of social leadership and military activity. Both groups of generals were well educated, though a somewhat higher proportion of those in the eastern theater had attended the United States Military Academy.† From the point of view of social position, the two groups were virtually interchangeable.

* The median age of generals, lieutenant-generals, and major-generals commissioned in 1861 was 51 years; the median age of those appointed in 1864 was 37. Of the 12 men commissioned at these ranks in 1861, 10 had attended the United States Military Academy; of the 29 commissioned in 1864, only 14 had been at West Point.

† Of the 38 generals, lieutenant-generals, and major-generals clearly identified with the western theater of operations, 57 per cent had attended the United States Military Academy; their mean age at the date of appointment to their highest rank was 40.7 years. Of the 50 top commanders identified with eastern operations, 64 per cent had been at West Point; their mean age at achieving highest rank was 39.8 years. Generals like Samuel Cooper, who were identified with neither theater of action, and those like Joseph E. Johnston, who fought for long periods in both, have been omitted from these computations.

The class line which separated field commanders from lower, elective officers was not completely impassable, but it was virtually so. The few who crossed it were made to feel conspicious as social misfits. Nathan B. Forrest, the West's most daring calvary leader, was never allowed to forget that he was "wholly without formal education" and that he had been in civilian life a trader in horses and slaves.[51] A Mississippi gentleman placed under Forrest indignantly expressed his "distaste to being commanded by a man having no pretension to gentility—a negro trader, gambler,—an ambitious man, careless of the life of his men so long as preferment be *en prospectu.*" "Forrest may be," he added, "the best Cav officer in the West, but I object to a tyrannical, hotheaded vulgarian's commanding me."[52] Forrests in the Confederacy were few; the southern army offered only limited opportunities for social mobility.

The Confederate army was, thus, at the same time an extraordinarily democratic military organization and an extraordinarily aristocratic one. The paradox was the reflection of the basic ambivalence of southern society itself, which believed in the equality of all white men and simultaneously recognized sharp gradations between the social classes.

At the outbreak of the war this ambiguous southern attitude toward democracy proved a major asset to the Confederate cause. There was little time to convert civilians into proper soldiers, and it was an advantage that southern recruits were sturdy, independent-minded individualists. Their subaltern officers often lacked training and knew "nothing of details or how to look after the thousand wants which arise and must be met."[53] Even the West Pointers at first needed experience in handling large numbers of men. In 1861 when General R. S. Ewell, who had previously commanded a company of dragoons on the Indian frontier, was told that the countryside around Manassas was bare of supplies for his men, he sallied forth on a cattle hunt himself. Late in the day he returned to camp triumphantly leading one bull to the slaughter. When one of his fellow officers "observed that the bull was a most respectable animal, but would hardly afford much subsistence to eight thousand men," the general ruefully exclaimed, "Ah! I was thinking of my fifty dragoons."[54] Under the circumstances it was just as well that southern recruits were not army regulars.

At the same time it was a decided southern asset to have recognized, trained leaders who required merely time and experience to develop into expert army commanders. There was some grumbling at times against the upper-class professional officers who pre-empted the high positions, particularly the staff officers, "young sprouts with bob-tailed coats and vast importance, . . . who obviously thought the war was gotten up that they might dazzle the world by their talents."[55] Occasionally President Davis had to yield to popular prejudices and appoint political generals of no very great military knowledge or aptitude, such as "Extra Billy" Smith, former governor of Virginia, who "was equally distinguished for personal intrepidity and contempt for what he called 'tactics' and for educated and trained soldiers, whom he was wont to speak of as 'those West Pint fellows.' "[56] But the Confederacy never saw an organized attempt to oust the military experts comparable to the northern Radical Republicans' campaign against the West Pointers in the Union army. In the South training, tradition, and social postion kept qualified officers in control.

But what was an advantage in the opening days of the war became a serious handicap later. When both opposing armies were little more than armed mobs, the Confederate soldier, fighting on his own terrain, could ignore orders, rely on his wits, and still achieve victory. But as gigantic and highly disciplined northern armies pressed forward, the Confederate, though still a magnificent individual fighter, was disadvantaged by his indifference to discipline. These differences must not be exaggerated; northern armies too were shockingly undisciplined by modern standards. But the Confederacy, with its shortages of men and materiel, could poorly afford the high price of individualism. In February, 1865, General Lee sadly concluded; "Many opportunities have been lost and hundreds of valuable lives have been uselessly sacrificed for want of a strict observance of discipline."[57]

The rigidity of social structure which had provided the Confederacy with a secure, trained top command at the outbreak of the war also became a disadvantage as the conflict continued. The Confederate high command showed a remarkable continuity through the four years of war. While the Army of the Potomac was led successively by McDowell, McClellan, Pope, Burnside, Hooker, and Meade, the southern forces in northern Virginia had only two generals-in-chief—Joseph E. Johnston and Robert E. Lee. As the war progressed and death or incapacity made room for fresh leaders, there were, of course, new faces in the Confederate high command, but these were from the same social class, with the same kind of training, and the same social outlook as their predecessors. Had the art of war remained unchanged, this continuity in Confederate leadership would have been only an advantage, but the Civil War, the first truly modern war, witnessed technological changes of an unprecedented nature—new kinds of rifles, new uses for artillery, new possibilities for railroad warfare. The northern winning team of Lincoln, Grant, and Sherman came from a more openly structured society, and was trained to improvise and adapt. Confederate leadership had an aristocratic hostility toward change.[58]

The Southerner as a fighting man, then, was a product of the paradoxical world that was the ante-bellum South, devoted to the principles of democracy and the practice of aristocracy. And to compound the paradox, the Southerner's assets at the outbreak of the war became his liabilities by its conclusion. Historians in seeking the reasons for the collapse of the Confederacy have correctly pointed to inadequate southern resources, poor transportation, unimaginative political leadership, and state rights. All these, and more, deserve to be taken into account; yet perhaps more basic to the Confederate failure was the fundamental ambivalence in the southern attitude toward democracy. Because of that weakness, the Southerner made an admirable fighting man but a poor soldier.

CHAPTER FIVE

RECONSTRUCTION: INDEX OF AMERICANISM

By GRADY MCWHINEY

UNTIL THIRTY YEARS ago scholars agreed that the decade following the Civil War was a tragic era, especially in the South. Ruled
by carpetbaggers, Negroes, and renegade scalawags instead of
by "decent white men," that section of the country was "reduced
to the very abomination of desolation." "It was the most soul-
sickening spectacle that Americans had ever been called upon to
behold," wrote John W. Burgess. "Every principle of the old
American policy was here reversed. In place of government by
the most intelligent and virtuous part of the people for the benefit
of the governed, here was government by the most ignorant and
vicious part of the population for the benefit, the vulgar, materialistic, brutal benefit of the governing set."[1]

Today most historians still consider the postwar period a tragic
one, but usually for a different reason. Products of an age that
is not shocked by Negro suffrage, they are inclined to deny
that Reconstruction was an unmitigated disaster for the South.
Revisionists have taught them to see some evidence of democratic
advance in the achievements of the Reconstruction regimes in the
fields of public education and internal improvements.[2]

But the democratic advance seems to many a modern eye to
have been painfully limited and compromised. The real tragedy,

in this revisionist view, was that the national reconstruction program was only insincerely democratic. It gave the Negro nominal political power without giving him economic power, and so condemned him to virtual reinslavement. The tragedy of Reconstruction was that it did not really reconstruct.

One may well puzzle over this peculiar Reconstruction that did not reconstruct, with its peculiar Southerners (presumably feudal-minded racists) who accepted more colorblind democracy than they could have been expected to, and who would have accepted more than they were forced to, and with its peculiar Yankees (presumably democratic idealists) who abandoned all too quickly any effort to make colorblind democracy stick. If one puzzles long enough, he may begin to perceive that these Southerners and these Yankees were acting in peculiarly similar ways. He may begin to suspect that Reconstruction was not so peculiar after all, that it may not have been so tragic after all—except as a reflection of the contradictions of Americanism.

Today Americans are remarkably alike. Their values and aspirations are similar. With few exceptions, they believe in democracy, progress, success, universal education, equal opportunities for all citizens, Mother, God, and country. Their tastes in literature, art, music, food, drink, clothing, houses, furniture, automobiles, and entertainment vary only slightly. According to the Kinsey reports even their sex lives are similar.

American society is so mobile that economic, social, or intellectual status is frequently difficult or impossible to determine. Salesmen dress like celebrities. Cadillacs are accessible to plumbers. By following advice readily available in newspapers and magazines, garbage collectors can learn to dress, talk, and even smell like bankers. A coal miner can fly to South Bend for a football game between Pitt and Notre Dame and, if his fingernails are clean, be mistaken for an industrialist. Fashion journals tell secretaries how to outdress executives' daughters. For a nominal price every American can obtain a product which allegedly prevents tooth decay.

Such opportunities were not always present. Nor was such homogeneity. In colonial America a man's class could be recognized by his dress and, as late as 1815, gentlemen still wore ruffles and silk stockings. Nineteenth-century technological developments, however, soon allowed the poor to ape the rich. The presidency of James Monroe marked the end of an era. He was the last chief executive to wear a wig. By the end of the ante-bellum period nearly all Americans dressed alike.

Aiding technology in effecting this revolution were two of the most pervasive themes in American history: the ideology of progress and the democratic dogma. Brought to the colonies by Europeans, both doctrines were subtly shaped by Americans and have enjoyed almost universal approval since the Jacksonian period. The majority of Americans, without having heard of the Enlightenment, accepted unquestioningly the belief that men and institutions (especially American men and institutions) could attain here on earth a state of perfection once thought possible only for Christians in a state of grace, and for them only after death. Not to believe in both material and individual progress quickly became un-American. By hard work any man could become successful. The newer religions even promised earthly salvation for the most miserable sinner. A man born in a log cabin could become president. Indeed, for a time, it was hard for a man not born in a log cabin to become president.

Complementing the ideology of progress was the liberating tendency of American democracy. To develop their talents, it was argued, men must be free from traditional restraints. They must have freedom to get ahead, to make something of themselves, to start a new business, religion, or poltical party. But democracy was also a leveling process. If the race to perfection was to be run fairly, the participants must start together. Men must have equal opportunities.

Combined, the progressive and democratic doctrines have encouraged (among other things): the accumulation of wealth, westward expansion, "manifest destiny," immigration from Europe, extension of the suffrage, political demagoguery, "common man" culture, crime and violence, religious diversity and religious conformity, erosion of the family unit, sundry reform movements, and technological development.

One of the great myths of history is that somehow the South escaped the intellectual forces which shaped American thought and action. Tied to slavery from colonial times until 1865, Southerners supposedly developed a separate nationalism, glorified and practiced the plantation ideal and its concomitant philosophy of aristocracy and white supremacy. Democracy and progress found no supporters in the Old South. Even the failure to win independence in the 1860's scarcely changed the Bourbon attitude of white Southerners, who continued to exploit the Negro and follow a reactionary policy of racial discrimination.

The preceding essays have belabored this myth, insisting that in most ways faith in democracy developed in the South as it did in other parts of America. Southerners were likewise just as devoted as other Americans to progress, especially material progress. The whole colonial experience of Southerners was one of improving themselves by acquiring farms near the Atlantic coast, or moving westward. The westward trek of Southerners continued throughout the antebellum years. Like their Yankee cousins, southern migrants were men on the make, driven to the frontier by the ideology of progress and the liberating theme of democracy. They knew that in America individual progress was measured in dollars and cents, and they had faith in their ability to succeed in the virgin land beyond the Appalachians. The industrious and lucky ones were not disappointed. Aided by technological discoveries which improved agriculture, transportation, and manufacturing, many Southerners prospered during the ante-bellum period. Particularly in the lower South, cotton was a great democratizing influence before 1860. It could be cultivated profitably on a few acres by one man, or on large plantations by many slaves. Men could climb to riches over bales of cotton.[3]

Southerners joined other Americans in the Jacksonian rebellion against entrenched privilege. In fact, Andrew Jackson received some of his largest majorities in the South, where popular culture, universal suffrage for white males, and other leveling developments also won victories. Before the Civil War southern "men of the people" like W. R. W. Cobb, Alabama's "friend of the poor against the rich," who sang such original compositions as "Uncle Sam is rich enough to give us all a farm," were unbeatable politicians. According to recent studies, by 1860 white Southerners enjoyed a large measure of political, social, and economic democracy.[4]

If most Southerners believed in progress and democracy, why were Negroes denied liberty and equality in the Old South? Part of the answer is that throughout the nineteenth century there was an aberration in the thinking of all white Americans about the Negro. Nowhere is this better demonstrated than in the diaries and letters of Union soldiers.[5] Although considered human, "colored" peoples (such as Negroes, Indians, and Orientals) were regarded as inferiors by most Americans. Ironically, Americans believed in equality, but they also believed that some men were more equal than others. This perversion of the doctrine of equality was more apparent in the South because of its large Negro population, but it also existed in the North.

Knowing that few Yankees practiced equalitarianism, Southerners nevertheless had an uneasy conscience. True, they sought religious, philosophical, scientific, historical, and sociological justification for slavery. But the Southerner was too American to be convinced by his own arguments. One thing he did know, however: slavery was profitable. Without slaves, Southerners were certain they would fall behind the rest of America in the progressive race. As businessmen, they did not want to lose their investments or gamble with the uncertainties of a free labor supply. They were as grasping as their northern kinsmen. The indulgent master, the fabled southern planter of cavalier extravagance existed more in the mind of Henry Timrod than in fact. Plantation mansions were exceptions in the architectural pattern of the Old South;[6] most planters lived in rather crude houses and enjoyed few luxuries. None were as wealthy as the richest Northerners. Southern slaveholders were not knights of the round table, but men of the market place. Intellectually, their culture was as sterile as the dreary romances their wives and daughters read. Planters damned the dry or rainy weather when they met, and talked about the price of staples, land, and slaves, not about the philosophy of Plato or Aristotle. Clearly, ante-bellum Southerners were men of progress. They favored better methods of cultivation, improvements in transportation and technology, and higher profits. "No class of people in the world are so dependent on Science . . . as the planter," wrote a slaveholder in 1859.[7]

The great majority of Southerners owned no slaves (nearly three-fourths of all free Southerners had no connection with slavery through either family ties or direct ownership), yet even these non-slaveholders had practical, thoroughly American reasons for defending the "peculiar institution" to the end. Owning slaves was the way to wealth and success in the ante-bellum South, and men who did not own slaves hoped to acquire human chattels some day. In a real sense, emancipation would endanger their chance of success. Thus, Southerners faced an intellectual dilemma: how to be at the same time progressive and democratic and yet dominate the Negro.

Ironically, one reason why Southerners lost their struggle to preserve slavery was because they were too democratic. "Universal suffrage—furloughs & whiskey, have ruined us," wrote a high-ranking Confederate general.[8] The extreme liberty practiced by state rightists, the frequently malicious criticism of civil and military officials by the unmuzzled Confederate press, the lack of discipline in the army (fostered by the election of numerous officers), and the high rate of desertion by soldiers and disaffection by civilians contributed more to the destruction of the Confederacy than stronger northern armies. Superior to the South in resources, the North could afford democracy. Lacking a distinct nationalism, the South could not.

Throughout their entire history down to Appomattox, then, Southerners had shown an unshakable devotion to both democracy and material progress, and, in case of conflict between the two, a disposition to bend their democratic ideals to accommodate their progressive appetites. But were the Yankees so different? While marching to "The Battle Hymn of the Republic" it had been easy for them to picture the Civil War as a struggle between their own democratic idealism and the South's materialistically-based racism. But Appomattox was not the end of the story; in a sense it was but the prelude to its climatic and most revealing phase. For in the sequel of Reconstruction white Northerners and white Southerners discovered a spiritual brotherhood which, however unedifying to a later generation, resulted in a durable reunion. In this spiritual brotherhood material progress took precedence over democracy.

Southerners opened the drama of Reconstruction by manifesting a disposition—such was the paradoxical situation created by defeat—to accept a large measure of democratization, including a goodly dose of colorblind democracy, in order to get back on the progress road. "The war being at an end, . . . and the questions at issue . . . having been decided, I believe it to be the duty of every one to unite in the restoration of the country, and the re-establishment of peace and harmony," wrote General Robert E. Lee. "By doing this and encouraging our citizens to engage in the duties of life with all their heart and mind . . . our country will not only be restored in material prosperity, but will be advanced in science, in virtue and in religion."[9]

Southerners were so anxious for a share in American material prosperity that they complied with every demand made upon them for readmission to the Union. Arguing that actually they had never been out of the Union, they renounced secession, abolished slavery, repudiated the Confederate debt, and, as a result of demands by such determined congressional leaders as Thaddeus Stevens and Charles Sumner, even temporarily consented to try Negro suffrage. "I was not disappointed at the result of the war," wrote a Georgian. "Thad. Stevens would be as safe here as in Pennsylvania," said a Virginian. "Should you visit Mississippi I would be pleased to have you at my house," a stranger informed Senator John Sherman.[10] James L. Alcorn, a former brigadier who had suffered financial ruin during the war, admitted: ". . . you were right Yankee! You have established your power; . . . we are and ever have been in the Union; secession was a nullity. We will now take the oath to support the Constitution and the laws of the United States. . . ."[11] As proof of his sincerity, Alcorn became the Republican governor of Mississippi in 1869 and a Republican member of the United States Senate in 1871. He also recouped his financial losses and increased his property holdings.

Of course, not all Southerners were as easily reconstructed as Alcorn. Many able men were disenfranchised and prohibited from holding office. Some, like Judah P. Benjamin, left the South and found economic opportunities abroad. Edmund Ruffin, one of the most determined secessionists, committed suicide; John J. Pettus,

Mississippi's war governor, spent the remaining two years of his life as a disillusioned recluse.

But Ruffin and Pettus were exceptions. Eventually, only seventy-one of the 656 prominent Confederates who lived long enough to make postwar readjustments "failed to recover a substantial portion of the position and prestige they had enjoyed at the Confederacy's peak."[12] Denied the right to hold public office, Jefferson Davis sought to rehabilitate himself economically. For a time he served as president of a life insurance company. When it went bankrupt, he tried to start a steamship line. Only after repeated economic failures did he return to his plantation and devote himself to glorifying the Old South and the Lost Cause.

A number of leaders joined the carpetbag and Negro governments and returned to power sooner than others. In Mississippi Albert G. Brown, a former governor, advocated political expediency and submission to Radical Reconstruction. By 1868 such prominent Alabama Democrats as Lewis E. Parsons, Alexander McKinstry, Judge Samuel F. Rice, and Alexander White had joined the Republican party. Motivated partly by personal political ambition, they also believed that as Republicans they could best help their own as well as their state's economic recovery. General William C. Wickham, of Virginia, endorsed the Republican party less than a month after Appomattox. He soon became president of the Virginia Central Railroad, and three years later president of the Chesapeake and Ohio. In New Orleans General James Longstreet actually led an army of Negroes against Confederate veterans. His reward was lucrative posts from successive Republican administrations. James L. Orr, of South Carolina, marched into the National Union Convention in 1866 arm in arm with a Massachusetts general. When President Andrew Johnson's candidates lost the fall congressional elections, however, Orr changed his allegiance to the victorious Radicals. In North Carolina James G. Ramsey, Richmond M. Pearson, and General Rufus Barringer were early advocates of Negro suffrage and industrialization. General George Maney, of Tennessee, became president of the Tennessee and Pacific Railroad and a Republican.

Clearly, not all of these scalawags were renegade "poor whites." Many of them were former Whigs, seeking a new political home. Others were simply trying to adjust to the new order or to get ahead politically and financially.[13] That they were not always concerned with the means by which success was obtained is illustrated by the case of Josephus Woodruff. A native South Carolinian, Woodruff deserted the Democratic party to become clerk of the state senate, and to insure that his company received all the state's official printing business. In 1874 he confided to his diary a conversation in which the influential Negro legislator Robert Smalls "Said if anyone was to offer him $50,000 to vote against me he would indignantly decline." Woodruff replied that he "Was pleased to hear it, but would be glad to see the offer made and accepted, and the amount equally divided between us." Three years later Smalls was convicted of having accepted a $5,000 bribe from Woodruff to vote for a printing bill.[14]

The Radical regimes in the South lasted only a few years, however, and many scalawags either lost their positions of power and privilege or in order to save them were forced to become Democrats. After abandoning the Republican party Joseph E. Brown not only weathered investigations of his honesty, but remained one of the most powerful politicians in Georgia and one of the leading industrialists in the South. Generals P. G. T. Beauregard and Jubal A. Early had yielded to the blandishments of the Republican-supported Louisiana Lottery Company and received substantial sums for presiding over the drawings. "Ever since Longstreet feathered his nest, there has been an itching about Beauregard's stern for a similar application, and, to those who know him, it was evident time would find him in the radical camp," wrote an impoverished Confederate general.[15] Yet both Beauregard and Early managed to retain their posts after the Democrats returned to power in Louisiana.

Without consistent Federal support, torn by internal conflicts within their own state parties, and hurt by a nation-wide depression, Republican officeholders were driven from the South in the 1870's. Charged with fraud and corruption, they were ousted by pragmatic Democrats who did not shrink from using violence, intimidation, and stuffed ballot boxes.   *896/8*

The Radical Reconstruction experiment failed for a number of reasons, but foremost, perhaps, was northern disillusionment with the Negro. "In spite of all their efforts, the abolitionists . . . failed to create widespread determination in any part of the nation to grant to the freedman social or political or economic equality," writes a perceptive scholar.[16] For the most part Negro suffrage was a political expedient which was endorsed by northern voters only because politicians "waved the bloody shirt." Senator T. O. Howe wrote in 1875 that the Civil War was not "fought for the 'nigger' " and the Negro was not "the end and aim of all our effort."[17] James H. Paine tried to insert a promise of suffrage for southern Negroes into the platform of the Wisconsin Republican Convention in 1865, but the delegates voted overwhelmingly against his proposal.[18]

When Northerners discovered that former Confederates would defend Yankee railroad and industrial interests as vigorously as they fought Yankee armies, the Negro vote became less important. "There can be no way so sure to make the late rebels of the South loyal men and good citizens," declared the New York *Commercial and Financial Chronicle* in 1865, "as to turn their energies to the pursuits of peace, and the accumulation of wealth."[19] By the 1870's Southerners had proved that they were willing to help bring the American dream of a materialistic utopia to fulfillment. Newspapers throughout the South reflected and helped shape their readers' enthusiastic devotion to material progress. "Country papers gave those patron saints of the New South . . . a wide reading public. Liberal news space was devoted to excerpts from the *Manufacturer's Record*. In many areas . . . there was something of religious fervor in the numerous editorials on immigration and on exploitation of land, timber, and mineral resources. Since 1867 country editors have told their readers that they were living in a land of golden opportunity. Their section . . . needed only population, capital, industry, and mechanical knowledge to make it wealthy."[20]

The struggle for power in the South, as well as in the rest of the country, during the Reconstruction period should not be treated as a contest between the forces of good and evil. Rather it should be considered as an encounter between rival economic interests seeking exclusive privileges and trying to control the various states through two different political parties. After 1868 financiers, not radicals, dominated southern politics. According to Horace Mann Bond, "the Louisville and Nashville Railroad, the Alabama and Chattanooga Railroad, . . . the banking houses of the Cookes, of Russell Sage, of the Morgans and the Drexels, loom more significantly in Alabama Reconstruction than do the time-honored figures of the history books." In the struggle for state bonds and land grants, Democrats supported the L. & N., whose president was backed by August Belmont, national chairman of the Democratic party and the American agent for the Rothschilds. In turn, Republicans supported the A. & C., which had the backing of Russell Sage, Henry Clews, and William D. ("Pig Iron") Kelley. Initially, the L. & N. got the upper hand, but after Republicans took over the state the A. & C. put pressure on them to eliminate the L. & N. During the depression of the 1870's, however, the A. & C. went bankrupt, and when the Democrats returned to power in 1874 the L. & N. was assured of success.[21]

In Virginia railroad promoters also played an important role in the state's reconstruction. One of the leading figures in this struggle for power was General William Mahone, who in order to protect his railroad interests successively shifted his political allegiance from the Radicals, to the Conservatives (Democrats), to the Readjusters.[22] Even General Robert E. Lee, who was named president of the Valley Railroad a few months before his death in 1870, succumbed to the promotion fever.

By the time the Reconstruction experiment ended, Southerners were thoroughly Americanized. Every southern state was controlled by businessmen or the friends of business.[23] The dream of an industrial millennium captivated nearly every mind. "The South found her jewel in the toad's head of defeat," said the most famous southern apostle of progress.[24] The Lost Cause was not forgotten, but the Yankee was forgiven. Instead of lynching Congressman Lucius Q. C. Lamar for eulogizing Charles Sumner, Mississippians made him a United States senator.

Though the Negro once again was relegated to a subservient position in the South, he too pursued the goal of material progress. Booker T. Washington, the most famous Southerner of his day, advised his people: "Cast down your bucket where you are—cast it down in making friends in every manly way of the people of all races by whom we are surrounded. Cast it down in agriculture, mechanics, in commerce, in domestic service, and in the professions. And in this connection it is well to bear in mind that whatever other sins the South may be called to bear, when it comes to business, pure and simple, it is in the South that the Negro is given a man's chance in the commercial world."[25] If Washington's thoroughly American and materialistic plan to raise his race to equality was not entirely successful, it was nevertheless applauded by white Southerners.

Twentieth-century international developments have helped shape a New Reconstruction program. Today many Americans, aware that their future prosperity as well as the fate of their country may well be determined by an overwhelmingly "colored" world, insist that national survival depends upon practicing colorblind democracy. A number of white Southerners recognize the logic of this argument, but most of them are still too American either to endorse racial equality or to renounce their democratic pretenses. Like most Americans, they boast of being common men while they admire eliteness. They see no inconsistency between the doctrine of personal equality and the selecting of beauty queens. They admire the Queen of England more than the wife of their own chief executive. They send their children to schools that do not educate so that they will not be maladjusted in a society that reveres television and movie stars. They suspect that integration is a diabolical scheme to destroy not only their present social and economic status but their chance of future success. The white ladies of Montgomery, Alabama, who chauffeured their bus-boycotting maids to and from work, are merely comfort-loving Americans, not integrationists.

Aware that white northerners also indulge in democratic hypocrisy, white Southerners fear that they will be jim-crowed by other Americans if Negro equality is practiced in the South. Subconsciously, Southerners realize that the genius of America is inequality. They will accept colorblind democracy only if convinced that the alternative is loss of status and the chance of future success. Briefly this was the situation during the Old Reconstruction, when the white Southerner was ready to acquiesce in Negro suffrage; and now the New Reconstruction seems to promise a similar but more lasting acquiescence in a limited amount of school desegregation. The great segregationists' bastion at Little Rock has fallen because those ultra-typical Americans, the members of the Downtown Businessmen's Association, hold racial exclusiveness less dear than the good name and the continued growth and prosperity of their fair city. For Governor Faubus' constituents, like other Southerners and other Americans, are more devoted to the ideology of material progress than to either racial superiority or the democratic dogma.

CHAPTER SIX

THE CENTRAL THEME REVISITED

By George B. Tindall

It is now more than thirty years since Ulrich Bonnell Phillips defined the unifying principle of southern history as "a common resolve indomitably maintained" by the white man that the South "shall be and remain a white man's country." "The consciousness of a function in these premises," he said, "whether expressed with the frenzy of a demagogue or maintained with a patrician's quietude, is the cardinal test of a Southerner and the central theme of southern history."[1]

The search for monistic central themes is a quest that has attracted thinkers in all times, and one that seems to have a special fascination for students of the South, but it is also one that has been confounded repeatedly by the diversity of human experience, in the South as well as elsewhere. In its geography and history, in its society and economy, in its politics and ideology, the South has experienced a diversity that resists synthesis under any all-encompassing concept yet found, whether it be in some unfortunate phrase like "sowbelly and segregation" or in the grandiose schemes of romanticism, economic determinism, or the ideology of white supremacy—although each of these may throw considerable light upon the character and history of the South.

At the same time, however, it cannot be denied that a preoccupation with the issue of race, its mythology and its symbolism has been one of the major themes of southern history, with innumerable ramifications into every aspect of southern life. Every Southerner of the present generation can recognize the continuing validity of James Weldon Johnson's observation in 1912 that "no group of Southern white men could get together and talk for sixty minutes without bringing up the 'race question.' If a Northern white man happened to be in the group, the time could be safely cut to thirty minutes."[2]

But to speak of a preoccupation with issues of race is not to say that there is or ever has been a monolithic unity in the thought or practice of southern whites on the subject. For attitudes have ranged from the anti-slavery Negrophobia of Hinton Rowan Helper to the liberal equalitarianism of George Washington Cable. Nor can it be said that either the theory or social reality of race relations in the South has been constant. They have, in fact, gone through numerous changes: from the uncertain status of the first Negroes in early Virginia through the evolution of slavery, from the post-Revolutionary liberalism to the pro-slavery argument, from emancipation and Radical Reconstruction to Redemption and the rise of the twentieth-century system of white supremacy, and into accelerated change in the present generation.

Yet, underlying the diversity of southern experience, certain lines of continuity are apparent. Theory and practice with respect to race relations have moved chiefly in two broad channels developed in the eighteenth and nineteenth centuries. The first of these is what Gunnar Myrdal has labelled "the American Creed." It stems principally from the eighteenth-century philosophy of the rights of man, but has important sources also in Christianity and English law. The ideals "of the essential dignity of the individual human being, of the fundamental equality of all men, and of certain inalienable rights to freedom, justice, and a fair opportunity," says Myrdal, "represent to the American people the essential meaning of the nation's early struggle for independence."[3]

The existence of these ideals, he maintains, has set up a tremendous ideological conflict, which he pictures as largely a psychological struggle within the individual who recognizes that racial prejudices and discriminatory practices do not conform to the generally accepted creed. But in the South, resistance to the "American Creed" has been bolstered by a counter creed which has supplied the white Southerner with racial sanctions that are somewhat more than the expression of individual racial prejudice.

If Myrdal's "American Creed" was primarily a product of the struggle for independence, then what Howard W. Odum has called the "credo of the South with reference to the Negro"[4] was in large part the product of sectional conflict. Thrown on the defensive by the vigorous abolitionist assault of the 1830's, the southern leadership perfected an elaborate philosophical justification for the "peculiar institution" of slavery. Whether or not the masses of southern whites were aware of its existence, its influence was pervasive and they accepted most of its basic tenets.

Although the Civil War and Reconstruction shattered the institutional basis upon which race relations had rested in the South for more than two centuries, even this profound upheaval failed to undermine the prevailing patterns of thought on race—pro-slavery doctrines had penetrated too deeply into southern thinking. During the brief period when President Andrew Johnson was able to leave conservative whites in charge of southern state governments, most of them adopted more or less elaborate "black codes," which sought to retain as much white control over the civil and economic status of Negroes as the new conditions permitted.

As soon as the northern radicals established their dominance, however, the black codes were wiped out. It was now clear that the prevailing southern ideas on race would have to find new modes of social expression. By the time white southern Democrats secured control of their states in the 1870's, new constitutional amendments guaranteed certain rights to Negro citizens. The national Democratic party in 1872 announced its acceptance of these amendments as a *fait accompli*. And while the southern Democrats' rise to power had come about in campaigns characterized by the intimidation of Negroes, those campaigns and the Compromise of 1877 had also been accompanied by Democratic commitments to respect the newly-won legal rights of the freedman.

The Democratic Redeemers represented white supremacy, which they believed to be the supremacy of intelligence and character, but they also represented a measure of moderation that did not equate white supremacy as yet with Negro proscription. For a number of years, as Professor C. Vann Woodward has pointed out, certain forces operated as elements of restraint against the triumph of extreme racism. These forces were southern liberalism, a weak thing at best; northern liberalism and the threat of renewed intervention; the conservative spirit of the Redeemers; and the radicalism of the agrarian movement, which for a time united whites and Negroes in their common economic grievances.[5]

With the collapse of these restraints in the 1890's, something endemic in southern thought asserted itself with new vehemence. Because of new circumstances and because of the Reconstruction amendments it found expression in new instrumentalities, but by the first decade of the twentieth century the main patterns of a new "peculiar institution" of white supremacy had become clear. These patterns embodied the now familiar forms of economic subordination, disfranchisement, segregation, and proscription.

One basic aspect of this new peculiar institution, the economic subordination of Negroes under systems of tenancy and wage labor, had never been challenged seriously even by Radical Republicans, whose abundant gifts to enterprise were for the most part distributed to petitioners better organized to push their claims than were the freedmen. Southern whites remained in control of the land and the chief agencies of economic activity, and the labor laws after Reconstruction increasingly reflected the domination of the landowning and merchant classes, sometimes reducing laborers to peonage even with the connivance of the law. Later, with the rise of industry, Negroes found themselves either excluded or limited to the more menial jobs. Even in traditional "Negro jobs" they were faced with the growing competition of white workers. These patterns have remained fairly consistent even into the middle of the twentieth century, with mechanization in agriculture now threatening the Negroes' position in the most traditional of all "Negro jobs."

Other developments were somewhat slower in coming, their evolution stretching out over the generation that followed Reconstruction. Disfranchisement of Negroes was accomplished by the use of fraud and intimidation until such methods became institutionalized in the development of literacy tests and other legal qualifications for the vote and, what was eventually more important, the white primary. The proscription of Negroes from public office was increasingly required until, after the turn of the century, Negroes disappeared entirely from the picture except for a few scattered Republican appointees.

So far the movement constituted a true reaction. Economic subordination, disfranchisement, and political proscription involved a return to conditions roughly approximating those before emancipation. But the keystone of the whole new structure may be found in the caste symbolism of racial segregation. The patterns of segregation were somewhat longer in developing because they represented something rather new. Racial segregation as known in the twentieth century was not a necessary accompaniment of slavery, for that institution in itself provided the necessary symbols and instrumentalities of white supremacy. Segregation as a general civil institution and as a hallowed social myth is essentially a phenomenon of the twentieth century.[6]

When the forces of white supremacy had completed their work, the product was remarkably similar in purpose and appearance to the slave codes of ante-bellum days, even more complex and thoroughgoing in application, yet different because of new circumstances and especially because of the Reconstruction amendments. If the Negroes' caste status could not be defined legally in terms of slavery or of laws with specific racial discriminations, it could be defined in terms of economic legislation, the establishment of restrictions upon the suffrage, and certain other formal restrictions under the convenient legal doctrine of "separate but equal" facilities, although segregation in practice seldom meant equal facilities and often involved the complete ostracism of Negroes from community activities.

Looking upon their work and finding it good, the authors of the new dispensation saw little need for developing new rationalizations. Rather they found that "Numerous theories, already well-worn in the ante-bellum period, were at hand to justify the caste system."[7] These were the ingrained doctrines of the pro-slavery argument. The Scriptural justification of slavery, for example, reappeared in later years as an argument for discrimination and segregation. The letters column of almost any southern white newspaper will reveal citations of the curse called down by the drunken Noah upon his son as evidence that the divine plan ordained the descendants of Ham to be the servants of servants. St. Paul's declaration that God has "made of one blood all nations of men for to dwell on all the face of the earth" is modified, the Scriptural segregationist insists, by the additional revelation that He has "determined . . . the bounds of their habitation."[8]

The economic justification of slavery similarly re-emerged in the contention that subordinated Negroes afforded a superior supply of "mud still" labor. "With all their faults and short-comings," one Southerner remarked, in echo of ante-bellum sentiments, "there is at least no Anarchist-making material in them."[9]   The idea that slavery was a school of civilization was completely transformed after emancipation into the argument that Negroes must now find the opportunity for progress in their own institutions, in the development of their own leadership, even in the development of a separate culture.   Thus a contemporary southern governor has defended school segregation "in order that we might maintain the older culture of the white race and encourage the growth of the new and rapidly developing culture of the Negro race . . . through good will and pride in the integrity of our respective racial cultures and way of life. . . ."[10]

Some points of the pro-slavery argument were actually charged with added potency by postwar developments.   In a variety of unpremeditated ways, the ante-bellum web of personal association between whites and Negroes broke down following emancipation. The tenant system disrupted the plantation community; residential segregation gradually came to be accepted as the natural pattern in the newer sections of southern towns and cities; a pattern of segregated schools was set by northern missionary agencies bent upon supplying the supposedly peculiar educational needs of a people newly freed from slavery; and Negroes found opportunities for independence and responsibility in their own separate churches. As the races drew apart and as opportunities for personal acquaintance, even in a paternalistic setting, diminished, the ante-bellum argument that the Negro was biologically distinct from and inferior to the white man gained an acceptance which had been prohibited during the slavery regime by the opposition of churchmen and by the more intimate knowledge of Negroes.   By the end of the nineteenth century a number of writers had carried the argument to its ultimate extreme, in the "Negro a beast" school of thought. While the majority of southern whites have doubtless preferred a more moderate version, which regards racial differences as simply predisposing the races to different functions in society, there can be little doubt that the biological argument has been fundamental to the justification of caste in its changing forms.[11]

Just as the institutional and personal estrangement of the races gave new currency to the biological inferiority argument, so the bitter controversies of the Reconstruction years, which were viewed largely as race conflicts, exacerbated the ante-bellum assumption of a fundamental antagonism of race. Even Jefferson had been frightened by the potentialities of race conflict if the restraints of slavery should be removed; and the appeal to social stability became one of the most potent weapons in the pro-slavery arsenal.* In like manner, the new peculiar institution, especially its segregation feature, came to be defended as essential "in the interest of orderly government and the maintenance of Caucasian civilization."[12]

White Southerners interpreted almost any exercise of the freedmen's new physical and social mobility as a bid for "social equality." The precise meaning of the term was uncertain, but the hypersensitivity of white men to the remotest suggestion of sexual relations between Negro men and white women charged it with overtones of fear. By the 1890's ambitious politicians were play-

* "Deep-rooted prejudices entertained by the whites," wrote Thomas Jefferson, "ten thousand recollections, by the blacks, of the injuries they have sustained; new provocations; the real distinctions which nature has made; and many other circumstances, will divide us into parties, and produce convulsions, which will probably never end but in the extermination of the one or the other race."— Jefferson, *Notes on the State of Virginia,* edited by William Peden (Chapel Hill, 1955), 138. A certain confirmation of this was offered by Alexis de Tocqueville, who observed in the 1830's that "the prejudice of race appears to be stronger in the states that have abolished slavery than in those where it still exists," and predicted, "that the abolition of slavery in the South will, in the common course of things, increase the repugnance of the white population for the blacks."— Tocqueville, *Democracy in America* (Knopf Vintage Edition, New York, 1954), I, 373, 390.

ing upon the frustrations generated by the agrarian depression to arouse against the helpless Negroes that old fear of racial conflict which had made rumors of Negro insurrection such a terror to the ante-bellum countryside.

How simple, then, to seize upon the principle of separation as a means of lessening the possibility of conflict and "amalgamation," at the same time making it a symbol of the Negroes' permanent subordination! Our scanty knowledge of the movement for segregation laws indicates that arguments for their passage emphasized most of all their contribution to public tranquility. Alfred Holt Stone, of Mississippi, looking back over the early movement for legal segregation in 1908, concluded: "In almost every instance of separate car legislation, public sentiment was crystallized into law as the immediate result of intolerable local conditions, not infrequently accompanied by concrete acts of violence."[13] And in subsequent controversies the argument has been advanced time and again that any relaxation of the color line would lead inevitably to incidents and bloodshed. Whether uttered in terms of the potentialities of the situation or in terms of an agitator's threat, the danger of race conflict has been one of the chief justifications for white supremacy in its various forms.*

In addition to theories derived from the pro-slavery argument, there were also certain new factors that could be called into the defense of white supremacy. Out of the sectional conflict there had arisen powerful symbols of Southernism: the romantic picture of the old plantation, the cult of the Confederacy and its heroes, and especially the memory of Reconstruction. By the turn of the century the great traumatic experience of Reconstruction was being rehearsed in ever more macabre terms by politicians, his-

---

* J. Strom Thurmond, for example, stated in his campaign for president in 1948 that the enactment of President Truman's civil rights program would lead to "the greatest breakdown of law enforcement in the history of the nation." New York *Times*, August 1, 1948, quoted in Sarah Lemmon, "The Ideology of the 'Dixiecrat' Movement," *Journal of Social Forces*, XXX (December, 1951), 163.

torians, and novelists. It was probably the novelist Thomas Dixon, Jr., who more than any other person—aided by Hollywood's all too faithful translation of one of his books into *The Birth of a Nation*—fixed the popular view of Reconstruction as a period of unparalleled horror.

And while the new dispensation was being established, certain new sociological concepts were seized upon eagerly and incorporated into the rationale of white supremacy. A new school of sociologists, led by Franklin H. Giddings, spoke of "innate racial instincts" and the universal "consciousness of kind," phrases that found their way into the speeches and writings of southern leaders. Another contribution was William Graham Sumner's concept of folkways, immutable and unchangeable except by the geological processes of time.[14] This was brought quickly into play as a support for the new peculiar institution, even for the recently passed segregation laws, which were rationalized as the ancient folkways of the South. This idea became perhaps the chief popular support for the way of the South, and had the superior merit of eliminating the necessity for any moral justification.

In the long run, however, these new supports for the new peculiar institution were less significant than the white South's continuing reliance on the pro-slavery argument; and even the persistence of the older theories seems less significant than the fact that the white South so rarely defended its new peculiar institution by any arguments whatever. "I do not think the [Southern racial attitude] needs any defense," declared Alfred Holt Stone in 1908. "All it needs is to be understood."[15]

Even during the inflamed decade and a half around the turn of the century, when the new peculiar institution was being established, the politicians and publicists who led the white supremacy campaign relied almost wholly on irrational appeals to popular emotions and fears long conditioned by the old pro-slavery arguments, without attempting to refurbish these arguments, or even necessarily to repeat them. No sooner was the campaign won, and segregation and proscription of the Negro firmly embedded in public policy, than a powerful sentiment developed to dampen the rekindled fires of racial feeling and to discourage any further public discussion of race. Politicians who continued to exploit the racial issue were condemned as demagogues by respectable opinion in the South as well as in the North.

The white South's reticence in defending its new peculiar institution can be explained in part by the absence of any effective attack on southern racial practices remotely comparable to the earlier abolitionist or Radical Republican offensives. Influenced by dynamic forces of Social Darwinism and imperialism, the whole country was drifting closer to the white South's racial attitudes. The cult of Anglo-Saxonism, in fact, won its first triumphs in the North before finding a secure repository in the South—which had sometimes pictured itself as a Norman chivalry doing battle with the boorish Saxon. With the increasing respectability of racism and the growing willingness to let the southern whites handle the Negro as they saw fit, white Southerners felt less need to justify their social system.

What was equally important in the failure to elaborate new justifications was the fact that the new peculiar institution of the South did not provide any convenient ganglion, like the institution of slavery, about which a philosophy of justification could cluster. The new dispensation was not an institution clearly defined in law and in the minds of men, as slavery had been, but rather an ill-defined mélange of diverse factors of economic domination, repression by force and intimidation, political disfranchisement, segregation, and proscription either by private or public imposition. Nor was there any cohesive group like the old slaveholders whose leadership and immediate interests demanded eternal vigilance in the defense of their peculiar institution. The result was that the defense of white supremacy was never fully reformulated, but remained essentially the lengthened shadow of the pro-slavery argument.

Looking back over the first half of the twentieth century, it becomes clear that a whole series of developments was beginning imperceptibly to undermine the ideological defenses of white supremacy almost as soon as its new institutional patterns became established. The doctrine of biological inferiority was questioned by anthropologists and geneticists who could find no conclusive evidence for it, and their ideas seeped into the public consciousness. Tortured interpretations of the Scriptures were taken less and less seriously by literate Southerners. The need for a mudsill labor force was reduced by the development of mechanization in agriculture and industry. The argument for a separate Negro culture ran up against the manifest fact that Negroes could and did assimilate the general southern and American patterns, even in their separate institutions. The fear of race conflict with any relaxation of caste barriers eventually was found to be exaggerated as Negroes were re-enfranchised and segregation was ruled out in some areas without the predicted blood bath. And finally, these matters were opened up for discussion and debate in countless classrooms and organizations.

It would not be feasible within the scope of this essay to attempt a survey of all the forces and factors in the twentieth century that have contributed to the erosion of the ideological defense of white supremacy. Professor C. Vann Woodward has offered a tentative catalog which includes the following: the N.A.A.C.P. and other national reform organizations, the Harlem Renaissance, religion and the social gospel, the American Creed, the Southern Regional Council and similar organizations of Southerners, the migration of Negroes to the North and into the cities and their subsequent increment of political influence, a growing prosperity in the South, the struggles against Nazism and Communism, and the rise of the spirit of nationalism since the nineteen-thirties.[16]

In times of change it is only natural to look for new factors as explanations, and most of the above come in that category. Yet equally important was the traditionally ambiguous nature of the southern position, for it was this that made the new peculiar institution vulnerable to the twentieth-century challenges. The spell cast by the Southern Credo and the widespread assumption that it constitutes the central explanation of southern character have obscured the equally fundamental role of its antithesis, which in the larger Southernism has been a continuing source of disquietude about the Southern Credo.

For while the American as Southerner has been unable to shake off the pro-slavery argument, the Southerner as American has never abandoned the American Creed. Southern liberals have repeatedly argued that the liberal traditions of American nationalism are to a considerable degree southern in their origins, and national heroes of southern birth like Jefferson and Jackson have been invoked to lend respectability to their views. Even in the period of slavery, white Southerners found themselves unable to agree upon, or even fully to accept, the ingenious social theories advanced to justify the original peculiar institution. The biological inferiority argument collided with the Christian view of human personality that white Southerners could not help extending to their slaves; and their Jeffersonian liberalism was still too ingrained to permit them to accept the argument for a rigid caste society, rising tier on tier from the "mud-sill" of the happy slave to the planter at the top. "[T]hey never entirely freed their subconscious minds," W. J. Cash has written, "from the old primitive democracy of outlook bequeathed by the frontier."[17]

If few ante-bellum Southerners could really assimilate the neo-feudalism of the pro-slavery argument, fewer still could be found in the New South willing to attack frontally the valuations of the American Creed by attempting to build a general theory of society on a mudsill foundation, however implicit the idea may have been in their general outlook. Inhibited by moral taboos, Gunnar Myrdal has suggested, the Southerner has found it impossible to think *"constructively along segregation lines"* or "to think through carefully and in detail how a segregation system could be rationally organized. For *this would imply an open break with the principles of equality and liberty.*"[18]

This experience would seem to confirm the observation of Eric Voegelin that "the racial symbolism has comparatively little chance in a society which has gone through an 18th century revolution, because the collective element of racialism is hardly compatible with the belief in the value of the sovereign person and the indestructible soul, and its rights and liberties; and because the biological determinism is incompatible with the idea of reason as a spiritual substance independent of the qualities of the body which houses it. . . ."[19]

The force of Voegelin's observation has become apparent in the last three decades, during which the South's new peculiar institution has come under severe attack. The changes already brought about by the effects of attack and criticism would seem to necessitate some re-examination of the widely-held view largely based upon the history of the nineteenth-century sectional conflict, that "outside" criticism weakens the forces of moderation within the South and generates nothing but intransigence, which in turn generates further criticism and so on into a deepening whirlpool.

Granting some force to this argument, it remains to be recognized that criticism has other effects in a libertarian society, especially when the criticized share many of the assumptions on which the criticism is based. Where those who are free from the pressures of the new peculiar institution have spoken or acted forcefully and judiciously, they have sometimes raised the problem to a level where conscious recognition of basic incongruities becomes inescapable. It is true that psychologists have recognized the possibility of an individual's holding several incompatible views at one and the same time, but Myrdal has suggested that "A need will be felt by the person or group, whose inconsistencies in valuations are publicly exposed, to find a means of reconciling the inconsistencies. This can be accomplished by adjusting one of the conflicting pairs of valuations."[20] Thus criticism of southern racial practice has repeatedly generated temporary intransigence, but in the long run and more significantly it has also compelled self-justification and a slow but steady adjustment by white Southerners in the direction of the American faith in equality of opportunity and rights.

This is, in part, evidence of the lasting victory of those earlier critics who wrote the fourteenth and fifteenth amendments into the Constitution. While there have been dire predictions of violence and bloodshed to come from any tampering with southern folkways, there has been a widespread acceptance of Negro suffrage in places where it would have been unthinkable a generation ago. Political leaders, even in the midst of growing tensions (and perhaps because of them), talk increasingly in terms of equal facilities and opportunities. Measures of segregation have generally been defended under the legal fiction of "separate but equal" facilities; and where the attack has come white leaders have generally capitulated to a movement to give at least a semblance of reality to the principle of equality. Whereas in 1940 a Gallup poll showed that about half of the white Southerners frankly opposed "equal" education for Negroes, today even the segregationist leadership avows equality as its goal and has taken important steps towards it.[21] This has been a truly profound change in the thinking of white Southerners, albeit somewhat obscured in the blood and thunder of newspaper headlines.

In emphasizing the significance of the American Creed and the pressures brought in its name, it is not intended to say that changes in southern thought and action have been brought about only by the operation of outside forces, for criticism has also originated in the South, nor can it be said that the South is a peculiar repository of the eighteenth-century Enlightenment. Other traditional factors have persisted with equal or greater tenacity in the South and have imparted a distinctive flavor to its culture and heritage.

One of the factors has been Christianity. "Conservatism in religion," one historian holds, "did not rank far behind traditional racial attitudes as significant causes for the South's retention of its regional distinctiveness."[22] The effect of the social gospel movement has undoubtedly been a factor in the advanced pronouncements of major southern church bodies on issues of race. Yet the southern churches, on the whole, have remained wedded to orthodoxy in spite of cynical jibes at the "Bible Belt." One result of this has been a deep-seated moral-religious consciousness that has always proved troublesome to the Southern Credo from the day of primitive anti-slavery among backwoods Methodists and Baptists to the day of the outstanding practitioner of contemporary evangelism, a native Southerner who has sought and has had unsegregated audiences at his meetings in the South.

A consciousness of God's justice and a sense of sin have always been sources of uneasiness among Southerners about their peculiar institutions. If Jefferson could tremble when he reflected that God's justice could not sleep forever, or Kate Stone, a Louisiana Episcopalian, could be oppressed with worry about "the moral guilt of it" and "how impossible it must be for an owner of slaves to win his way into Heaven," so white Christians in the New South, according to Bishop Atticus G. Haygood, found themselves "in a state of mental unrest as to their present attitude toward the negroes."[23] Finally, a sense of the importance of the individual, however humble, and his responsibility to the judgment of God have constituted the very core of Christianity, especially in its Protestant expression. These concepts are practically identical with "the belief in the value of the sovereign person and the indestructible soul" described by Eric Voegelin as inhibiting the development of "the collective element of racialism."

The churches have never been the spearhead of social change in the South, it is true. "With all its mighty influence," said Howard Odum, "the power of the church has been in its ideologies and conditioning attitudes and not in its program."[24] But these ideologies and conditioning attitudes have, with few exceptions, functioned as an important restraint upon the most extreme expressions of racism, and have thereby contributed importantly to the erosion of the Southern Credo.

Not only the church, but also the lingering influence of frontier and agrarian society, have contributed to that "exaggerated individualism" which W. J. Cash found to be one of the essential characteristics of the Southerner. Respect for the individual personality and a certain easy-going "personalness" in human relations have continued to carry a significance in the South that has not been wholly undermined by the encroachments of industry or urbanism.

A northern visitor to South Louisiana in 1945 discovered that "The habits of both frontier and plantation days are still real along the Mississippi. . . ." Among these habits was a sort of institutional kindness that "flows from a thoroughgoing personalness in the aristocratic style of living in the South, and does not exist in the North anywhere."[25] Here was a survival in almost pure form of the patrician attitude of personal affinity between whites and Negroes. Despite the paternalistic and exploitative connotations of this attitude, it has been both a source of interracial good will and sometimes of intimate personal contact across the barriers of caste. The kindlier attitudes of ante-bellum paternalism, surviving among upper-class whites of the New South, gave rise to the tradition that no southern gentleman engages in the harrassment of Negroes, but rather regards them with a certain affection and finds a certain affinity of interest with them.   He may even take pride in their social and educational progress and attempt to help them in the process, as did J. L. M. Curry of the Peabody Fund and other leaders in the southern education movement.

The neighborly spirit of human relations in the South also has democratic as well as aristocratic implications, stemming in some measure from the historical influence of frontier and agrarian democracy that has been as much a part of the southern tradition as the feudal heritage of the plantation.   In the southern experience recognition of a community of interest between whites and Negroes has been manifested by individuals and groups other than those with pretensions to gentility.   During any period in southern history since the Civil War some instances of interracial action may be found in the labor movement, among craftsmen, longshoremen, miners, factory workers, and others.   In the agrarian revolt of the eighties and nineties the "wool hat boys" found themselves allied with Negro farmers in the struggle against their common economic grievances, and since the nineteen-thirties an indigenous organization of tenant farmers and agricultural laborers has existed without racial barriers.   Middle-class manifestations of a community of interest have appeared in various projects for community improvement such as Community Chest drives.

The older notions of southern gentility and the newer concepts of a community of interest did not expire with the rise of Negrophobia, but on the contrary survived into the twentieth century to give rise to fair-play sentiments and policies.   While assuming the inevitability of white supremacy, these movements sought to give Negroes a measure of justice within the system and to keep open the avenues of communication across the barriers. This may be seen in the southern education movement that was

developing at the turn of the century, and which inspired even
North Carolina's white supremacy leader, Charles Brantley Aycock, to a defense of "the equal right of every child born on earth
to have the opportunity 'to burgeon out all that there is within
him.' "[26]   It may be seen in Edgar Gardner Murphy's conference
for the discussion of race problems at Montgomery in 1900.   The
same spirit motivated the interracial commission established in Atlanta by the efforts of Booker T. Washington after the riot of 1906,
and the South-wide movement of the Commission on Interracial
Cooperation, established after the First World War for ". . . the
creation of a better spirit, the correction of grievances, and the
promotion of interracial understanding and sympathy."[27]   The
chief organizational repository of this tradition (by no means the
only one) since 1944 has been the Southern Regional Council, an
interracial group of Southerners which has moved from moderate
expressions of fair-play sentiments to outright affirmations of equal
rights for all Southerners.

Last of all, the intellectual and economic progress of Negroes
has nurtured the seeds of change by developing Negro institutions
and enterprises and professional occupations, with leaders dependent upon the Negro community and relatively independent of
white control.   Such leadership has frequently provided the spearhead of the most effective actions against discrimination, sometimes
through tactics of adjustment and at other times through tactics
of protest and criticism.

This indigenous leadership has been of supreme importance
and increasing ability, but it has been forced of necessity to operate
in a situation requiring a high degree of white sympathy and support.   One of the most militant Negro leaders, W. E. B. Du
Bois, no less than Booker T. Washington, long ago recognized
that Negro leadership must address itself ultimately to the better
consciences of white men who, "Deeply religious and intensely

democratic . . . feel acutely the false position in which the Negro problems place them."[28]

A gradual diminution in the force of the Southern Credo has now been apparent for several decades. Though persisting in most of its aspects, the new peculiar institution itself began to show signs of strain under pressure in the thirties, in the forties it began to crack, and now, in the fifties, its chief symbol and support, Jim Crow, has come under virtual sentence of death by the federal courts. The threatened collapse of any institution, however, may bring forth a stubborn defense. Hostile reactions to civil rights programs and especially to the Supreme Court decision in the school segregation cases demonstrate that the old ideas are held with remarkable tenacity. They have even experienced a certain revival, born in the late nineteen-thirties and mounting to a peak of intensity in the fifties.

This new reaction invites comparison with the defense of slavery. The white Citizens' Councils and similar groups, for example, had their counterpart in the vigilance committees of the Old South. Some political spokesmen of the white South have revived the dormant ante-bellum theory of nullification in a new form. Other segregationist leaders—like the secessionists of Charleston, who "adopted as an article of faith the propagation of slavery" with all the zeal of "the Mormons or early Mahometans"[29]—have sought to erect the temporary *modus vivendi* of segregation into some kind of eternal moral principle. Analogies of the sort could be pursued at great length, but at several important points the comparison breaks down.

In the first place, the slavery interests of the eighteen-fifties were to some extent on the offensive, actively seeking the extension of slavery into the territories. The tone of the new reaction is decidedly defensive, seeking only to hold the ground already occupied, or even to retreat to the line of separate but equal.

In the second place, the oratory and literature of the new reaction have shown no serious promise of developing a positive
philosophical justification of the new peculiar institution. An intellectual leadership of the sort that perfected the pro-slavery argument is conspicious by its absence. Such efforts at rationalization
as have appeared lean heavily upon charging the opposition with
questionable motives and susceptibility to insidious influences.*
This observation may seem to place an excessive emphasis upon
the rationality of human motivation in an area where irrationality
has often ruled. Yet the lack of a reasoned defense may very well
constitute a serious long-range vulnerability of an institution that
conflicts with so many values deeply imbedded in the traditions
and thought of the people.

In the third place, the solid front of southern whites in the
eighteen-fifties has been splintered in the nineteen-fifties. What
George Washington Cable once called the "Silent South" is now
articulate. Church organizations, citizens' groups, individuals, even
prominent political leaders have demonstrated publicly their indifference or hostility to the old Southern Credo.† Assertion of the

* Examples of the literature may be found in Theodore G. Bilbo, *Take Your
Choice: Separation or Mongrelization* (Poplarville, Miss., 1947); Tom P. Brady,
Black Monday (Brookhaven, Miss., 1954); Charles Wallace Collins, *Whither
Solid South?* (New Orleans, 1947); W. E. Debnam, *Then My Old Kentucky
Home, Good Night!* (Raleigh, 1955); Stuart Omer Landry, *The Cult of Equality*
(New Orleans, 1945); Herman E. Talmadge, *You and Segregation* (Birmingham,
1955). The book by Landry is the only one of these that offers a lengthy positive justification of the new peculiar institution, largely in terms of Negro
inferiority. Landry, Bilbo, and Collins offer as an ultimate solution to the
problem the establishment of a forty-ninth state in Africa, thereby offering
some confirmation of Myrdal's observation regarding the inability to think
through rationally how a segregation system might work. Debnam's little volume
offers an interesting example of a man who is willing to abandon segregation
laws in public transportation, parks and playgrounds, even the prohibition of
interracial marriage, but insists upon the maintenance of segregation in public
schools, 101-11.
† Examples of literature illustrating a range of such opinion include Harry
Ashmore, *An Epitaph for Dixie* (New York, 1957); James MacBride Dabbs,
The Southern Heritage (New York, 1958); Brooks Hays, *A Southern Moderate
Speaks* (Chapel Hill, 1959); Henry Savage, Jr., *Seeds of Time* (New York,
1959); Lillian Smith, *Killers of the Dream* (New York, 1949), and *Now Is The
Time* (New York, 1955); Wilma Dykeman and James Stokely, *Neither Black*

American Creed in the face of serious pressures makes it difficult
to assume that the old spell of unanimity will ever be revived. Even
spokesmen for the new reaction seem in many cases to have adopted
in private the attitude, which sometimes crops out in public utterances, that their function is in the nature of a rear guard delaying
action rather than a lasting revival of white supremacy doctrines.

Adequate appraisal of contemporary developments is an uncertain business. But one southern historian has been "so bold as
to maintain that recent changes are of sufficient depth and impact
as to define the end of an era of Southern history."[30] If the dy-
namics of recent events can inspire so bold an observation, they
must also lead us to consider whether we may be witnessing the
disappearance of the South as a conscious entity.

For if we accept the analysis of U. B. Phillips, that day when
white supremacy should be no longer the cardinal tenet and primary aim of white Southerners would be the day in which the South
would become but another geographical part of the United States,
for the central theme of its history and the chief source of its unity
would have come to an end. It would be a rash prophet indeed
who would forecast when that day might come, but in view of
general trends over the past three decades and the direction of
public policy today, it can no longer seem so completely outside
the range of possibility as it must have seemed to Phillips in
1928.[31]

But would a decline and fall of white supremacy necessarily
reduce the South to merely another geographical part of the United
States? Only if we must accept the dictum of Phillips that white
supremacy is the central and indispensable determinant of southern
peculiarity. Though for a century and a half the issue of race has

Nor White (New York, 1957); and Robert Penn Warren, *Segregation* (New
York, 1956). See also files of the Southern Regional Council's periodical, *New
South* (Atlanta, 1946-   ), which reproduces selections of such materials and gives
references to others.

been an important key to southern character and one of the chief issues on which other elements of Southernism and Americanism have interacted, we cannot in the light of recent events continue to regard it as an immutable feature of southern life.

Present perspectives suggest, indeed, that the "credo of the South with reference to the Negro" can no longer be regarded as the indispensable key to southern distinctiveness—just as, for that matter, the American Creed fails to explain fully the broader national character. The Southern Credo has never summarized the diverse aspects of the southern heritage. This is recognized in popular thought, for popular stereotypes of the Southerner have flourished and have been readily recognized without any overt reference to the issue of race. Southerners themselves have time and again manifested intense regional loyalties in situations dissociated from an emphasis on the issue of race—the cotton mill campaign of the 1880's, for example, the Southern Education Movement around the turn of the century, the campaign against freight rate discrimination, the Agrarian manifesto of 1930, and the development of an academic ideology of southern regionalism by Howard W. Odum and his disciples.

The historian can report, too, that the Negro has been a Southerner. The point is seldom comprehended in the general usage of the term "Southerner," but the records and literature of the South bear voluminous recognition of the fact. In making the culture of the South, W. J. Cash asserted, "Negro entered into white man as profoundly as white man entered into Negro—subtly influencing every gesture, every word, every emotion and idea, every attitude."[32] In shaping patterns of speech, of folklore, of music, of literature, and in the manifold products of their labor, Negro Southerners have everlastingly influenced and enriched the culture of their region. To overlook this contribution would be to neglect much that has made the South distinctive.

The Negro has been a Southerner. The Negro, too, has been an American. In the promises of the American Creed, rather than in programs of escape or revolution, he has found the fundamental key to his aspirations. According to a Negro Georgian, "Negroes are really more American than most whites. Actually they are more loyal. Negroes are trying to achieve their full status as American citizens. . . . This fight forces Negroes to be nationalistic."[33]

In the perspective of the Southerner as American, then, we may gain insight into the Negro Southerner as well as the white. The Negro Southerner, like the white, has been moving on the momentum of slavery but also on the momentum of the American Creed. Starting with tremendous handicaps from slavery—social, economic, psychological, and intellectual—his patterns of adjustment to the situation have sometimes been modeled after the patterns of slavery, in the submissiveness of the old time "darky" or even in the limited progressivism of Booker T. Washington's "Atlanta Compromise." But at the same time there have been other patterns of Southernism and of more militant striving after the promises of the American Creed.

Finally, we return to U. B. Phillips' central theme of southern history. To recognize the Negro as a Southerner is perhaps to deliver the *coup de grâce* to the Phillips thesis, but before abandoning it precipitately, we must render a proper deference to its great validity in explaining much about the South. Phillips' essay dealt chiefly with the ante-bellum South and in that context it emphasized the importance of slavery, as a race issue, in forging that consciousness of southern unity which culminated in secession and the Confederacy. It was reprinted, most appropriately, at the end of a volume entitled *The Course of the South to Secession*. At the time of Phillips' writing it was an interpretation that was losing favor in many quarters, but more recent historians like Allan Nevins and

Arthur M. Schlesinger, Jr., have tended to turn back to slavery and racism as the fundamental issue in their explanations of the sectional controversy and Civil War.

In this essay, however, we have tried to view the subject in a broader context than politics, which Phillips scarcely did, and also in the perspective of a New South now older than the Old South ever was while it existed. In this perspective a larger Southernism is an unquestionable reality, especially to those who have grown up in the South, and the historian can list some of the objective factors that produced it: a distinctive historical experience involving defeat and poverty; the climate and physical setting with their effects on life, tempo, emotion, and character; the presence of the Negro and his pervasive influence on the whole life of the region; the powerful religious heritage and the knowledge of good and evil; and finally, the persistence of an essentially rural culture with its neighborliness in human relations.

Yet the historian who is also a Southerner knows that the reality of Southernism—like so many important aspects of experience—defies precise definition or objective analysis. This reality he knows best as a Southerner, for whom it is a subjective experience of land and people and ways of living, which has become a ground for attachment and loyalty. As an historian he can only report that the many different kinds of people living in the South's many widely different parts find a large degree of common meaning in their infinitely various personal experiences.

He can report, in short, that the southern way of life has involved infinitely more than a system of segregation and proscription. And more and more frequently, as time passes, he can report that a consciousness of loyalty to the South may even take the form of opposition to the old Southern Credo. More than one white Southerner has experienced the same change that came into the life of Katherine DuPre Lumpkin, who, after abandoning her native heritage of racial beliefs and practices, was "haunted by the old dogma, that but one way was Southern, and hence there could be but one kind of Southerner." "I could still half believe this," she said, "even as late as the 1920's, perhaps partially remain under the spell of its old authority. . . . But then I learned that this was not so. It could not be. What had altered me was the South's own doing. The beginning of the beginning for my change lay far back in our history."[34]

CHAPTER SEVEN

THE NEGRO AS SOUTHERNER AND AMERICAN

By L. D. Reddick

THE NEGRO IN THE South is a study in attachment and alienation. For him, identification has always been a problem. Inescapably he has found himself to be a "Southerner." He may not have preferred the term, but the objective fact could not be denied. As everyone knows, the majority of Negroes, historically and currently, have been born in the South and lived out their lives there. By way of residence and experience, the region has set its mark upon all of its people.

Likewise the Negro has set his mark upon the South. It is difficult to imagine this part of the country without colored people —their presence, their labor, their music and humor, and their challenge. What would be left of southern literature, for example, if we took away the black man as subject and creator?

Negro and white Southerners are reluctant to admit their kinship, not merely at times when it is biological, but more generally when it is regional. They tend to stress their differences, while in fact they are in so many ways brothers under the skin. Their similarities are remarkable—especially in speech, gait, food habits, and orientation toward life. Often, when the person we just heard over the telephone appears before us, we are surprised to find his skin color different from what we expected. One perceptive white Southerner, sensitized to this by his residence in the North, has "noted again and again how often we laugh at the same things, how often we pronounce the same words the same way to the amusement of our hearers, judge character in the same frame of reference, mist up at the same kind of music." "All men, to be sure, are kin," concludes Charles L. Black, "but Southern whites and Negroes are bound in a special bond. In a peculiar way, they are the same kind of people. . . . [Even] their strife is fratricidal."[1]

Southerners—black and white—tend to exhibit an open, sprawling friendliness, yet strongly emphasize family ties and personal loyalties. To them it is the man that counts, rather than the idea he represents. Talk runs to conversation, not discussion. Orators are everywhere. Church going is habitual and regular, manifesting a religion that is active and demonstrative. The womenfolk move about the home, but the menfolk take to the woods and rivers. Perhaps not quite so well armed as the mythical American Westerner, the Southerner is, nevertheless, notably quick with his fists. In a word, the people of Dixie are still relatively rural and folkish, encouraged in this by the open country, blue skies, and warm weather.

This is true for blacks as well as whites and is fairly obvious to any observer who can see beyond skin color. On almost any summer's Saturday afternoon he could view a scene that would be re-enacted in the thousands of sleepy little county seats scattered south of Washington and east of San Antonio:

"In the town square stood the courthouse, with the customary columns infrequently white-washed or painted, and surrounded by a low, flat-topped wall on which the folks in from the country sat when they became tired of milling around. On a bright Saturday afternoon, the white and colored people—looking very much alike, with the whites perhaps a little better dressed—filled the square, moving slowly in and out of the stores, talking and laughing, sitting and looking."[2]

Of course, there is that other South, of Atlanta, Miami, and Houston. In the cities, some may argue, the South has lost much of its regional flavor. And yet the southern metropolis somehow retains its regional accent and exposure. Atlanta can never forget Sherman or the Talmadges or "Gone With The Wind" or "Uncle Remus," even if it should want to. The southern urbanite, white or Negro, readily doffs his three-button jacket for a game of horseshoes.

Almost every adult treasures the vivid moments of his own childhood—the bend of the road, the swimming hole, chums and relatives, holidays, trips and other well-remembered sights and sounds. And so the Negro Southerner, even when he is in revolt or far away from the land of his birth, betrays his attachment for the South and will own up to it, whenever he can avoid or forget about bad race relations. "It is not that I love Maryland less, but freedom more," wrote the celebrated fugitive slave Frederick Douglass to his former master. If the slaves were all emancipated, he went on, rather than flocking to the North, "you would see many old and familiar faces back again to [sic] the South. The fact is, there are few here who would not return to the South in the event of emancipation. We want to live in the land of our birth, and to lay our bones by the side of our fathers'; and nothing short of an intense love of personal freedom keeps us from the South. For the sake of this, most of us would live on a crust of bread and a cup of cold water."[3]

And that is where the alienation comes in. Because the South for so long has denied the Negro his essential manhood, he has become, in a sense, a sort of anti-Southerner. Thus, when fourteen-year-old Emmett Till was allegedly murdered for "wolf-whistling" at a white woman, a Negro ex-Southerner snarled:

"When I hear the word Mississippi, I spit." School teachers from Alabama were embarrassed in New York City when it was noticed that their automobile license tags bore the state legend, "Heart of Dixie." One Negro to another: "Man, where are you going if you ever decide to leave Detroit?" Answer: "Anywhere but South!"

At the first meeting of a graduate class in southern history at a Negro college, two questions were raised: What is the South? and Who is a Southerner? The ensuing discussion was most animated. Almost all of the students admitted that they were Southerners but only half of them appeared to be happy about this. Most were sharply critical of the treatment of Negroes in Dixie but invariably became defensive whenever they told of aspersions that were cast on their homeland by northern Negroes. Apparently, Negro as well as white Southerners—especially while on visits "up North"—can be embarrassed by the reputation that their region has acquired.

Within the section itself, the two extreme and opposite reactions to the hostile forces that bear down upon the Negro have been typified by the "Uncle Tom" and the "Bad Nigger." The former accepts his inferior status passively, or for internal peace or special favors actively cooperates in the subjection of himself and his people. The latter fights all the way—with his fist, knife, or gun—boisterously aggressive or sullenly silent, in either case violently protecting himself and family against "anything white" that crosses him. He has no respect for a law not made by or for him. He expects no justice from the courts. The police are his natural enemies. Between these two poles may be found the intermediate types, mixtures in varying proportions of the extremes.

The conflict between embracing and rejecting the South has set up a war within the persons of Negro Southerners as well as in the social order. Some of them hate the South; others, despite everything, love it. Most, however, alternate their love and hate, while a few seem to be capable of loving and hating at the same time. It is a great and confusing frustration. Most southern Negroes, apparently, attempt to accommodate themselves to the realities and, as with other problems of life, struggle to improve their situation. But behind this realism linger big questions that cannot always be pushed aside: Is "staying South" worth the price? How much betterment is possible or likely?

The negative anti-Southernism of the Negro helps give him the basis of a positive national outlook. He realizes that in his success as an individual, a friendly, white southern neighbor may lend him a helping hand, but that the large advances of Negroes as a group have come by way of national rather than regional or local attitudes and policies. The abolition of slavery, the granting of citizenship and whatever of civic equality the Negro has obtained have come largely through federal action. Even education for dark-skinned children in the South received its original impetus from New England school ma'ams and the Freedmen's Bureau.

Thus, unlike many of his white fellow Southerners, the Negro in the South (as in the North) has stood with Daniel Webster rather than Robert Y. Hayne, Lincoln rather than Jefferson Davis, Franklin D. Roosevelt rather than Senators Bilbo and Eastland. A "State's Rights" Negro is indeed a rarity. Freedom of speech being what it has been in the South, much of the Negro Southerner's political attitude is expressed in gesture and deed rather than in word. Perhaps a more graphic illustration of this could not be found than that of the Negro South Carolinian, who, just before leaving his native state for New York, took his five-year-old son to urinate at the statue of John C. Calhoun.

This rejection of State's Rights broadens into a general liberal Americanism. As Gunnar Myrdal has shown in his *American Dilemma,* the basic American and Negro creeds are identical. The Declaration of Independence and the Constitution of the United States are radical enough for most Negro Americans. Their "rights" campaigns are thus constitutional and legal, and the only qualification that they would tie to patriotism is that it not be Jim Crow. Federal aid to public and social services is also highly regarded. Similarly Negroes may be counted upon as allies of organized labor and other such economic and social action groups—unless they draw a color curtain around their programs of "progress." In collecting the essays for his *What The Negro Wants* (1944), editor Rayford W. Logan found that Negroes north and south want no more, no less than what all other Americans want. In a word, the southern Negro (as well as his northern brother) favors the welfare state and liberalism if he himself is not discriminated against en route to Utopia.

The Negro's inner conflict and outer ambivalence are nothing new. Through each historic period he has revealed himself as Southerner and as American, behaving according to his southern conditioning and his national aspiration. Under the shadow of naked power, he had little choice but to remain a slave. That bondsmen were at times merry may not have meant, as some historians and orators would have us believe, that they were contented with their enslavement; rather, this might have been one more evidence of the durability of the human spirit, of a deep-seated human capacity to make the best of a difficult situation. Moreover the Underground Railroad to the North, the slave revolts, the arson and threats of well-poisoning that swept over the land from time to time suggest further that the stereotype of the "happy slave" may have been a creature of wish-fulfillment on the part of slave-owners and their propagandists.

During the ante-bellum days, the free Negro at times tried very hard to prove that he, too, was a Southerner. For instance, the colored creoles of New Orleans held themselves aloof from the blacks—at least publicly, though here again, the discerning observer will notice that many a free Negro was yanked into court for "harboring" runaways. When the Civil War broke out, these free persons of color, as they were called, were eager to show their loyalty to the southern cause—apparently. They joined in a general parade through the city and volunteered to shoulder arms. However, about a year later, as soon as the federal forces captured the city, these same Negro freedmen were among the most enthusiastic supporters of Union General Butler.

Southern orators love to make much of the "undying devotion" of the slave to old massa and missus during the War Between the States. Often this is proclaimed as an argument that the Negro was "satisfied" with his status. Perhaps the slaves should be complimented for not assaulting the women and old men who may have been left in the big house on the plantation; yet both house servants and field hands, by a wide range of activity, demonstrated that they really understood the issues involved. The researches of Bell I. Wiley, W. E. B. Du Bois, and others show that southern Negroes deserted the plantations in droves, gave valuable information to the invaders, and joined as laborers and camp followers wherever federal troops appeared, and that over a hundred thousand of them fought as soldiers on the Union side.[4]

When the Civil War was over, Negroes and others assumed that a new social order would come into being in the South—a colorblind democracy. Its three requirements were: (1) distribution of land so as to create small free holders; (2) universal manhood suffrage; and (3) civil rights for all. Looking back, we can speculate that the nation would have been spared many tears if this three-ply program had been carried out. How much further along would we be as a united people and a thoroughgoing democracy, if the federal government had thrown its full force behind these proposals, and if official and non-official agencies had carried on pro-equalitarian education?

For a moment it looked as though this would happen. After the 13th, 14th, and 15th amendments had been adopted, Congress in 1875 enacted a comprehensive Civil Rights Act. It provided that: "All persons within the jurisdiction of the United States shall be entitled to the full and equal enjoyment of the accommodations, advantages, facilities, and privileges of inns, public conveyances on land or water, theaters, and other places of public amusement; subject only to the conditions and limitations established by law and applicable alike to citizens of every race and color, regardless of any previous condition of servitude."[5] And so the Negro and much of the nation assumed that the new order was well on its way. But we know that the fates decreed otherwise.

During the tumult and confusion of the Reconstruction period, national policy zig-zagged in contradictory directions. The death of Lincoln may have been a calamity to Negroes—no one really knew what he would have done for the social revolution. The "poor white," Andrew Johnson, was distrusted, but his successor in the White House, General Grant, would, it was felt, see to it that "right" prevailed. This was confirmed when Grant made it clear that he would use federal troops to restore order and re-seat Negro legislators who had been ousted in the southern states.

Despite the speeches and gestures, the retreat of the nation from the idealism of the later war years became, after a while, apparent to all. And when the clear line of policy emerged, it was obvious that the holders of power in the nation had no social revolution in mind.

In the first place, the South would get no homestead act such as did the northern poor man in 1862 when he was sorely needed as a common soldier in the Union Army. The idea of confiscating and breaking up the big southern plantations was even more repugnant to the defenders of private property, North as well as South. Industrialism had realized its objectives. The war had broken the hold of the southern landed aristocracy on the federal government, and the South as well as the West was now open to economic penetration. The southern Negro definitely would not get his forty acres and a mule.

In the second place, the Negro voter was no longer needed after 1876 to consolidate the war gains of big business through the Republican party. If the anti-Negro elements of the South insisted upon disfranchisement and subordination of the Negro, this was allowable and could be made a part of the good-will bargain between the erstwhile warring sections.

In the third place, the United States Supreme Court, in 1883, declared the Civil Rights Act of 1875 unconstitutional. This meant that it was all right for the southern states to erect a wall of segregation between Negro and white Southerners in public facilities and services. This relatively new structure was given a more positive legal sanction in the much better known *Plessy vs. Ferguson* decision of 1896.

It is impossible to exaggerate the dismay of the Negro as democratic Reconstruction was undone. When the Court killed the Civil Rights Act, protest meetings were held throughout the nation by angry or saddened Negroes and their sympathizers. Bishop Henry McNeil Turner, for one, was so disconsolate that he had copies of the decision printed at his own expense and distributed among Negro leaders so that they could read for themselves just how this branch of the national government had let the Negro down. Turner advocated migration to Africa and swore never to die on the soil of a land that had rejected his people. Though his stay in Africa was short-lived, Turner kept his promise, for when he felt that death was near, he dragged himself from the United States over the Canadian border, dying in the little town of Windsor, across from Detroit.[6]

For others the dénouement was equally dispiriting. They did whatever was possible and appealed to the few remaining humanitarians in and out of Congress. But the decisive force in race relations was not so much what the Negro and his friends—or his enemies—wanted; rather, whatever was required for the triumph of big business and national expansion to the Pacific Coast and beyond to Hawaii, the Philippines, and down to Cuba and the Caribbean. The knife of imperialism carried as its cutting edge the doctrine of white supremacy, which was at once a national version of southern racism and an American version of what was best known in Europe as "the white man's burden." Asia, Africa, and the islands of the seas would be taken over by merchants and the military, while Christian missionaries and poets like Kipling provided the balm to conscience.

The reaction of the Negro during the period from the Civil War to the first World War, revealed more deeply than ever his dilemma as a Southerner. His faith that the federal government would not desert him died a hard death. He had wanted so much to prove himself a worthy citizen. Economically, he had squatted on the land where it had been abandoned and was willing to work and save his meager earnings to purchase and possess a farm. Politically, he was so proud to be a voter that contemporary accounts show him getting up at dawn on election day in order not to be late at the ballot box. Educationally, he gave us an example of a self-initiated campaign against illiteracy the like of which had never been seen. Many a dark-skinned plowman stopped his mule at the turn of the furrow to take another look in his blue back speller. Religiously, he set up churches and denominations of his own in addition to those provided for him by white brethren; and the Fisk Jubilee Singers introduced the "Negro spiritual" to the world. Militarily, the Negro organized himself into authorized militia units, for he wanted to be a citizen-soldier. He did not push for integration as an individual, but he did expect that his unit would be integrated as such into the state guard and the national service. In brief, the southern Negro intended to remain in the South and make an excellent record, if given an equal chance. And he expected from the federal government a guarantee of that chance.

When this assumption was disproved, many other Negroes besides Henry McNeil Turner considered leaving the South. Frederick Douglass and Richard T. Greener, Harvard's first Negro graduate and briefly a professor at the University of South Carolina, debated the issue in 1879, attracting national attention.[7] That same year "Pap" Singleton of Tennessee led a migration of Negroes to Kansas; others followed. But such efforts were more dramatic than effective because the West and the North were hostile to Negro newcomers, and southern Negroes generally did not have the means of financing and effecting a new settlement.

Douglass, who consistently contended for equal rights under the Constitution, died in 1895. In that same year, Booker Taliaferro Washington came to the fore at the Atlanta Exposition with a new rationale for southern race relations. He de-emphasized political action and the drive for equality, leading a retreat to economic usefulness and the cultivation of southern employers and neighbors. "Cast down your bucket where you are," he said. This was the philosophical acceptance of segregation. *Plessy vs. Ferguson* came the next year. Perhaps Washington felt that such a withdrawal was a skillful strategem in a battle that was wasting men and resources in futile defense of a position that was untenable without support from the federal government. And as we have seen, no such federal support was forthcoming after Grant left the presidency. Moreover, Booker Washington could see that the effort to unite the poor white and the poor Negro on the basis of their common class interests was being broken in the defeat and dismemberment of the Populist movement. Meanwhile lynchings were more numerous than ever during the 1890's, and middle-class Negro society was subjected to the ridicule of low comedy and the coon song.

When the Spanish-American War came, the Negro militia units that had so confidently marched up and down the streets of southern cities were not accepted and utilized for combat duty. Except in a few cases they were declassified and converted into laborers, if used at all. Hostility in the southern states was at its height, and the nation as a whole did not seem to care. Professor Rayford W. Logan has correctly named the period 1877-1901, "The Nadir."[8] Contemporary Negro newspapers and the speeches of prominent Negroes were infused with defeatism, religious fantasy, and resignation in the hope that perhaps things would be better after we "cross over Jordan."

It was 1910 before the Negro was able to re-group his forces and launch a movement that was based on an ideology different from Booker T. Washington's. Crying out against the Tuskegee philosophy in *The Souls of Black Folk,* W. E. B. Du Bois had launched a counter-movement with a small group of leaders at an all-Negro convention at Niagara Falls in 1905. But organizationally nothing much happened until the interracial NAACP (National Association for the Advancement of Colored People) was founded five years later. With headquarters in New York City, these equalitarians soon had branches in most of the urban South. This meant that the Booker T. Washington retreat was over, having failed to stem the anti-Negro tide. Washington himself seemed to realize this failure during the last years of his life, 1910-1915. This mood was reflected in his letters and in an article that he wrote the year he died, attacking segregation.[9]

Here again, it should be remarked that the attitudes of Negro and white Southerners were important but hardly decisive. World and national affairs were taking a new turn at the second decade of the twentieth century, and the first World War accentuated the shift establishing the pre-conditions for a new phase of the struggle for equality. The United States was becoming a creditor nation, expanding industrially and exporting capital and ideas. But all this was taking place while world-wide imperialism had passed its high tide and was already beginning to recede. By mid-century

Asia had freed itself from European domination, and Africa was starting down that same freedom road.

Indirectly this meant as much to the Negro in the "backward" South as it did directly to the colonials in "backward" lands overseas. The southern Negro now found it possible to leave the South in considerable numbers, to exert political pressure upon the national government, and to pick up unexpected allies at home and abroad.

No doubt Negroes of the 1880's and 1890's had just as much motivation to move northward as their sons and daughters did a generation later, but it was 1910 before noticeable numbers were able to get away. The ravages of the boll weevil in the Southeast had "liberated" thousands of Negro workers from the cotton plantations, and these "new freedmen" moved on to southern and northern cities. And when World War I cut off European immigration to the United States, the black trickle of migrants from the South to northern industries became a flood.

During the war thousands of Negroes, going to France as soldiers and laborers experienced an even more radically different brand of race relations from that encountered by their brethren who went North. Shortly afterwards, hundreds of thousands of blackfolk, under the hypnotic oratory of Marcus Garvey, at least vicariously responded to the call to leave "white America" forever and go "home," "back to Africa." Many applauded, but few took the boat.

The three million Negroes who went North between 1910 and 1930 gradually gained a political balance of power in the great cities. Soon their strength would be felt in the nation's capital when the fight was launched to recover the franchise and civil liberties below the Potomac.

Increasingly, the confluence of economic and social forces favored the Negro in his struggle. The great depression chastened big business and gave impetus to consideration of "the forgotten man." Industrial as well as craft unions were organized. In the South the Southern Conference for Human Welfare, beginning in the mid-thirties and lasting a decade, served to kindle the bright though finally illusory hope that Negro and white Southerners could unite for social action. The more conservative interracial committees that antedated the Conference were willing to work against racial *discrimination* but would not face up to, as the Conference did, the more controversial issue of racial *segregation.*

During this period, America's Negro community experienced a cultural renaissance. Alain Locke's *New Negro* was mainly northern and urban, but over half of the contributors to this famous anthology were born or had lived in the South. Later, Mississippi's Richard Wright, after migrating to Chicago (and later to New York and Paris), led a phalanx of tough depression-bred literati who projected the images of "Bigger Thomas" and the "Invisible Man"—symbols of men who would not be denied their humanity, even if to get it they had to murder, "go Communist," or live underground. Some of the same vitality characterized the art of painters like Aaron Douglas and Hale Woodruff, sculptors like Richmond Barthe and musicians like William Dawson, William Grant Still, and Hall Johnson.

With the coming of World War II, Negroes again streamed out of the country as soldiers and out of the South as war workers. This time the migrants went west as well as north. Negro-white relations moved to our Pacific Coast, where already race patterns involving Japanese, Chinese, Mexicans, and American Indians had been established.

To mobilize people all over the world against Hitler, the United States and its allies carried on a vast campaign against racism. Roosevelt spoke of the Four Freedoms that should prevail "everywhere in the world." And these were precisely what American Negroes had been contesting for—especially in the South.

The voting strength of the Negro in the other-than-southern parts of the country helped the home-front fight down South. No section of the nation, to be sure, had clean hands in racial matters, but in the North and West all of the weapons of democratic contention could be utilized, whereas this was seldom the case in most of the South.

As for the current, or post-World War II, phase of the story, it is strange that the United States Supreme Court has been most sensitive to the need of the American government and people for a new racial policy. In the mid-thirties the Court began to whittle away the legal basis of racial segregation, and as everybody knows, on May 17, 1954, destroyed it completely. This has been looked upon as a "Negro" decision; in fact, it is much more an "American" decision, because it did more for the American economy and foreign relations than it did for the colored man.

As a nation, we are now perhaps the number one world power at a time when European-American or Western or "white" imperialism has reached ebb tide. Africa is following Asia so rapidly in getting free of the colonial yoke that it becomes difficult to keep count of the new self-governing nations that are appearing so rapidly upon the map. Liberia has been there for more than a century and a half, and the ancient kingdom of Ethiopia was only reliberated from Mussolini's conquest. But since the second great war, the erstwhile dark continent has as new nations—Egypt, Sudan, Libya, Tunisia, Morocco, Ghana, Guinea, Nigeria and, surprise of surprises, the Belgian Congo, which probably will soon be followed by the territories previously known as British East Africa, French West and Equatorial Africa and perhaps Algeria. (White South Africans say that they're Africans, too).

At the same time, America is confronted by a rival world power, a communist state that has revealed startling scientific and military achievements and has begun to challenge us in the production of consumer goods. Moreover, Soviet Russia projects an ideology of national liberation—especially for the colonies of capitalist nations—and condemns racial segregation and discrimination unceasingly. The cold war between the political giants is acompanied by a propaganda barrage. Our Supreme Court must have noticed that some of the direct hits of the Soviets were on our vulnerable and explosive race relations.

As a nation, not only can we no longer export white supremacy, we cannot afford even to display it. Racial arrogance will win us no friends or allies in Afro-Asia. Even Europe nowadays seems to prefer Negro Americans to some of our other citizens who visit there. Nobody loves the white, "ugly American."

Accordingly we have had to abolish Jim Crowism in our armed forces, not so much for the sake of our Negroes as for national policy, realizing that a separate black and white army advertised to the world that we did not practice our democratic preachments. Little Rock has embarrassed our State Department no end, and the late John Foster Dulles found it necessary to write the Governor of Alabama that our mail bags from American embassies were loaded with protests about a scheduled execution of a colored man for the relatively insignificant crime of robbing a white woman of $1.95. Today a lynching in Poplarville, Mississippi, becomes an international incident. It is difficult for provincial Southerners to realize this. And as they exhibit their cultural shortcomings, lawlessness and prejudices before the TV and newspaper cameras, fellow Southerners join in the question the world asks: Is this America?

Consequently our federal government, from considerations of national security alone, will have to do something about civil rights, will have to clean up the racial situation. It may respond fitfully or reluctantly, but the political necessity is there, if the United States is serious about maintaining and advancing its position as a world influence.

Thus history is on the Negro's side. He has a good chance now to achieve what he has always wanted and what he envisioned during the radiant promise of Reconstruction—colorblind democracy. At last economic and political forces dictate what idealism would have chosen almost a century ago.

The procedural problem for the Negro Southerner, therefore, is to push forward toward his and the nation's goal in race relations but to do this without generating resentment and a residue of hate among his white fellow Southerners. Already we have had too many embittering lost causes. Perhaps the secret of non-violent social change has been found in the theory and practice of the Montgomery, Alabama, bus boycott. Here for a year, December 5, 1955, to December 21, 1956, the Negro community demonstrated well disciplined collective action, successfully boycotting the city's segregated bus system and at the same time projecting a philosophy of social humanitarianism that was based upon Christian ethics and the thought of Henry David Thoreau and Mohandas K. Gandhi.[10] If the Montgomery spirit could be applied generally, it is quite probable that the transition from a racially segregated to an integrated society might be made with a minimum of frustration.

One more possible aid to a peaceful transition might be supplied by educators, publicists, and scholars—including historians. It is not necessary to contend that the structure of ideas shapes the social structure to realize that what people believe influences greatly the way they behave. W. I. Thomas, the sociologist, has said that howsoever people define situations as real, they are just that. Like the nation, the South has always lived under powerful social myths, some of which have had no foundation in reality. However, this has not kept persons from *acting as though* these notions were true. We recall, for example, that the pro-slavery argument was based upon what went for science and scholarship as well as upon distortions of the Bible. Similarly the sociologists, anthropologists, novelists, political scientists, and historians, as well as theologians, have contributed to the rationalizations of segregation.

We must admit that all of this was, in a way, logical—if not scientific or scholarly—for it fitted in with the imperatives of a society that was based upon separation of the "races." So long as white and Negro Southerners were living separately, it was perhaps inevitable that their differences should be emphasized and exaggerated.

But the national necessity now demands an integrated American society, South as well as North. At this juncture, when very soon we must begin to live together in civic unity, what could be more nonsensical than a continued over-emphasis on our differences? If scholarship and education—in the South particularly—are to play a constructive social role in the great transition now going on, they must do what fidelity to truth has long demanded and reverse some of their traditional tendencies. Our similarities need to receive attention.

To many, change is frightfully difficult. Our social and natural scientists, historians, men of letters, editors, orators—all who communicate information and ideas—could help ease this pain if they would remind our nation, our section, our people, of the values, experiences, and dreams that we share. Therein we might discover at the least a common humanity and a universal destiny.

CHAPTER EIGHT

AN AMERICAN POLITICS FOR THE SOUTH

By Dewey W. Grantham, Jr.

THE THEME OF impending political change runs like a bright thread through the course of modern southern history. The South it seems has always been on the verge of entering a new era in politics. As Walter Hines Page said long ago, "Every year of our lives the new era was just about to begin."[1] Such wistful expectations were perhaps a manifestation of the South's haunting search for social identity, a symptom of its political schizophrenia; but, whatever their deeper meaning, they usually turned out to be illusory. Now, after three quarters of a century, the forces making for political change have been so powerful as to mark an epoch in the region's politics.

The ambiguous character of southern politics has been obscured by the myth of a monolithic South.* For fifty years liberal Southerners, disheartened by their section's continuing attachment to the one-party system and to "the old, dead issues of a past generation," have themselves contributed to the myth. But behind its façade of one-party uniformity the South has steadily and vigorously

* C. Vann Woodward has recently pointed out how certain developments of the past century have given rise—with considerable assistance from politicians who have found it politically profitable to obscure internal cleavages—to a false historical image of a monolithic South. *Reunion and Reaction: The Compromise of 1877 and the End of Reconstruction* (Doubleday Anchor Edition, Garden City, 1956), xi.

practiced the kind of competitive politics that is the guarantee of a liberal society. Rampant factionalism within the southern Democratic party has paralleled or exceeded the two-party strife in other sections, and more often than not the issues and cleavages in southern politics have been those of the larger American politics. Of course the South has been the most stubbornly sectional part of the country, and the most aberrant from national norms in its political attitudes and behavior. Yet Southerners, while often uncomfortable in the presence of the nation's liberal traditions, have never ceased to think of themselves as Americans and as democrats. For a long time after Reconstruction, their leaders could not bring themselves to attack openly the theories of democracy and equality established by the Civil War amendments; and even when they were disfranchising the Negroes and formulating a new defiinition of the suffrage, they sought to justify their actions in terms of the American democratic creed. Their tortuous efforts to achieve such a reconciliation reveal how difficult it was for them to surrender the heritage of liberal principles they shared with other Americans. Louis Hartz, in describing an earlier attempt by the South to repudiate its Americanism, has put it well: "When the guns of the Civil War were stilled the liberal self that the South could not sublimate even in the age of its great 'reaction' would gradually come to the fore again and, as in the days of Jefferson, would unite it to the North."[2]

The South's great ideological aberration, the dogma of white supremacy, is obviously related to its institutional aberration, the one-party system. Yet the basic ingredients of southern politics have been, not doctrines of race, but socio-economic groupings like those outside the region—business-minded conservatives, agrarian radicals, middle-class progressives, and the like. Each of these groups has one time or another used racism as a potent weapon against its competitors, but racism has never imposed sufficient unity on the white majority to override for long the fundamental pattern of group conflict.

The interaction between racism, conservatism, and agrarian radicalism in the last decade of the nineteenth century has been analyzed brilliantly by C. Vann Woodward.[3] Exploiting the racism of the white masses to overthrow the Reconstruction regimes, the business-minded Redeemers consolidated their power by preaching total allegiance to the one-party system. These Bourbon Democrats, though gilded with the leadership of ex-Confederate brigadiers, were not unlike their conservative counterparts, Democratic and Republican, who dominated northern politics in this period. Both groups showed marked favoritism to business enterprise and both encountered growing opposition from hard-pressed farmers.

The agrarian revolt assumed its most radical form in the South, where the Populist movement challenged the "New South" system and threatened a combination of the dispossessed farmers and Negroes along economic and social lines. It brought into sharp relief long-time cleavages which the Redeemers had never been able completely to suppress, no matter how assiduously they played upon the themes of race and tradition. The small farmers and inhabitants of the hill regions disliked the political domination of the white minorities in the Black Belts and the powerful alliances between the Black Belt leaders and the city politicians that often controlled the state governments. These small farmers, as well as many larger operators, resented discriminatory taxes, unfair railroad rates, high interest charges, and the big business orientation of the Bourbons; they joined the western farmers in castigating the eastern plutocracy, the Wall Street bankers, and the monopolistic corporations. The fury of the rebellion was strong enough to liquidate the Bourbon regimes in the southern states but it failed to bring about any fundamental alterations in the one-party system. The conservatives hurriedly invoked the race issue, rang the changes on the dangers of bolting the party, and fell back on skillful election maneuvers and tricks to win threatened districts. Even so, they found it necessary to present themselves as a sacrificial offering to prove their good intentions; they allowed themselves to be absorbed by the radical wing of the Democratic party led by William Jennings Bryan.

In this way the purity of the one-party system was preserved, the threat of extreme radicalism on the local scene was contained, and the possibility of deciding future issues on a more realistic basis was removed. Such immediate reforms as the agrarian radicals obtained did not result from Populist successes but from the leadership of insurgent Democrats like Benjamin R. Tillman of South Carolina and James S. Hogg of Texas who joined forces with the Farmers' Alliance but were careful to remain in the Democratic party. Bryan's defeat in 1896, improved economic conditions during the McKinley administration, and the South's patriotic response to the Spanish-American War served further to dissipate the force of the agrarian revolt. There remained much, moreover, to give strength to those who preached southern unity: racial considerations, the magic of Confederate and Reconstruction incantations, a predominantly agricultural economy based on cotton and tobacco, and the pervasive faith in the gospel of southern industrialization. Yet among rank-and-file Southerners no man since Lee had been more popular than Bryan, and Populist principles survived to leaven the factional politics of the South during the early years of the twentieth century.

A more immediate result of the Populist movement was the stimulus it gave to Negro disfranchisement. Both the conservatives and the radicals agreed that the political corruption of the 1890's was demoralizing and must be ended. The conservatives were profoundly shocked by the possibility of a political alliance between the humbler whites and the Negroes on the basis of common economic interests; the radicals bitterly contended that Negro votes had been used by the conservatives to defeat them. Although they approached the question from different points of view and were inclined to be suspicious of each other's motives, they tended to agree that the Negro was a source of trouble and that he must be disfranchised. In some states white farmers, eager to throw off Black Belt domination based in part on Negro votes, took the lead in calling for constitutional changes. Yet the poorer whites, who inhabited the mountain and hill regions in large numbers, looked with suspicion upon disfranchisement proposals which might be turned in their own direction. In the end the disfranchisement advocates carried the day, though not without a fight; Louisiana, North Carolina, Alabama, Virginia, and Georgia soon joined Mississippi and South Carolina in adopting a series of cleverly designed devices that quickly disfranchised such Negroes as still voted.* The long-range effect of the disfranchisement measures was to deprive large numbers of white men of the ballot, but contemporary white Southerners were inclined to view the suffrage restrictions as a necessary step, even a reform.†

Another important heritage of the Populist era was what Roger W. Shugg has called the "uprising of the poor whites."[4] During Populist days agrarian leaders like Tom Watson and Ben Tillman ignited the spark of political consciousness among common white men, and when the direct primary came into widespread use shortly thereafter, partly in response to their demands, these little men awoke to the fact that they possessed a new political power and that politicians were beginning to court their affections. The dis-

* Oklahoma adopted a constitutional disfranchisement provision in 1910. Other southern states accomplished virtual disfranchisement by means of such devices as the poll tax and the white primary.

† Edwin A. Alderman asserted in 1908, for example, that one of the most constructive acts of "Southern genius in reference to the negro, has been the limitation of the whole idea of manhood suffrage, thus removing the blacks from politics, and centering their thought on industrial life, removing frightful temptations from the politics of the white people, and in a large way, placing the whole idea of suffrage on the highest plane possible in a Republic."—*The Growing South. An Address Delivered before The Civic Forum in Carnegie Hall, New York City March 22, 1908* (New York, 1908), 12.

placed patricians might regard them as "a people who carry pistols in their hip pockets, who expectorate upon the floor, who have no toothbrushes and comb their hair with their fingers,"[5] but there was considerable point to the observation of a "redneck" farmer in Mississippi following one of James K. Vardaman's victories. "Wall," he remarked sagely, "the bottom rail's on top and its gwiner stay thar."[6]

Demagogues like "Cotton Tom" Heflin of Alabama, Cole Blease of South Carolina, and Theodore G. Bilbo of Mississippi, understanding the pains and frustrations of the common man on the farm and in the village, were quick to recognize the potentialities involved in the "rise of the poor whites." They proclaimed their belief in the power and wisdom of the masses and began to give expression to the social and economic grievances—and to the prejudices and passions—of the "rednecks" and the "wool hat boys" whose number was legion in the early twentieth-century South. "You can look at the back of my neck and see that I am a Vardaman man," declared a Mississippian in 1910.[7] The demagogues had no trouble in spotting such men and in speaking their language. They pictured themselves as men of action who would attack the rich and destroy the trusts. According to Wilbur J. Cash, Tillman brought forth the "whole bold, dashing, hell-of-a-fellow complex precisely in terms of the generality themselves," while Blease exemplified "the whole tradition of extravagence, of sectionalism and Negrophobia in Southern politics."[8] Once elected these men usually proved less rebellious, often making peace with the political hierarchy and the business interests they had recently denounced and threatened. Even so, they evoked a fierce loyalty from their supporters, and at least most of them served a cathartic function by acting as a "safety valve for discontent."[9]

These men of the people did not include that other downtrodden element, the Negroes, in their appeals. Instead, the Negro question supplied an issue that aroused the average white man even more powerfully than economic and class exhortations, and the defenseless black man became the chief stock-in-trade of such politicians. They never forgot that many white men identified the Negro as an economic competitor. An authentic hillbilly in Carl Carmer's *Stars Fell on Alabama* provides a perfect illustration. "We don't like niggers in this neck o' the woods," Tom Nabors explained. "We ain't ever liked 'em. I can remember my father standin' on the mountain where you can look off down toward the Black Belt an' the flat country an' sayin': 'Them black-bastards is takin' the food out'n our mouths. We oughta be down there workin' that black land but we got too much pride to work for nothin'.' They're down there sharin' the good things with the rich while good white folks in the hills have to starve."[10]

Following the Populist upheaval the supremacy of the Democratic party in the South became complete, but within the confines of one-party politics something happened during the decade and a half preceding the First World War to quicken the spirit of southern politics. For one thing, Populism and Bryanism served as powerful influences in the formation of election alliances. Then, too, "the revolt of the rednecks," even when led by demagogic opportunists, emphasized social, economic, and geographic cleavages in the party and promoted a dual factionalism that possessed some discipline and continuity. In addition to these developments, an urban-sponsored, middle-class reform movement emerged in the South which was somewhat in line with the progressivism of other regions. In the towns and cities, especially, there was a tendency to see the South through new and more critical eyes and a yearning to see it participate in the national reforms. "The old moss-backs will soon be gone, thank the Lord," declared an Atlanta minister in 1908. "Here, then will come a generation of young men and women to be transformed by the quickening forces of a new environment."[11] Edwin A. Alderman, president of the University of Virginia, voiced the new interest in a more responsible politics when he urged Southerners never again to vote for a candidate "who does not have some well-worked-out program for conserving and developing our rural communities, for constructing good roads throughout the State, for placing a respectable school house and good school in easy reach of every child . . . and for making our institutions of charity and higher education equal to any."[12]

Political "reformers" arose in every state in the South to take advantage of such sentiment. Some of these men were demagogues and some were conservatives masquerading as progressives. Others were genuine liberals, ranging in type from moderate humanitarians, concerned about such things as penal reform and public education, to agrarian radicals who talked like Populists. The most comprehensive of these reformers had a certain sectional cast, since they identified the evils they saw in an unrestrained capitalism with the railroads and other corporations of the Northeast. Southern progressives resented the colonial status of the South's industry and commerce, and their first coalescence in many states came with movements for railroad regulation and rate reductions. Successful leaders like Thomas M. Campbell, Braxton B. Comer, Hoke Smith, and Napoleon B. Broward combined their anti-corporation radicalism with humanitarian programs. Such issues as railroad and public utility regulation, public education campaigns, child labor legislation, penal reform, prohibition, internal improvements, and the extension of state control over primary elections and campaign contributions they used effectively to secure support from farmers and city voters. They also knew the value of publicizing their opposition to the "machine" elements and of dramatizing their campaigns. The conservative Democrats, usually allied with the railroads and other business interests, fought savagely to retain control of the party in the various states of the South and to block progressive measures. In North Carolina, for example, the conservative machine of Furnifold M. Simmons cease-lessly opposed North Carolina progressives. One of the reformers recalled years later, "For those of us who espoused the liberalism of Jefferson, followed the leadership of Bryan, admired the judi-cial statesmanship of Walter Clark, and opposed machine-con-trolled politics, Simmons had little respect and no regard."[13]

Southern progressives added a good deal to the functions of government and secured a substantial body of reforms, but their successes varied from state to state and they neglected some funda-mental questions, including the worsening problem of farm tenancy and the condition of the Negroes. Southern progressivism was for "whites only" and some of the progressives could not refrain from invoking the race question in their political contests. They even contended that this was necessary to break the business dom-ination of politics. William E. Dodd pointed out in 1907 that "in order to break the hold of J. P. Morgan on Georgia the radical wing of the Democratic party felt constrained to appeal once again to the ever-present race hatred." As Dodd said, ". . . while we go forward with one foot we are drawn backward with the other."[14] There was always the temptation to follow Joseph W. Bailey's campaign confession: "I believe more in the purity of the Anglo-Saxon race than I do in the principles of democracy."[15]

The progressives learned, just as they did in other parts of the country, that it was one thing to win elections and quite another to secure the passage of progressive legislation. They also discov-ered that even after reforms were adopted they often failed the test of administrative effectiveness. There were still other barriers to reform. Spurious issues had a surprising habit of turning up at the most inopportune moment. Farmers were often hostile to-ward city folk and ready to follow local demagogues who sought to set the country against the city. Furthermore, the country "radi-cal" of Populist persuasion and his urban cousin, the middle-class "liberal," tended to approach such questions as railroad regulation and business control from different directions and with different degrees of political intensity.   The city voter characterized some of the agrarian proposals as "class" legislation, and he was more likely than the farmer to consider industrialization the *sine qua non* of southern progress.   Indeed, the current of southern progressivism was slowed and often turned aside by the shoals of the old yearning for industrial advances.   Prohibition also diverted the liberal movement.   In some southern states it became the *raison d'être* of the reform movement, smoothing over the more natural patterns of conflict in the body politic and shifting attention from more pressing economic and social problems.   Finally, the southern progressives learned, or at least the more advanced of them did, that on some issues they were simply too far ahead of the people to be successful.   It was no lack of faith in the people, no failure of the democratic spirit within him, that led North Carolina's Walter Clark to admit during the latter part of his long career that Southerners were too conservative from habit and training to accept the most advanced progressive ideas.[16]

Whatever their limitations, the more effective of the southern progressives did much to encourage a widespread bi-factionalism in the Democratic party and to present the voters in the primaries with a real choice between conservative and liberal candidates. So strong was the factional division in some of the southern states during the progressive era that it is possible even today to find evidence of those old cleavages.   But inevitably, the liberal factions generated by the progressive movement in the South had to pay the heavy cost of too-great reliance on personal politics.   It was a cruel handicap and one over which the progressives had little control. In order to be successful they must needs have powerful and colorful leaders, but when they were successful the leaders often loomed larger in the minds of the people than the reforms they advocated. Even more important was the inability of strong progressives to pass on their leadership to equally effective successors.[17]   There was no system to recruit and train leaders and no sure restraints in such an amorphous politics that would preserve discipline and coherence for any length of time. With leaders and lieutenants of each faction going off at various tangents, and even joining the opposition, the voters often found it difficult to determine just what a candidate stood for. The obstacles to a continuous political registering of the existing social and economic differences under a one-party system have only occasionally been surmounted. The latent class conflict in Louisiana provided the setting for Huey P. Long, whose regime in turn established the basis for a durable and well-disciplined bi-factional system.[18] But even the effects of Longism may be expected to wear off in time, unless new developments occur to perpetuate the state's bi-factionalism.

Meanwhile, as the second decade of the twentieth century began, material and educational advances were encouraging many Southerners to believe that a new and better South was just around the corner. Walter Hines Page expressed the new optimism when he declared in 1911: "With 15-to-18 cent cotton, with profitable manufactures, with the broadening influence of trade, with the results of modern education, the old land is really just coming to its own."[19] It remained for a political development to convince such men as Page that the South had indeed come into its own; this was the nomination and election of Woodrow Wilson, the first southern-born president since Andrew Johnson.

During the years 1911-1912 the movement to nominate Wilson, who was then achieving a solid national reputation as a progressive governor of New Jersey, received the enthusiastic support of the liberal faction of the Democratic party in almost every southern state. The Wilson movement served to give the liberal factions—some of which had been thwarted on the state level—a kind of national base and to sharpen the bi-factional politics that had been developing in the South. Wilson's election also gave a new note of pride and satisfaction to millions of Southerners who could scarcely believe that a Southerner had won the highest office in the land. "Long ago I had despaired of ever seeing a man of Southern birth President," exclaimed a North Carolina judge, who felt that Wilson's election marked "an era in our national life. With it we have the ascendancy of men of Southern birth and residence to the seats of power and responsibility such as has never been seen in our day. . . . The world is looking on to witness the result."[20]

Five members of Wilson's cabinet were born in the South and southern congressional leaders assumed a prominent role in the enactment of the extensive domestic reforms that the Wilson administration pressed in the years 1913-17. A significant feature of the Wilson period was the preponderant control of congressional committee chairmanships by Southerners, whose seniority in service, growing out of the one-party system's operation, gave them precedence over non-southern Democrats in Congress.* Another aspect of the South's relationship to Wilson's New Freedom was the influence of several neo-Populist congressmen from such states as Arkansas and Texas in forcing the administration to sponsor more radical agricultural, banking, and anti-trust legislation than Wilson had at first recommended.[21] At the same time, Wilson was a strong president who did much to interest Southerners in national affairs and to pull southern politicians into the orbit of national politics. One of the most interesting developments of the Wilson era was the steady support given the President by many southern conservatives, who were perhaps more amenable than the liberals to the blandishments of federal patronage.

The retreat of southern sectionalism has generally coincided with the rise of strong Democratic administrations in Washington.

* During the Sixty-third Congress (1913-1915) ten of the fourteen major committees in the Senate were headed by Southerners, while thirteen of the sixteen principal House committees had southern chairmen.—*Official Congressional Directory*, 63 Cong., 2 Sess. (Washington, 1913), 161-70, 185-94.

During the Wilson years local and state politicians in the South—conservatives as well as progressives—suddenly found themselves under strong pressure to endorse the president and his reforms. The South firmly upheld Wilson's war diplomacy, although some dissatisfaction existed in the cotton belt in 1914-15, because of the administration's failure to adopt stronger measures to keep open the commercial routes to Continental Europe. After the war came, Southerners strongly supported it and they were equally staunch in their adherence to the President's peace proposals.

The liquidation of the progressive movement amid the fierce flames of World War I, the foundering of Woodrow Wilson's peace plans on the shoals of partisanship and normalcy, and the overwhelming repudiation of the Democratic party in 1920, had important repercussions on the politics of the region from the Potomac to the Rio Grande. For one thing, the powerful current forcing southern politicians into places of power and responsibility in a national administration, with the attendant pressures on state and local leaders in the South, was gone. This is not to say that southern influence in the Democratic party declined. In fact, just the opposite occurred; with the decline of Democratic strength in other parts of the country Southerners could more nearly dominate the shaping of party policy than had been possible during the Wilson period. But liberals throughout the South felt the loss of Wilson's leadership. Then, too, what had seemed important to reformers in the years before the great war often seemed unimportant and far away during its disillusioning aftermath. The most constructive politicians in the 1920's tended to emphasize administrative reorganization, highway development, and efforts to attract business to their states. The blandness of southern politics reasserted itself and the strong bi-factionalism and the fairly clear-cut cleavages of the prewar period threatened to disintegrate.

It would not be accurate, however, to picture southern politics in the twenties entirely in the somber colors of the Ku Klux Klan, prohibition, and Bible Belt fundamentalism, important as were those influences.   There were also constructive political leaders like Governor Austin Peay of Tennessee who sought to modernize the machinery of their state governments.   Most of the southern states joined in the national trend toward the expansion of state services, particularly for roads, schools, and public health.   There was much evidence of the South's overwhelming desire to share in the business prosperity of the times, whatever the cost.   But while they were endeavoring to revolutionize the face of the region through economic changes, Southerners held on grimly to old-time religious, moral, and social mores.   As Donald Davidson put it some years later, "The United Daughters of the Confederacy and the Kiwanis Club flourished side by side.   Mule-wagon and automobile, fundamentalism and liberalism, education and illiteracy, aristocratic pride and backwoods independence disproved the axiom that two bodies cannot occupy the same space.   Cities that preserved the finest flavor of the old regime had to be approached over brand-new roads where bill-boards, tourist camps, filling stations, and factories broke out in a modernistic rash among the water oaks and Spanish moss."[22]

In such seemingly paradoxical circumstances southern politicians sometimes found it difficult to be consistent.   But the men who cared most about "tourist camps, filling stations, and factories" took pains to demonstrate their social as well as their economic conservatism.   Indeed, the South's social conservatism made it possible for the economic conservatives to have their way more completely.   The bitter conflict between urban and rural Democrats, roughly symbolized by the northeastern and southern leadership of the party, was not so much an economic as it was a social clash.   Social conservatives in the South rebelled against the incipient orientation of the Democratic party toward the urban, Catholic, and foreign East.   The protracted struggle in the national convention of 1924 was only a prelude to the desertion of a Tammanyite presidential nominee four years later. Yet Herbert Hoover's victories in the South did not occur in the areas of strongest rural, prohibition, and protestant sentiment, but in those states with relatively few Negroes, traditional Republican strength, and economic interests that pulled them toward national integration. Thus, despite Republican efforts to capitalize on the discontent of social conservatives, they were successful only where they could exert an economic as well as a social attraction.

The depression and the New Deal brought a return of the Solid South. The effect of Franklin D. Roosevelt's program on southern politics can scarcely be overestimated; in some ways it was revolutionary. Addressing itself directly to the South's problems, the New Deal precipitated an unprecedented popular agitation on social and political issues in the region below the Potomac. It frightened the conservatives, shocked the section out of its normal complacency toward national politics, promoted the growth of organized labor, and encouraged the spread of liberal ideas throughout the South. It introduced codes and standards that did much to undermine the old faith in freedom of contract and state rights.[23] Those who opposed what they considered to be federal encroachments on state rights learned that they must assume responsibilities on the state level if they were to head off centralization. But most Southerners seemed willing enough to accept the federal largess offered to them.* State rights seemed less essential than federal assistance. As William Faulkner has recently said, "We—Mississippi—sold our state's rights back to the federal government when we accepted the first cotton price-

* While bitterly denouncing federal encroachments on state rights during the last few years, southern leaders have continued to appeal to Washington for all manner of financial aid. They do very well too. During the fiscal year 1950-51, the eleven ex-Confederate states contributed 12.52 per cent of all internal revenue collections, while receiving in return over 27 per cent of federal grants-in-aid. See Robert J. Harris, "States' Rights and Vested Interests," *Journal of Politics*, XV (November, 1953), 470-71.

support subsidy twenty years ago. Our economy is not agricultural any longer. Our economy is the federal government. We no longer farm in Mississippi cotton fields. We farm now in Washington corridors and Congressional committee rooms."[24]

During the New Deal years Roosevelt's leadership tended to broaden and nationalize the outlook of southern congressmen, much as had Wilson's administration. The Roosevelt administration also had its influence on the Democratic factionalism of the southern states, since it forced New Deal issues into state and local political contests. At the same time Roosevelt demonstrated his independence of the Democratic South by his powerful appeal to the masses of voters in other regions, and he even forced the South to acknowledge its loss of indispensability to the party by accepting the repeal of the historic two-thirds rule in the national convention of 1936. But the relationship between the New Deal and southern Democrats worked both ways, for Roosevelt found that he still had to depend upon the cooperation of southern party leaders, who once more monopolized the important committee chairmanships, in the enactment of his program.*

Some southern leaders played important roles in the passage of New Deal legislation; such men as Joseph T. Robinson, Hugo Black, Alben W. Barkley, William B. Bankhead, and Sam Rayburn were invaluable in their legislative assistance to the President. But not all southern congressmen were as cooperative. The abolition of the two-thirds rule and, especially, Roosevelt's attack on the Supreme Court unsettled many of them and gave them an excuse to oppose the administration. The threat of an anti-lynching bill and the last major domestic reform surge of the New Deal in 1937-38 precipitated increasing conservative opposition from southern congressional leaders like Walter F. George. Many of

* During the Seventy-third Congress (1933-1935) nine of the fourteen major Senate committees and twelve of the seventeen most important House committees had Southerners as chairmen.—*Official Congressional Directory.* 73 Cong., 1 Sess. (Washington, 1933), 175-80, 191-203.

these men spoke for southern business interests, and their bitter opposition to such New Deal measures as the wages and hours bill in 1937-38 reflected the South's fear that it would lose certain regional advantages in its efforts to industrialize. Roosevelt's one real effort to take an active hand in eliminating some of the more obdurate southern conservatives, in the congressional elections of 1938, failed, and the administration's drive for domestic reform was soon engulfed in the larger concern with World War II.

The war, which was strongly supported by the South, moderated southern discontent with certain aspects of the administration's program. Party loyalty and economic considerations involving foreign trade, as well as such factors as military tradition, ethnic composition, and psychological make-up, stimulated southern internationalism.[25] Nevertheless, while supporting the war, large numbers of southern congressmen opposed many of the President's proposals, reassured no doubt by his recent defeat in the 1938 elections and encouraged by his difficulties since that time.* The defeat of many northern Democratic congressmen in 1942 and 1946 further strengthened the influence of the southern conservatives in the party, and Roosevelt's death, which temporarily cast southern liberals adrift, added to this supremacy. In the early forties, moreover, a group of southern anti-New Deal governors, led by Eugene Talmadge and Sam Houston Jones, launched violent attacks on various parts of Roosevelt's program.

Still, there were evidences in the forties that southern liberalism was not dead. Young Ellis Arnall of Georgia won a notable record for progressivism during the war years, and in the postwar period Kerr Scott of North Carolina and Sid McMath of Arkansas achieved considerable success as New Deal-Fair Deal governors.

---

* In 1944, for instance, three-fifths of the northern Democrats in Congress were more than 90 per cent loyal to their party while less than one-twelfth of the Southerners achieved that degree of party regularity. In the 1920's, on the other hand, when Southerners dominated the party in Congress, they were more loyal than were northern Democrats. See Julius Turner, *Party and Constituency: Pressures on Congress* (Baltimore, 1951), 134-36.

Proven liberals like Claude Pepper, Lister Hill, and Estes Kefauver continued in Congress. During the first three or four years following the war a great many Southerners still thought of themselves as New Deal Democrats, but President Truman's forthright advocacy of a civil rights program caused many to draw back and allowed those who wanted to repudiate the Truman administration, for whatever reason, to seize the initiative.

The Dixiecrat movement in 1948 and subsequent Republican successes in the South were the culmination of two streams of protest which had long been building up against the Roosevelt and Truman administrations. Many Southerners responded to the States Rights Democrats because of their hostility toward New Deal economic policies. But despite its tender regard for business interests and all its talk about state rights and constitutional government, the Dixiecrat movement gathered most of its strength from the racism and traditional sectionalism that had long frustrated political realignment and perpetuated the Solid South.[26] The States Righters made their strongest appeal in those Black Belt areas which V. O. Key describes as the hard core of the Solid South, the areas that had stood by the Democrats in 1928. Long disturbed by the New Deal's "coddling" of the Negro and troubled by the implications of American war aims, as well as by such wartime innovations as the federal commission on employment practices, many Southerners had their worst fears realized in Truman's civil rights recommendations. The southern leaders apparently hoped that Truman would be more responsive to the "southern bloc" in Congress. They assumed that he would be defeated in 1948 and, having foreseen that northern liberals would raise the civil rights issue in the national convention, they seized upon the election as a favorable time to frighten the party leadership into a more cooperative attitude.

Perhaps the most significant thing about the Dixiecrat revolt was its failure—a failure that came in spite of fervent appeals to the South's most cherished shibboleths. Even in the states which they carried, the States Righters appropriated the official Democrat label on the ballot. The most substantial political leaders in the region shied away from the Dixiecrat radicals and were careful to keep lines of communication open with the national party leadership. Following the election the question of party loyalty became an issue in some southern states along the general lines of the old liberal-conservative cleavage. The fact that white-supremacy politicians like Herman Talmadge and Olin D. Johnston would have no part of the third-party movement indicated the anachronistic character of the old sectionalism. No politician interested in national politics could afford to campaign on such a sectional basis. Sectional politics could not control national politics, but rather must be adjusted to them. Most issues had become national issues, and the major social and economic divisions extended throughout the country, causing Southerners and Northerners to be arrayed against Southerners and Northerners. As H. C. Nixon said some years ago, "In our political arithmetic national denominators are gaining in importance in comparison with regional denominators."[27]

If the Dixiecrat movement of 1948 gave expression to pressures serving to retard political change in the South, the elections of 1952 and 1956 reflected long-accumulating forces pushing toward a political realignment in the region. What happened in 1952 and 1956 was not unrelated to the schism of 1948, for there was a noticeable "Dixiecrat to Ike" trend in the states that had been carried by J. Strom Thurmond. But the basic explanation of the Republican victories in the South lies in the long dissatisfaction, primarily for economic reasons, on the part of many southern Democrats with New Deal policies. This southern distaste for New Deal liberalism had already begun to reveal itself in such sporadic movements as the "Constitutional Democrats of Texas" in 1936, the "Jeffersonian Democratic Party" of South Carolina in 1940, and the "Texas Regulars" in 1944. By 1952 this Democratic discontent had grown strong enough to burst out of its old bounds in vigorous fashion, and in doing so it brought to light some of the profound social and economic forces on which it rested.

The most significant of the new factors in southern politics are associated with the economic revolution that is industrializing and urbanizing the South, diversifying its economy, and effecting a large migration into and out of its borders. Rejuvenated by the New Deal and vastly stimulated by the war, the southern economy is experiencing the flush days of a boom. The South's relative position among the major regions has improved in almost every category of wealth since 1930.[28] Factories and assembly plants have sprung up from Richmond to San Antonio; agriculture has been increasingly mechanized and diversified; sharecroppers and agricultural workers in large numbers have left the farm for the cities of the North and South, while a growing stream of technicians, managers, and businessmen has flowed into the region. As the current quip has it: "Cotton is going West, cattle are coming East, Negroes are going North, and Yankees are coming South." Most Southerners are enjoying a degree of unaccustomed prosperity; and a broad new middle class, extremely business-minded, as well as a liberal sprinkling of *nouveau riche,* has emerged in the cities.*

One measure of the transformation under way in the South is the growing urbanization of the region, a process now taking place

* A significant commentary on the economic revolution under way in the South is the fact that in 1950 only about one out of every five southern workers was employed in agriculture. It is also interesting to note that cotton now furnishes one-fourth instead of one-half of the agricultural income in the South. See Rupert B. Vance, "The South," *Collier's Encyclopedia 1957 Year Book* (New York, 1957), 663.

relatively more rapidly than in the Northeast. Between 1930 and 1950, for example, the growth of cities of 50,000 or more in the South proceeded at a rate three times the national average. As late as 1920 the South was only about one-fourth urban, whereas today one-half of its population lives in cities and towns. In their assiduous efforts to industrialize their section, Southerners seem curiously unable or unwilling to perceive the likelihood that economic innovations will ultimately change their social and political institutions. Yet the economic revolution in the South is surely breaking the cake of social custom and diluting the homogeneity of the region. New jobs and new faces mean new ideas and new habits. Urbanization means the decline of ruralism and the creation of an atmosphere in which the old loyalties and prejudices are less potent; in which workers are likely to join labor unions and Negroes begin to vote.[29]

An important consequence of these developments, as Alexander Heard has pointed out, is the creation of divisive influences in southern politics and the sharpening of social and economic issues in such a way as to cut into the traditional domination of the Black Belts.[30] The recent changes in a state like Texas, during an era of phenomenal prosperity and population growth, would seem to provide a solid basis for such political divisions. The "respectable" elements of a rapidly-growing middle class, as well as the wealthy oil promoters and cattlemen, have found the policies of Harry S. Truman anathema and the ideas of Robert A. Taft more and more attractive. Negroes, farmers, and urban workers, on the other hand, tend to support liberal candidates. These economic and social cleavages also find expression on the state level within the one-party system, but in a halting and confused fashion.

When viewed against this background the Republican victories of 1952 and 1956 in the South become far more than Eisenhower victories, though many Southerners rationalized their Republican votes on the ground that General Eisenhower was above party, or by asserting that there were no real differences between the two parties—only between their candidates.* Republican successes represent what Professor Key calls "the political fulfillment of demographic and economic trends" in the region. The number of "Presidential Republicans" in the South grew steadily in the 1940's, but the election of 1952 was the event that set off the explosive forces long building up there. The most significant thing about 1952 is not that it inaugurated a real two-party system in the South, which is clearly not the case, but that an analysis of the election returns shows that Southerners, especially in the cities, divided their votes much as did other Americans, and for pretty much the same reasons. In city after city in the southern states Eisenhower carried the upper-income precincts by handsome majorities (and a great many of the middle-income precincts by less generous majorities), while Adlai E. Stevenson carried the lower-income districts by equally substantial margins.[31] The same trends are evident in the returns for 1956, when the Eisenhower-Nixon ticket made an even better showing in the urban South. In two out of every three southern counties containing a city of at least 25,000 people, the Republicans actually increased their percentage of the vote. They carried no less than sixty of the approximately ninety-six such urban counties in the eleven ex-Confederate states.[32]

A recent study of political behavior in a representative "white" precinct in a southern city would suggest that President Eisenhower's personality appeal did not operate in a random fashion among Dixie Democrats. Such factors as socio-economic status and migration patterns revealed significant differences between "Eisencrats" and "Stevencrats."[33] Loyalty to the Democratic party

* In announcing that he would support President Eisenhower in 1956, Governor Allan Shivers of Texas declared: "I believe he has proved himself to be a bigger and better man, by any and all the political, moral and spiritual standards by which we judge men, than his opponent of 1952 and 1956."— Nashville *Banner*, September 24, 1956.

remains a major consideration in southern politics, but changes in class identification are clearly laying the groundwork for shifts in party affiliation.

Another significant aspect of the Republican victories in the South was the way in which the recurrent cleavages within the Democratic party there spilled over into the national contests between the major parties. In Louisiana, for example, the Long forces supported Stevenson while the anti-Long voters crossed party lines in large numbers to cast their ballots for Eisenhower. In Texas the Republican vote in 1952 and 1956 was similar to the Shivers vote in 1954 and the anti-regular vote in 1958. Even in Florida, where a multi-factional system has long prevailed, the traditional liberal-conservative division in Democratic primaries is being translated into a Democratic-Republican division in national elections.[34]

The return of Negroes to the polls during the past decade and a half is another development that is likely to have a significant bearing on future southern political affairs. The large increase of Negro voters in the South, following the famous *Smith vs. All-wright* decision of 1944, which opened the white primaries to Negroes, is nothing short of a revolution in southern voting habits. Negroes still find it difficult to exercise the franchise in many places in the Deep South,[35] and only about 25 per cent of the southern Negroes of voting age are registered, as compared with 60 per cent of the eligible whites in the region, but they are voting in every southern state. The Southern Regional Council estimated the Negro registration in the former Confederate states by the end of 1956 at 1,238,000. More than 163,000 Negroes had registered in Georgia by that time, as compared with 10,000 in 1944.[36]

Although the Negro vote in the South has not become the balance of power the demagogue spoke of in his old-time warning, it has become too important to ignore. A student of Louisiana politics has pointed out, for instance, that it is "statistically proveable that the Negro vote was a crucial element in Adlai Stevenson's narrow victory in Louisiana in 1952; in Earl Long's first primary triumph in the 1956 Democratic gubernatorial primary; and in Eisenhower's precedent-shattering conquest of Louisiana's electorial vote in 1956."[37] Urban politics in particular reflects the Negro's new political role. Negro members of city councils and school boards have been elected, Southerners of darker skin have suddenly begun to acquire an unaccustomed leverage in obtaining a fairer share of municipal services, and local politicians increasingly are taking Negro voters into account. The mere fact that southern Negroes are voting in such spectacular numbers is full of meaning, but it may be equally significant to note that they tend to join the liberal factions of the Democratic party. It was almost as if another of the old Populist dreams was coming true. Fifty years ago W. E. B. Du Bois declared that "The Negro voter . . . has in his hand the tremendous power of emancipating the Democratic Party from its enslavement to the reactionary South."[38] It would be ironic indeed if his claim should materialize.

The growing participation of Negroes in the Democratic primaries, usually on the side of the liberal factions, may well influence the movement of white Southerners into the Republican party. Many Southerners are disturbed by the claims that Negroes vote in blocs. Samuel Lubell found that Negroes voted heavily for Frank P. Graham in North Carolina and Claude Pepper in Florida in the 1950 senatorial primaries, but that the large Negro vote for these southern liberals provoked an even larger opposition turnout by whites.[39] The situation is complicated, however, by the new upsurge of race feeling in the region, which is being used in an effort to keep the South solid, presumably in the Democratic party. The Eisenhower administration, tarred with the integration brush and stamped with the stigma of Little Rock, has unquestionably become less attractive to Southerners. Furthermore, the current preoccupation with racial difficulties is likely to gloss over the economic and social divisions that would normally promote the chances of a two-party system. "Not since the last act of Hamlet," observes Professor Denis W. Brogan, "has there been such mixed scuffling as in the South since 1948. . . ."[40]

Examples of how racial tension and the "New Know Nothingism" in the South are obstructing the incipient transformation of southern politics are not hard to come by. One of the most drastic shifts in the presidential election returns of 1956, as compared with 1952, was the manner in which Negro voters left the Democratic party to support the Republicans. This shift was nowhere more pronounced than in the South, where civil rights and the slogan, "A vote for the Democrats is a vote for Eastland," proved effective in overcoming the attraction of economic considerations offered by the Democrats. In twenty-three southern cities Negroes increased their vote for Eisenhower and Nixon by 36.8 per cent over 1952. Thirty-eight Negro precincts in Memphis which had returned 68 per cent of their votes for Stevenson and Sparkman in 1952, gave 54 per cent of their ballots to the Republicans in 1956—and probably threw the state to the G.O.P. In 1952 Stevenson carried the Negro precincts in Atlanta by more than two to one, but four years later he received less than 15 per cent of the votes in those precincts.[41]

If southern Negroes are returning to the party of Lincoln, at least in national elections, to show their dissatisfaction with racial demagoguery, many white Southerners are finding it difficult to resist the campaigns of racist rabble-rousers. The Arkansas gubernatorial primary of 1958 provides an excellent example. In a campaign in which Little Rock and school integration overshadowed all other issues, Orval E. Faubus, who had faced a bleak political future less than a year before, was swept back into office by determinedly wrapping himself in the mantle of white supremacy. In Virginia the respectable Byrd machine, threatened on the left by liberal Democrats and on the right by a revived Republican party, suddenly discovered that school segregation was the magic road to white solidarity in the state. Yet the very existence of the racial crisis, so often foretold by southern politicians, is an indication of progress and an illustration of the way in which national and international pressures are working to bring provincial practices into line with American ideals. The quickening pace of change in race relations will certainly make for a more genuinely American politics for the South.

Political changes seem to proceed much more slowly than economic and social changes. The South's history shows how powerful tradition can be in the realm of political ideas and behavior. Those automobile stickers in 1952, proclaiming that "I'm a Democrat but I like Ike," had their own special meaning. There is still much truth in what Virginius Dabney wrote in 1942. "Many Southerners who currently profess allegiance to the Democratic party," observed Dabney, "would be far more congenially situated as Republicans if they could but forget Thad Stevens and Ben Wade, and put out of their minds the fact that to their grandfathers the Democratic party was only slightly less sacrosanct than the Army of Northern Virginia."[42] There is also a practical question to be considered. Except for the presidency, why should conservatives in the South vote for the Republican opponents of men like Harry Flood Byrd and Richard B. Russell? Why, especially, when these and many less responsible southern congressmen, operating from powerful committee positions,* have so often allied

* In addition to the chairmanship of the Democratic Policy Committee and the Speakership of the House of Representatives in the Eighty-fifth Congress (1957-1959), eight of the thirteen major Senate committees and ten of the fifteen principal House committees were headed by Southerners. *Official Congressional Directory,* 85 Cong., 2 Sess. (Washington, 1958), 231-36, 241-49.

themselves with Republicans in Congress on questions that involve federal spending and domestic welfare programs. The extent and the effectiveness of the Southern-Republican coalition may have been exaggerated,* but it has demonstrated its strength by destroying the O.P.A., by passing the Taft-Hartley bill over the president's veto, and by generally frustrating liberal plans. The growing Dixie revolt against the reciprocal trade program, which finds some southern politicians talking like latter-day William McKinleys, will no doubt ultimately promote southern Republicanism, but at the present time it may well be having the opposite effect by converting "free-trade" Southerners into champions of "protectionism."†

As long as conservatives who call themselves Democrats can control the state governments in the South, there is no place for a separate conservative party led by Republicans. For the most part, Republican leaders, satisfied with Democratic control on the state level and primarily interested in convention politics and

* A *Congressional Quarterly* analysis of the roll call votes in the first session of the Eighty-fifth Congress (1957) showed that a majority of the southern Democrats in the two houses opposed the stand taken by a majority of the non-southern Democrats on 64, or 31 per cent, of the roll calls. By contrast, the southern Democrats disagreed with the Republicans on 103, or 50 per cent, of the session's roll calls. The disagreements between the Democrats from the South and their party colleagues from other sections included not only the issue of civil rights but fundamental questions of foreign policy, domestic welfare, and the proper limits of federal activity. Mississippi, Virginia, and South Carolina were the states where disagreement with the policies of northern Democrats, as reflected in Congressional votes, was most marked.—"How Big Is the North-South Democratic Split?" *Congressional Quarterly Almanac*, 85 Cong., 1 Sess., (1957), XIII, 813-17.

† An analysis of the votes in 1951, 1952, 1955, and 1958 to extend the Reciprocal Trade Agreements Act reveals that the South has become the center of defection from the historic low-tariff position of the Democratic party. The most rebellious states, strangely enough, were in the deep South, until recently the most devout part of the region in its "free-trade" faith. Every member of the House and Senate from South Carolina and Georgia, for instance, voted to kill the 1958 measure to extend the reciprocity program. But for the region as a whole, more than two-thirds of the southern Democrats in the two houses voted for the bill on the crucial votes.—*Cong. Record*, 85 Cong., 2 Sess., 9782; *Congressional Quarterly Weekly Report*, XVI (July 25, 1958), 955, 979; Richard A. Watson, "The Tariff Revolution: A Study of Shifting Party Attitudes," *Journal of Politics*, XVIII (November, 1956), 682-91, 698-700.

patronage in Washington, have not wanted to win elections at home. Significant as were the Republican successes in 1952 and 1956, it is well to remember that few Republican congressmen and local officials were elected in the South during those years. Still, the bi-factional cleavages in the Democratic party offer a good basis for party realignment. A sustained period of state control by a liberal faction such as the anti-Shivers wing of the party in Texas would probably act as a powerful incentive for conservative Southerners to enter the Republican party. But southern liberals, forced for so long into a Procrustean bed with the dominant conservatives, have no place to go and, ironically, are actually "hugging the one-party system with might and main."[43] Their polar star must remain the Democratic party at the national level.

In the final analysis, the fortunes of the Democratic party outside of the South will have much to do with southern politics. A resurgent Democracy in the western and northern states will almost certainly impose its will on the party more vigorously than in the past, despite the Southerners' parliamentary adroitness. This would encourage southern liberals and make the Republican party more attractive in the eyes of many conservatives in the region. It might also stimulate another third-party movement in the South, although Senator Russell, the leading spokesman for southern Democrats in Congress, declared in mid-October, 1957: "Unless a third party movement can be sold to other states, it would be a terrible mistake. We are better off with the Democrats."[44]

It is extremely improbable that the shock registered in the South as a result of the large Republican gains in the last two national elections will entirely disappear. Despite the persistence of sectionalism, there is less and less need to be a crypto-Republican. According to a Mississippi congressman, writing in 1955 about southern politics during the past decade, "The one big change is the increasing respectability of the Republican party."[45]

President Eisenhower's intervention at Little Rock no doubt represents a setback for the Republican party in the South, but that episode will never rival the Reconstruction legends. There is too much pressure within the Democratic party in favor of a strong civil rights policy for that to happen. The new urban middle class will perhaps be more impervious to the debilitating effects of white-supremacy politics than most Southerners have been. The emergence of a two-party system in the South will probably proceed by a series of spurts, as in 1928 and 1952, with each movement ahead being followed by a partial loss before the next advance takes place. Republican successes may also depend upon the priority assigned to the region by national party leaders; the South may become so necessary for Republican success on the national front that it will develop into a real party battleground. At any rate, it seems safe to say that during the next few years Republican gains in the South will likely occur only on the national level, with occasional state and congressional victories coming first in the border states like Florida, Tennessee, and Texas, where the party is organized, has considerable strength, and benefits from economic and social conditions most favorable to political change.[46]

A wise Southerner has recently reminded us that "The Solid South has always been cracking from within. . . ."[47] The South can no longer be called a one-party region, at least not in national politics. It is plain enough that under the impact of an economic revolution, a world war, and the New Deal, the last quarter of a century has witnessed what V. O. Key terms the steady "erosion of sectionalism" in the southern states. Urbanization, industrialization, and the movement of people across the face of the country are undermining the old sectional attitudes and pointing toward a more complete political integration of all parts of the country. While retaining many of its accustomed habits and beliefs, the South has reflected the increasing homogenization of American society. Indeed, one of the neglected aspects of southern history is the manner in which the region has responded and adjusted to the major developments and the dominant moods of the country during the last seventy-five years. Certain economic and social conditions have caused parts of the South to resist these homogenizing and unifying forces more stubbornly than others, and in some cases the result has not been good. Professor Nixon has pointed out, for example, that the most militant pro-segregation agitation in the school integration controversy has been brought about by the inhabitants or spokesmen of regions of relative or absolute decline in population or of unbalanced economy. The frustration and prejudice produced by such conditions easily finds expression in demagoguery and race-baiting. "It is unfortunate for the cause of civil progress and the sense of moderation," declares Nixon, "that in most Southern states a disproportionate and undeserved political power is exercised by static or declining counties and communities. . . ."[48]

This is not entirely a southern problem. In fact, the most fundamental political problems in the South today are not vastly different from the fundamental political problems in other parts of the United States. The internal arrangements of state politics throughout the country appear to be growing more and more alike. It is true that few areas in the South have a competitive party system, but "one-partyism" is far from being a monopoly of the southern states. Fewer than half of the states outside the South have a real two-party system, and in many of those that do, responsible government is consistently frustrated by the divided control guaranteed through staggered elections, the bicameral system, and the separation of powers. The functions and political importance of the states have increased since the Progressive period, but effective state government is seldom achieved in the

United States. The conditions that explain this failure are as
prevalent in many non-southern states as they are in the South.
The exaggerated influence of rural areas, perpetuated by out-of-
date apportionment practices, is a problem almost everywhere.
The absence of a responsible opposition party and the lack of
interest and participation by most voters in state government seem
to be characteristic of a majority of the states, North and South.[49]
The problem everywhere is how to quicken the interest of the
voters in state politics, how to recruit able people to go into state
and local government, and how to make the political process at these
levels more responsive to the actual differences and divisions of
the people and to the majority opinion. The persistent failure to
secure responsible government on the state and local levels has
been a major cause of federal action.

It is not easy to dispel the myth of the monolithic South or to
unravel the threads woven into the old clichés about southern
politics. Of course the South's politics has differed in important
respects from the politics of other regions but, even so, it has always practiced a more American politics than is usually recognized. I have suggested that social and economic groupings, similar to those outside the South, have been of primary importance in
southern politics, and that profound changes of an economic and
social nature within the region have joined with compelling forces
of national and international origin to give these groupings new
meaning and gradually to bring about a political realignment.
Once the current racial tension diminishes, this process will go
forward rapidly and the promise of southern political traditions
can be more nearly realized. A habit of conservatism, strengthened by recent economic developments, should assert itself in a
more forthright and constructive fashion. A liberal tradition—
a "strain of protest and experimentation in the search for economic

equality"*—should make a more meaningful contribution to southern and American politics. One would also like to think that in the days ahead the old excitement over political matters, the belief in the value of individual control, the tradition of political leadership, and the concern for international affairs will be perpetuated in future southern politics.

* "The tragedy of the South," says Dean Acheson, "has been that racism has corrupted an otherwise respectable strain of protest and experimentation in the search for economic equality, dating back to Jefferson, Mason, Randolph, and Jackson." *A Democrat Looks at His Party* (New York, 1955), 44.

CHAPTER NINE

THE SOUTHERNER AS AMERICAN WRITER

By C. Hugh Holman

APPROACH IT HOWEVER you will, you will find at the heart of the Southern riddle a union of opposites, a condition of instability, a paradox. Calm grace and raw hatred. Polished manners and violence. An intense individualism and intense group pressures toward conformity. A reverence to the point of idolatry of self-determining action and a caste and class structure presupposing an aristocratic hierarchy. A passion for political action and a willingness to surrender to the enslavement of demagogues. A love of the nation intense enough to make the South's fighting men notorious in our wars and the advocacy of interposition and of the public defiance of national law. A region breeding both Thomas Jefferson and John C. Calhoun. If these contradictions are to be brought into focus, if these ambiguities are to be resolved, it must be through the "reconciliation of opposites." And the "reconciliation of opposites," as Coleridge has told us, is the function of the poet.

The poet's method is remarkably congenial to the Southerner; for the Southerner lives, as Robert Penn Warren has pointed out, in "the fear of abstraction . . . the instinctive fear . . . that the massiveness of experience, the concreteness of life, will be violated."[1] This use of the concrete, this pluralistic tendency to see the immediate, the experiential, is the way of the artist. It is little wonder, then, that the paradoxes at the core of southern life, although they have produced misery and catastrophe on many levels, have formed the materials for a literary expression uniquely powerful in our time, and have found in that expression their only effective reconciliation.

The South, however defeated it may feel itself in other areas, has triumphantly taken possession of the American literary world. William Faulkner, John Crowe Ransom, Allen Tate, Katherine Anne Porter, Erskine Caldwell, Robert Penn Warren, Caroline Gordon, Carson McCullers, Eudora Welty, Flannery O'Connor, Truman Capote, William Styron, Shirley Ann Grau, and that loosely defined group called "The New Critics," who in the last two decades have soundly trounced the historical scholars in the battle for the classroom—such a body of writers is unrivaled in a single region of America since the New England transcendentalists in the second third of the last century made Concord, Massachusetts, for a while the intellectual capital of the nation. Few today would argue with the London *Times Literary Supplement's* assertion that "the literature [of the South] . . . has solidly established itself as the most important, the most talented, interesting, and valuable in the United States."[2] This is a group of writers who are not only able to live at ease with a paradox; they are able to value paradox as a primary element of art. Cleanth Brooks sees the depths of meaning in poetry in the paradoxes that are found in word, image, and structure.[3] Allen Tate finds meaning in the "tension" of the poem.[4] These writers have presented the paradoxes and the dilemmas of southern life and thought in the only way in which they can ultimately be comprehended—in concrete and particularized terms. They have dramatized the contradictions, the ambiguities and intolerable couplings in individual cases and have made of them high art as well as accurate statement.

Southern writing from its beginnings, although it produced few works of true distinction and received small critical shrift before the twentieth century, has been consistently centered on the concrete, the particular, the actual, and, with varying degrees of excellence, has busied itself with the representation of reality as seen through southern eyes. That reality has been, until recently, at serious variance with the reality witnessed by other Americans, and southern writers have suffered in reputation and attention the consequences of the difference.

As late as 1710 Cotton Mather, belatedly speaking the sentiments of seventeenth-century New England, could declare that schoolmasters should "let it be [their] grand design to instil into their [pupils'] minds the documents of piety . . . . The sanctifying transformation of their souls would be infinitely preferable to any thing in Ovid's metamorphoses."[5] The first literary work of significance produced in the South was a translation of Ovid's *Metamorphoses,* by George Sandys, made while he was treasurer for the colony at Jamestown and published in London in 1621—a translation praised by Dryden and Pope.[6] In the first half of the nineteenth century the New England mind fell captive to German Transcendentalism; but Southerners, although interested in German literature,[7] disliked transcendental philosophy. When the German scholar, Dr. Robert Henry, of South Carolina, died, the *Southern Quarterly Review* reported, "Though . . . well versed in German literature, he had no taste for the German philosophers. His estimate of Kant was precisely that of Dugald Stewart, and as to Kant's successors, we do not believe that Dr. Henry could ever be induced to read a line of their writings."[8]

As a result of these differing attitudes, the southern writer has functioned as an American with a difference, and that difference has been his unique—and very valuable—contribution to the character of American art and life. It has expressed itself in three major ways: in his conception of nationalism, in his artistic method, and in the picture of archetypal man which his art has portrayed for Americans.

The concept of regionalism as a sound basis of art has been so generally accepted today that it is difficult to see that the importance of region or even of nation in literature could once have been a serious question. Yet it was, and the southern writer and critic tended in the first half of the nineteenth century to adumbrate the future rather than stand with his present on the matter. New England writers, although courageous voices were raised from time to time demanding a native strain, tended to distrust American qualities in art and to feel that nationalism should not manifest itself in our literature with any vigor.[9] In the 1840's a literary war broke out between the group associated with the *Knickerbocker* magazine and those associated with the Duyckinck brothers and the *Literary World* over the issue of nationalism, the *Knickerbocker* writers attacking the idea and the Duyckincks and their followers, known as the "Young America" group, supporting a vigorously patriotic literature. The two most noted southern writers of ante-bellum times joined the Duyckincks in this war; they were Edgar Allan Poe, certainly the most important writer which the South produced in the nineteenth century, and William Gilmore Simms, who as novelist, poet, dramatist, essayist, critic, and editor was the representative man of letters of the Old South. Yet their position was significantly different from that of the other "Young America" critics.[10] Their idea can be best expressed, I think, by a few lines from Robert Frost's poem "The Gift Outright":

> The land was ours before we were the land's.
> She was our land more than a hundred years
> Before we were her people. She was ours
> In Massachusetts, in Virginia,
> But we were England's, still colonials,
> Possessing what we still were unpossessed by,

Such as we were we gave ourselves outright . . .
To the land vaguely realizing westward,
But still unstoried, artless, unenhanced,
Such as she was, such as she would become.[11]

Simms wrote E. A. Duyckinck, on July 15, 1845: "If the authors of Am[erica] will only work together we can do wonders yet. But our first step will be to disabuse the public mind of the Eng[lish] & Yankee authorities. . . . Longfellow, a man of nice taste, a clever imitator,—simply an adroit artist. W. Irving is little more than a writer of delicate taste, a pleasant unobtrusive humor, and agreeable talent."[12]

Repeatedly throughout his career, Simms was to declare that a nation was "denationalizing" itself if it modeled its art on foreign forms or neglected to treat its native subjects. In a letter to the editor of the *Magnolia,* August 12, 1841, he said, "It is the literature of a country which preserves the language and represents the morality of a period. . . . The authors of a country are its true authorities. . . . They preserve all that is preserved."[13]   Yet Simms was one with Poe in decrying "puffery"—the praise of a work because it was American—and he almost parted company with his friend Duyckinck because Simms could find only faint praise for the work of Cornelius Mathews and none at all for Melville's *Moby-Dick,* despite these authors' high standing in the "Young-America" group.

This was the age when the critical cry was for the "Great American Novel," the book that would encompass the breadth and depth of America in one volume. And here Simms stood sharply aside, for he saw in sectional writing the basis for a national literature. Because he was active as editor, author, and critic in the movement for a distinctively southern literature between 1830 and 1860,[14] Simms has often been accused of fostering a sectional literature at the cost of a national one, and indeed such charges were made by the editor of the *Knickerbocker* maga-

zine during his lifetime.   However, Simms praised Cooper's novels
for their "Americanism,"[15] and they were as "sectional" as his
own and certainly not southern.   In 1839 he praised James K.
Paulding for his novels of Dutch life in New York as "one of the
earliest pioneers in the fields of American letters . . . who has
never made any concessions to that foreign sway."[16]   He viewed
the northern monopoly of book publishing without great alarm
and believed that New York would become the publishing center
of America without American literature suffering as a result.[17]
As late as 1856, when the fires of rebellion were flaming redly and
Simms as southern patriot was talking secession and a Caribbean
Empire, he wrote in the "Dedication" to a new edition of *The
Wigwam and the Cabin:* "One word for the material of these
legends.   It is local, sectional—and to be *national* in literature,
one must needs be *sectional.*   No one mind can fully or fairly
illustrate the characteristics of any great country; and he who shall
depict *one section* faithfully, has made his proper and sufficient
contribution to the great work of *national* literature."[18]

   Simms followed in practice in his fiction the theory here enun-
ciated.   His novels were motivated in large measure by his desire
to help in creating a literature indigenous to the spirit, events, and
character of America by faithfully working with those distinctively
American materials which were his local and sectional heritage.

   In the period after the Civil War, when the local color school
captured American fiction, the average critic and reader arrived
at a view of sectionalism much like that of Simms.   The Middle
West became the focus of sectional talent, and the modern southern writer, finding "regionalism" everywhere noised abroad as a
virtue of incomparable stature, moved on from Simms's position to
a new one.   In 1945 Allen Tate, writing on the occasion of the
twentieth anniversary of the *Virginia Quarterly Review,* asserted,
". . . picturesque regionalism of local color is a by-product of nationalism.   And it is not informed enough to support a mature

literature. . . . Yet no literature can be mature without the regional consciousness." Then he went on to define *regionalism*
as opposed to the *provincialism* of local color: "I mean the writer
who takes the South as he knows it today or can find out about it
in the past, and who sees it as a region with some special characteristics, but otherwise offering as an imaginative subject the plight
of human beings as it has been and will doubtless continue to be,
here and in other parts of the world."[19]

The national impulse in the southern writer reached perhaps
its most intense expression in the works of Thomas Wolfe, who,
like his character Eugene Gant, sought to find and to express the
meaning of his nation, and one night in Dijon had awakened in
him "a suddenly living and intolerable memory . . . of a life he
had lost."—"The memory of the lost America—the America of
twenty years ago, of quiet streets, the time enchanted spell and
magic of full June, the solid, lonely, liquid shuffle of men in shirt-
sleeves coming home, the leafy fragrance of the cooling turnip-
greens, and screens that slammed, and sudden silence—had long
since died, had been drowned beneath the brutal flood-tide, the
fierce stupefaction of that roaring surge and mechanic life which
had succeeded it.

"And now, all that lost magic had come to life again here
in the little whitened square, here in this old French town, and
he was closer to his childhood and his father's life of power and
magnificence than he could ever be again in savage new America;
and as the knowledge of these strange, these lost yet familiar things
returned to him, his heart was filled with all the mystery of time,
dark time, the mystery of strange million-visaged time that haunts
us with the briefness of our days."[20]

Wolfe goes on from this moment of revelation to attempt the
representation of the nation through the experiences of an archetypal self, and yet in the closeness with which he confines himself to immediate experience, in the degree to which the concrete

fact is the material of his expression, he is at one with the regional impulse, when it is viewed as a method of giving expression to the nation. When Wolfe concludes his exploration of his land, "I think the true discovery of America is before us. I think the true fulfillment of our spirit, of our people, of our mighty and immortal land, is yet to come. I think the true discovery of our own democracy is still before us,"[21] he speaks both as Southerner and as American. Here, indeed "the land vaguely realizing westward, / But still unstoried, artless, unenchanced" has become ours. That is the goal of the regional writer, and that persistent pushing forward at the frontier of art which the Southerner has made— sometimes, perhaps, for ignoble reasons—has ultimately made him loom large as American, and has taught him and through him others the dignity and the beauty and the terror of the land to be possessed.

If the southern writer seems a little out of step with the national literary scene through the earliness and the intensity with which he espoused the representation of the nation as a proper aim of art and the use of the region as the tool for such representation, he is even more out of step when the methods and materials of his writing are examined.

Fundamentally the ways of looking at art may be considered to be two—Aristotelian, in which the art object is examined with an eye to finding its values and its meaning within it, and Platonic, in which the art object acquires value and meaning in relation to something else, something extrinsic to it. Although the use of the names of Aristotle and Plato here represents the grossest of overgeneralizations, the tendency of criticism is toward examining the work of art either in itself, as Aristotle does in the *Poetics,* or in terms of its service to something else, as Plato does in the *Republic.*[22] In these terms, American writing in the nineteenth century was Platonic, and much twentieth-century American writing has been, too. And in sharp contrast, southern writers were more likely to take an Aristotelian view of literature. Poe, for example, wrote often of the "heresy of the didactic," declared that a poem dealt with beauty rather than "truth." He studied seriously the emotional effect produced upon the reader by the separate elements of the poem, and tried to establish an objective standard for evaluating works of art; he was concerned with the psychology of the audience and the technical qualities of versification. The line which connects him with the "New Critics" is a direct one.[23]

For Simms, the great novelist is a professional man of letters, producing work whose utility rests on its satisfaction of man's desire to tell and hear stories, on the creation of myths to raise the real into the realm of the ideal, and on the building of national character.[24] Simm's criticism was analytical and objective; as Bernard Smith—who is fundamentally unsympathetic with Simms —noted, "He had a decided interest in the mechanics of composition—plot, invention—a greater interest by far than the famous critics of New England."[25] This interest in the intrinsic qualities and the technical aspects of literature continued in southern writing, a notable instance being Sidney Lanier's book-length study, *The Science of English Verse* (1880). Throughout the nineteenth century, this tendency of the southern writer met with little approval outside the region. Poe was the "jingle man"; his "Philosophy of Composition" was discredited as a hoax; and his "Rationale of Verse" was never read. Simms's criticism accumulated dust in unread periodicals, and Lanier's *Science of English Verse* was taken as proof of the madness of mixing music and letters.

In our time the wheel has come full circle. A group of southern poets and critics, "The New Critics"—among them John Crowe Ransom, Allen Tate, Donald Davidson, Robert Penn Warren, and Cleanth Brooks—have triumphantly carried the gospel of the self-contained and self-sufficient art object across the land. These critics in true southern style have never formulated a system and have written comparatively few general statements. As Allen Tate says, ". . . there was no Southern criticism; merely a few Southern critics."[26] The New Critics have usually exercised their judgment upon particular works of art, not indulging in abstract theories very often. Yet the teaching of literature in the colleges and universities of the nation and the criticism of literature in critical quarterlies and in scholarly journals have undergone a profound revolution as a result of the persuasive insistence of these men that the values of art are intrinsic, that literature is a valid way of knowing and expressing something rather than a mere ornament to something else, and that nothing can replace for the reader the painstaking analysis of the work itself. Small though it may seem in one way, it may be ultimately true that the poet-critics who founded the *Fugitive* and fathered the "New Criticism" will have had a more profound effect upon the thinking of a larger number of Americans than any other single small group of Southerners in history. Yet what they assert, with astringent wit and calm grace, is essentially what Southerners have been saying about writing for a hundred and fifty years. The southern critics have not only functioned as Americans; they have made an indelible impact upon the America in which they have functioned.

The southern sense of the particular and the southern distrust of the abstract early expressed themselves in a concern with reality as immediately discerned by the senses. As early as 1827, when fiction in America walked a genteel way, even on Cooper's frontier, Augustus Baldwin Longstreet began publishing the sketches of frontier Georgia life which, as *Georgia Scenes,* have given him abiding fame. When they appeared in book form in 1835, Poe praised them, but the realism and the aesthetic distance at which Judge Longstreet stood when he sketched a violent and impolite society found few imitators. As early as 1833 Gilmore Simms began publishing novels based on life on the "Border," rough tales of violent men of harsh actions and untutored tongues. The polite press of America found them shocking, as did his biographer as late as 1892.[27]

In 1841 Simms published a story, "Caloya; or The Loves of the Driver," in the *Magnolia* magazine. The story was attacked as obscene, low, vulgar, impure. In a spirited defense Simms wrote: "It is a tale of low life—very low life—that is true. . . . There is nothing surely very attractive in Negroes and Indians; but something is conceded to intellectual curiosity; and the desire is human, and a very natural one, to know how our fellow beings fare in other aspects than our own, and under other forms of humanity, however inferior. No race is so very low, as to deprive them of the power of exciting this interest in the breasts of men . . . there can be no substantial moral objection to the mere agents in the narrative. Their modes of life, passions, pursuits, capacities and interests, are as legitimately the objects of the analyst, as those of the best bred people at the fashionable end of London; and possibly, considering their superior wants, are more obviously the objects of a higher moral and Christian interest. . . .

". . . nearly all of the great writers that ever survive their day . . . employ the deadly sins of man, as so many foils to his living virtues and whether he falls or triumphs, the end of the moralist is attained, if he takes care to speak the truth, the whole truth, and nothing but the truth! In this, in fact, lies the whole secret of his art. *A writer is moral only in proportion to his truthfulness.* He is and cannot but be immoral, whose truth is partial and one-sided."[28]

This is an attitude toward material that we normally do not expect to see in American writing much before 1870, for it is practically a definition of realism. What Longstreet, Joseph Glover Baldwin, George Washington Harris, and Simms were doing—and what Simms was here justifying—is the same thing that Ellen Glasgow was to do and defend; it is what Erskine Caldwell does when he functions at his best; what Faulkner and Robert

Penn Warren do. In the last third of the nineteenth century this impulse was to fall into the trap of whimsy and sentimentality in the local color school, but the writers of the twentieth century in the South have exercised, sometimes to the Southerner's discomfort, the right which Simms asserted to treat truthfully all material. That some excellent realistic writing done in the nineteenth century by Southerners fell by the critical wayside should not blind us to the fact that it was done, and that those harsh celebrators of the crude vulgarity of the Southern and Southwestern frontiers were in a tradition which our age sees as American.

But the way in which the southern writer has been most significantly of service to his fellow Americans has been as the portrayer of an archetypal man sharply at variance with the standard American view. In holding up this archetypal man the southern writer has presented America with a valuable image of the unique southern experience, and at the same time he has offered himself as a scapegoat for the frustrations and guilts of modern America.

In the broadest and simplest sense, the southern writer has shown man as caught in a tragic dilemma, tragic in the older and traditionally European sense. This "tragic sense of life" is, of course, partly the result of the experience of the South since 1860. As C. Vann Woodward has cogently argued: ". . . the inescapable facts of history were that the South had repeatedly met with frustration and failure. It had learned what it was to be faced with economic, social, and political problems that refused to yield to all the ingenuity, patience, and intelligence that a people could bring to bear upon them. It had learned to accommodate itself to conditions that it swore it would never accept and it had learned the taste left in the mouth by the swallowing of one's own words. It had learned to live for long decades in quite un-American poverty, and it had learned the equally un-American lesson of submission. For the South had undergone an experience that it could share with no other part of America—though it is shared by nearly all the peoples of Europe and Asia—the experience of military defeat, occupation, and reconstruction. Nothing about this history was conducive to the theory that the South was the darling of divine providence."[29]

Such a series of experiences is in sharp conflict with a view of life dedicated to inevitable success, to plenty, to progress and perfectibility, or even to the doctrine of individualistic strenuosity in which man is master of his fate and captain of his soul. If we can set the Southerner's experience of life against the perceptive comments of Alexis de Tocqueville on the nature of the poetry that would normally be produced in a democratic nation, the contrast between the southern writer and his non-southern American contemporary is almost shocking: "I have shown," says Tocqueville, "how the ideas of progress and of the indefinite perfectibility of the human race belong to democratic ages. Democratic nations care but little for what has been but they are haunted by visions of what will be. . . . [Americans'] eyes are fixed upon another sight: the American people views its own march across these wilds, draining swamps, turning the course of rivers, peopling solitudes, and subduing nature. This magnificent image of themselves does not meet the gaze of the Americans at intervals only; it may be said to haunt every one of them in his least as well as in his most important actions and to be always flitting before his mind."[30]

In 1840 when Tocqueville was publishing this, long before the catastrophe to which Professor Woodward refers, southern writers were already viewing man as a limited creature, with evil as an active force in life. Poe was dramatizing in his short stories and evoking through a medley of almost surrealistic images in his poetry the sense of evil and intolerable anxiety at the core of life, and he was casting serious doubts upon democratic processes. Simms in 1859, even when his hopes were high for the successful establishment of a Confederate government, wrote: "We are of those who think that we have very little to do with happiness. We have a certain destiny to fulfill, certain duties to perform, certain laws to obey, and vicissitudes to encounter, with such resources of courage as we have—energy, industry, and patient submission, with working; and, these laws complied with, we are to trouble ourselves no further with the compensative in our lot."[31] In 1842 he had written "We are . . . only so many agents and instruments, blind, and scuffling vainly in our blindness."[32]

Perhaps one source of this sense of imperfection and evil is the fundamentally Calvinistic religious belief of much of the South. Certainly the religious patterns of the region were much more shaped by the Scotch-Irish Presbyterians who settled the back-country and fanned out to encompass the region except for the coastal plain than it was by that plain's essentially Episcopal quality. In any case the view of life which many Southerners took was basically grim.

After the Civil War this quality was deepened by the sense of defeat that War brought. Ellen Glasgow said that she could never recall a time when "the pattern of society as well as the scheme of things in general, had not seemed to [her] false and even malignant."[33] And she declared, "For as long as the human race remains virtually, and perhaps essentially, barbarian, all the social orders invented by men will be merely the mirrors of his favourite imperfections."[34]

In the closing years of the nineteenth century and the early years of the twentieth, American writers were generally arriving at a similar disillusionment with the concepts of progress and perfectibility and, bowing to the new voices of science—to Darwin, to Spencer, to Comte, to Marx—were formulating a literature of despair and calling into being an American equivalent of the French naturalistic novel in which man is seen as hopelessly trapped. In the southern writer, by and large, the sense of defeat and of imperfection resulted in a picture rather of tragic strength than of pathetic weakness. Again Ellen Glasgow is a good case in point. She summed up the doctrine of her novel *Barren Ground* in these words: ". . . one may learn to live, one may even learn to live gallantly, without delight."[35] A confirmed pessimist, confident that the happy end, either in fiction or in philosophy, was false, she was always writing in some form or other the kind of book which she called a "drama of mortal conflict with fate."[36] Defeat was inevitable, but in the "conflict of human beings with human nature, of civilization with biology . . . tragedy lies, not in defeat, but in surrender."[37] A Greek sense of fate hangs over her world, and nobility is the function not of actions or of effective alterations in the world but of the spiritual qualities called forth by the world's hostility.

She is not alone in this view. Indeed, the extensive use of southern history by serious southern novelists has been as a tragic fable of man's lot in a hostile world. From Poe's damnation to Faulkner's myth of the reduplicating tragic history of Yoknapatawpha County, to Wolfe's half lugubrious "Lost O Lost and by the wind grieved," to the ambiguous calamity of Robert Penn Warren's Willie Starke in *All the King's Men* and the dark destruction of Peyton Loftis in William Styron's *Lie Down in Darkness,* southern writers and their characters have known what it is like to surrender their best hopes to the worst disasters, then pick up the pieces with stoic fortitude, and begin to make another dream that though lesser is equally doomed. Yet man does not lose his tragic stature in the process; he retains, though soiled and common like the Bundrens of Faulkner's *As I Lay Dying,* the potential of being challenged by an obligation and of accomplishing the impossible in discharging it. In this world, dark with evil and torn with bloody violence, over and over an idea of human dignity and responsibility comes. For example, it speaks through the words of Ike McCaslin in Faulkner's "Delta Autumn," when Ike says, "There are good men everywhere, at all times. Most men are. Some are just unlucky, because most men are a little better than their circumstances give them a chance to be. And I've known some that even the circumstances couldn't stop."[38]

In the thoroughness and the consistency with which the southern writer has dramatized this tragic aspect of his experience he has differed most radically from his fellow American writers. It has been only in our time that the average American has begun to sense the possibilities for disaster with which life is filled, to see the likelihood that the path of progress leads to the edge of a precipice, to imagine himself trapped and doomed. In that moment of facing the possible end of his world, when he suddenly hopes that his world can end differently from T. S. Eliot's—"Not with a bang but a whimper"—he finds a previously unsuspected validity in the work of the southern writers.

And, although they are southern and have undergone, at least vicariously, the tragic experience, these writers are also Americans and democratic; they weave their tragedies around common people, sometimes contemptible people, characters lacking in the social or economic status that would give them significance. Upon the insignificant shoulders of an itinerant saw-mill worker with a trace of Negro blood, William Faulkner in *Light in August* lays the burden of human guilt and the painful need for expiation. In the frail, middle-class son of a decaying southern family in *The Sound and the Fury* he finds the sufficient image for a vicarious (although ineffectual) atonement. Warren's Willie Starke rises from the soil to almost tragic power in *All the King's Men,* but Amantha Starr, in *Band of Angels,* who must learn for all of us that no man is free except in the act of surrendering freedom, is herself a slave. Erskine Caldwell's decayed creatures, drawn with the humor and detached anger that was in *Georgia Scenes,* can hardly be considered tragic, except in the sense we have of how far they have fallen; and yet the outraged sense of human dignity is powerfully present in his harsh tales.

Considered in a broad sense, nineteenth-century America built a democratic dream upon the idea of perfectibility and progress, upon the belief that the freedom of the individual inevitably meant the building of a new, healthy, strong state. By the last quarter of the century the drift of American culture had begun to raise questions in the mind of the most devoted dreamer of the simple democratic dream, questions which men like Nathaniel Hawthorne and Herman Melville had raised by mid-century. Even for Walt Whitman the question of the possible conflicts of the demands of the social order and the realization of the individual had validity. In *Democratic Vistas* he wrote: "Must not the virtue of modern Individualism, continually enlarging, usurping all, seriously affect, perhaps keep down entirely, in America, the like of the ancient virtue of Patriotism, the fervid and absorbing love of general country? I have no doubt myself that the two will merge . . . But I feel that at present they and their oppositions form a serious problem and paradox in the United States."[39]

The southern writer suggests, along with Hawthorne, that there are other bases for fellow sympathy and democratic process than man's inevitable goodness, that a commonwealth of mutual respect and common constructive effort can be built upon an awareness of our inevitable evil rather than upon the realization of our perfectible selves. Like the lesson the Reverend Mr. Dimmesdale learned—" 'Be true! Be true! Be true! Show freely to the world, if not your worst, yet some trait whereby the worst may be inferred!' "[40]—the southern writer's message has often seemed to be "Acknowledge your own evil, plumb the depths of darkness possible to you, and then let us join in trying to save ourselves from disaster." He may be formulating a more acceptable basis for democracy than the old one was.

The southern writer has been uniquely equipped by his history to draw the symbol of guilt and to serve, himself, as an example. For there have been few times in southern history, early or late, when the fact of Negro slavery, the inequity of the freedman's case, or the taint of second-class citizenship for the black citizen has not darkened the world of thoughtful southern men. The early writers, down to the 1840's, tended to rationalize the fact of slavery and to point to its final eradication. For instance, John Pendleton Kennedy in *Swallow Barn* (1832), the first influential book in the "Plantation Tradition," writes of slavery with a clear sense of its injustice, although he regards it also as a necessary expedient. Meriwether, the owner of "Swallow Barn," explains to the narrator, as they visit the slave quarters: " '. . . I am sure the Southern sentiment on this question is temperate and wise, and that we neither regard slavery as a good, nor account it, except in some favorable conditions, as profitable. . .' " and he proceeds to outline a program of gradual emancipation.[41] It would, of course, be a gross error to assume that all southern writers secretly felt slavery to be evil—Henry Timrod, for example, would demolish such a contention—but it is true that throughout the writing of the ante-bellum period, the Southerner knew himself to be a part of a system almost universally condemned outside his own region and often he himself seemed to feel it to be wrong.

Thus the Negro becomes both the cause and the symbol of the Southerner's guilt, and the southern writer repeatedly has so used him. Faulkner has one of his characters express it this way: "A race doomed and cursed to be forever and ever a part of the white race's doom and curse for its sins. . . . The curse of every white child that ever was born and that ever will be born. None can escape it. . . . And I seemed to see the black shadow in the shape of a cross. And it seemed like the white babies were struggling, even before they drew breath, to escape from the shadow that was not only upon them but beneath them too, flung out like their arms were flung out, as if they were nailed to the cross."[42] This intense sense of guilt, inherited from the past and demanding powerful expiations that exceed our ability to give, is recurrent in

Faulkner. Joe Christmas in *Light in August* believes that he has an infinitely small trace of Negro blood which functions as a symbol of his guilt, and unreasonably it preys upon his mind until he must die in expiating it. Ike McCaslin refuses the inheritance of his fathers, in *The Bear,* because it has been bought with human injustice, and yet he is unable to stand upon his repudiation.

In some writers this sense of guilt expresses itself in broader terms. In Robert Penn Warren's poem "Original Sin: A Short Story," it relentlessly tracks the protagonist at home, in Omaha, in the Harvard Yard,

> But it never came in the quantum glare of sun
> To shame you before your friends, and had nothing to do
> With your public experience or private reformation:
> But it thought no bed too narrow—[43]

In "The Wolves," Allen Tate dramatizes this guilty evil as threatening

> wolves in the next room waiting
> With heads bent low, thrust out, breathing
> As nothing in the dark.

And the protagonist must go in fear to open the door and confront the evil

> —and man can never be alone.[44]

Time too becomes a frightful entity for many southern writers, whose concern with time reminds us of European rather than American authors. Time is Thomas Wolfe's great enemy. Ellen Glasgow said, "Within time, and within time alone, there was life,"[45] and thus the relentless passage of time is the decay of death. To Faulkner's Quentin Compson, in *The Sound and the Fury,* time as symbolized by the watch, is the arch enemy. In one of Warren's most original poems, "The Ballad of Billie Potts," it is time that gives us identity and carries us relentlessly away from lost innocence.

Now certainly it would be an error to assume that in the South and its treatment of the Negro resides the sum total of American guilt, and yet for a hundred and fifty years America has seen in the South its classic symbol of willful injustice. As gradually Americans as a whole have come to question their easy assumptions, to feel uncertainty and inadequacy, to see what Reinhold Niebuhr has called "the irony of American history," I think they have found in the acknowledgment of guilt, in the pervasive sense of evil, in the darkness, the terror, and the despair of twentieth-century southern writing an effective catharsis for their own fear and pity. In the bringing of peace to the soul and in the awakening of the spirit to right impulses and noble actions, religions have employed the symbol of the scapegoat, upon whom, symbolically, the sins of the group are loaded and who through his sacrifice expiates them. In a sense, the southern writer has been a scapegoat for his fellow Americans, for in taking his guilt upon himself and dramatizing it he has borne the sins of us all. I believe that the powerful impact which southern writing has made upon the tormented world of the twentieth century is a commentary on the painful extent to which our total experience makes the southern experience intelligible, so that the southern writer, who has faced the bitter paradoxes of his world and found in them the element of tragic grandeur, can speak as brother and friend to his troubled nation. In doing so he sometimes seems to betray the trust of his southern friends and to portray them in anger and harshly, but he does it as an American and in love.

Out of the cauldron of the South's experience, the southern writer has fashioned tragic grandeur and given it as a gift to his fellow Americans. It is possible that no other southern accomplishment will equal it in enduring importance. As urbanization and industrialization conspire to write an "Epitaph for Dixie," its greatest contribution to mankind may well be the lesson of its history and the drama of its suffering.

THE AUTHORS

DAVID DONALD, a native of Goodman, Mississippi, was educated at Millsaps College, the University of North Carolina, and the University of Illinois. He has taught at Smith and Columbia, and after holding the Harmsworth Professorship at Oxford during 1959-60 returns to a professorship at Princeton. He has held a fellowship from the Social Science Research Council and a Fulbright lectureship at the University College of North Wales. He has written a study of *Lincoln's Herndon* and a collection of essays under the title *Lincoln Reconsidered,* and is now completing a biography of Charles Sumner.

JOHN HOPE FRANKLIN, chairman of the history department at Brooklyn College, was born in Rentiesville, Oklahoma, attended Fisk University, and received his graduate training at Harvard. Before assuming his present position he had taught at Fisk, St. Augustine's College, North Carolina College, and Howard. He has been a Guggenheim and a Rosenwald fellow and a director of the American Council of Learned Societies. His published works include *The Free Negro in North Carolina, From Slavery to Freedom: A History of American Negroes,* and *The Militant South, 1800-1861.*

THOMAS P. GOVAN grew up in Atlanta and was educated at the Georgia School of Technology, Emory, and Vanderbilt. After teaching at Emory, Vanderbilt, Chattanooga, Sewanee, Virginia, and Tulane, he became Executive Chairman for College Faculty Work of the National Council of the Protestant Episcopal Church. He has published a biography of Nicholas Biddle and many articles on southern history.

DEWEY W. GRANTHAM, JR., a Georgian, attended the University of Georgia and holds the Ph.D. degree from the University of North Carolina. He has taught at North Texas State College and the Woman's College of the University of North Carolina, and is now associate professor of history at Vanderbilt. The recipient of fellowships from the Guggenheim Foundation, the Social Science Research Council, and the Fund for the Advancement of Education, he has published a biography of Hoke Smith and is now completing a study of the Progressive movement in the South.

C. HUGH HOLMAN, chairman of the English department at the University of North Carolina, was born in Cross Anchor, South Carolina. He studied at Presbyterian College and the University of North Carolina. The bibliographer for the American Literature Group of the Modern Language Association, he has published (with C. Floyd Stovall) *The Development of American Literary Criticism,* as well as many articles on southern literature. His biography of William Gilmore Simms is near completion.

GRADY MCWHINEY grew up in Shreveport, attended Centenary College and Louisiana State University, and completed his graduate training at Columbia. He has taught at Troy (Alabama) State College, Millsaps, and the University of California, Berkeley, and is now assistant professor of history at Northwestern. He edited (with Douglas Southall Freeman) *Lee's Dispatches to Jefferson Davis,* and is now writing a biography of the Confederate general Braxton Bragg.

L. D. REDDICK, a native of Jacksonville, did his undergraduate work at Fisk and his graduate work at Chicago. After teaching at Kentucky State College and Dillard, he became curator of the New York Public Library's famed Schomberg Collection of Negro history, lecturing at City College and the New School. His next position was chief librarian of the Arnott Library, Atlanta, and he is now chairman of the history department at Alabama State College. He has published *Our Cause Speeds On* (with W. Sherman Savage) and a biography of Martin Luther King, leader of the Montgomery bus boycott. During a recent visit to India with King he gathered materials for a study of untouchability.

CHARLES GRIER SELLERS, JR., grew up in Charlotte and studied at Harvard and the University of North Carolina. He has taught at the University of Maryland and Princeton, and is now professor of history at the University of California, Berkeley. He has published the first volume of a two-volume biography of James K. Polk.

GEORGE B. TINDALL, a native of Greenville, South Carolina, was educated at Furman and the University of North Carolina. After teaching at Eastern Kentucky State College, the University of Mississippi, the Woman's College of the University of North Carolina, and Louisiana State University, he returned to Chapel Hill as associate professor of history. The recipient of fellowships from the Guggenheim Foundation and the Social Science Research Council, he has published a study of *South Carolina Negroes, 1877-1900,* and is now completing the twentieth-century volume for the cooperative *History of the South.*

NOTES

CHAPTER ONE

1. William P. Trent *et al., The Cambridge History of American Literature* (3 vols., New York, 1917-21), II, 288; John W. DuBose, *The Life and Times of William Lowndes Yancey* (2 vols., Birmingham, 1892), I, 376.

2. Avery O. Craven, *The Growth of Southern Nationalism, 1848-1861* (Baton Rouge, 1953), 8.

3. See especially David Ramsay, *History of the Revolution of South Carolina from a British Colony to an Independent State* (2 vols., Charleston, 1785); John Daly Burk, *The History of Virginia from Its First Settlement to the Present Day* (3 vols., Petersburg, 1804-05); J. G. M. Ramsey, *The Annals of Tennessee to the End of the Eighteenth Century* . . . (Charleston, 1853); John H. Wheeler, *Historical Sketches of North Carolina, from 1584 to 1851* . . . (2 vols., New York, 1851).

4. Wesley Frank Craven, *The Legend of the Founding Fathers* (New York, 1956), 93.

5. John W. Higham, "The Changing Loyalties of William Gilmore Simms," *Journal of Southern History,* IX (May 1943), 211; Craven, *Founding Fathers,* 112.

6. Craven, *Founding Fathers,* 109-13.

7. For a discussion of the role of the historian in the growth of nationalism, see Louis L. Snyder, *The Meaning of Nationalism* (New Brunswick, 1954), 27 ff.

8. Lorenzo Sabine, *The American Loyalists* (Boston, 1847), 42.

9. For examples of refutations, see "Southron" [William Gilmore Simms], *South Carolina in the Revolutionary War: Being A Reply to Certain Misrepresentations and Mistakes of Recent Writers in Relation to the Course and Conduct of this State* (Charleston, 1853); Lawrence M. Keitt, "Patriotic Services of the North and South," *DeBow's Review,* XXI (November, 1856), 491-508; and Joseph Johnson, *Traditions and Reminiscences Chiefly of the American Revolution in the South* (Charleston, 1851).

10. W. Gilmore Simms, *The Sources of American Independence: An Oration, on the Sixty-Ninth Anniversary of American Independence; Delivered at Aiken, South Carolina, Before the Town Council and Citizens Thereof* (Aiken, 1844), 22.

11. "Southron," *South Carolina in the Revolutionary War,* 62.

12. Lawrence M. Keitt, *Address of Lawrence M. Keitt, Esq. on the Laying the Corner-Stone of the Fire-Proof Building, at Columbia, December 15, 1851* (Columbia, 1851), 8.

13. *Proceedings at the Inauguration of the Monument Erected by the Washington Light Infantry, to the Memory of Col. William Washington, at Magnolia Cemetery, May 5, 1858* (Charleston, 1858), 13.

14. See, for example, Thomas L. Jones, *An Oration Delivered on the Fourth Day of July, 1847, At the County Seat of Polk County, North Carolina* (Greenville, 1847), and William E. Martin, *The South, Its Dangers and Its Resources. An Address Delivered at the Celebration of the Battle of Fort Moultrie, June 28, 1850* (Charleston, 1850).

15. Rollin G. Osterweis, *Romanticism and Nationalism in the Old South* (New Haven, 1949), 138.

16. "The Difference of Race Between the Northern and Southern People," *Southern Literary Messenger*, XXX (June, 1860), 407.

17. A notable exception is R. R. Howison, whose *History of Virginia* was published in 1848. For a discussion of his views see Clement Eaton, *Freedom of Thought in the Old South* (Durham, 1940), 270-71.

18. *Southern Review*, I (April, 1867), 285.

19. Benjamin H. Hill, Jr., *Senator Benjamin H. Hill of Georgia: His Life, Speeches and Writings* (Atlanta, 1893), 405. See also E. Merton Coulter, *The South During Reconstruction, 1865-1877* (Baton Rouge, 1947), 181-83.

20. "The Want of a History of the Southern People" in Thomas Nelson Page, *The Old South, Essays Social and Political* (New York, 1892), 253, 257.

21. Wendell Holmes Stephenson, "John Spencer Bassett As A Historian of the South," *North Carolina Historical Review*, XXV (July, 1948), 299, 300.

22. W. Stull Holt, ed., *Historical Scholarship in the United States* (Baltimore, 1938), 245-47, and Michael Kraus, *A History of American History* (New York, 1937), 533-45. See also Alcee Fortier, "The Teaching of History in the South," *Iowa Journal of History and Politics*, XXX (January, 1905), 92-93, and William P. Trent, "Historical Studies in the South," *American Historical Association Papers* (Washington, 1890), 57-65.

23. Ulrich Bonnell Phillips, *Life and Labor in the Old South* (Boston, 1929), 201, 203.

24. Walter Lynwood Fleming, *Documentary History of the Reconstruction* (Cleveland, 1907), II, 328.

25. 13 volumes (Richmond, 1909-13).

26. Philip M. Hamer, "The Records of Southern History," *Journal of Southern History*, V (February, 1939), 3-17.

27. Wendell H. Stephenson, "The South Lives in History," *Historical Outlook*, XXIII (April, 1932), 153-63; Clement Eaton, "Recent Trends in the Writing of Southern History," *The Louisiana Historical Quarterly*, XXXVIII (April, 1955), 26-42. For a recent report by a committee of the Southern Historical Association calling attention to many still neglected areas of southern history, see "Research Possibilities in Southern History," *Journal of Southern History*, XVI (February, 1950), 52-63.

28. Eaton, "Recent Trends." See also The American Historical Association, *List of Doctoral Dissertations in History Now in Progress at Universities in the United States* (Washington, 1952).

29. Francis B. Simkins, "Tolerating the South's Past," *Journal of Southern History*, XXI (February, 1955), 3-16.

30. The most exhaustive studies of the non-slaveholding element of the South have been made by Frank L. Owsley and his students. The findings are conveniently summarized in his *Plain Folk of the Old South* (Baton Rouge,

1949). See also Kenneth M. Stampp, "The Historian and Southern Negro Slavery," *American Historical Review,* LVII (April, 1952), 613-24, and his *The Peculiar Institution* (New York, 1956).

31. Bell Irvin Wiley, *Southern Negroes, 1861-1865* (New Haven, 1938).

32. Benjamin Quarles, *The Negro in the Civil War* (Boston, 1953).

33. Howard K. Beale, "On Rewriting Reconstruction History," *American Historical Review,* XLV (July, 1940), 807-27, and Vernon Lane Wharton, *The Negro in Mississippi, 1865-1890* (Chapel Hill, 1947).

34. C. Vann Woodward, *Origins of the New South, 1877-1913* (Baton Rouge, 1951).

CHAPTER TWO

1. Frank L. Owsley, "The Irrepressible Conflict," in Twelve Southerners, *I'll Take My Stand* (New York, 1930), 72.

2. Samuel E. Morison and Henry S. Commager, *The Growth of the American Republic* (2 vols., 3rd ed., New York, 1942), I, 337-38.

3. Charles C. Tansill, ed., *Documents Illustrative of the Formation of the Union of the American States* (Washington, 1927), 371-72, 635.

4. *Annals of Congress,* 18th Congress, 2nd Session (1816-17), 351-88, quoted in John M. Anderson, ed., *Calhoun, Basic Documents* (State College, Pa., 1952), 11-12.

5. J. C. Calhoun to James Monroe, July 10, 1828, J. Franklin Jameson, ed., *Correspondence of John C. Calhoun, American Historical Association, Annual Report, 1899,* 266.

6. J. C. Calhoun to Christopher Van Deventer, March 20, 1830, *ibid.,* 270-71.

7. Charles M. Wiltse, *John C. Calhoun, Nullifier, 1829-1839* (Indianapolis, 1940), 351.

8. J. C. Calhoun to J. E. Calhoun, September 7, 1837, *Correspondence,* 377-78; F. W. Pickens to James H. Hammond, July 16, 1837, Hammond MSS., Library of Congress.

9. John P. King to a Friend, October 17, 1837, *Niles' Register,* LIII (Dec. 9, 1837), 229.

10. Thomas Jefferson, *Notes on the State of Virginia,* ed. by William Peden (Chapel Hill, 1955), 163.

11. Tansill, *Documents,* 163, 590.

12. *Ibid.,* 372, 588, 589, 617, 618.

13. Extract to R.S.N. from Edward Coles to Nicholas Biddle, March 21, 1815, microfilm (Historical Society of Pennsylvania from manuscripts in private library of Edward C. Robbins, Paoli, Pennsylvania.)

14. Second Inaugural Address in Roy P. Basler (ed.), *The Collected Works of Abraham Lincoln* (8 vols. and index, New Brunswick, N. J., 1953-1955), VIII, 332.

CHAPTER THREE

1. David Ramsay, *The History of South-Carolina, from Its First Settlement in 1670, to the Year 1808* (2 vols., Charleston, 1809), II, 384.

2. Fletcher M. Green, "Listen to the Eagle Scream: One Hundred Years of the Fourth of July in North Carolina (1776-1876)," *North Carolina Historical Review,* XXXI (July, October, 1954), 36, 534.

3. *A Selection of Eulogies Pronounced in the Several States, in Honor of Those Illustrious Patriots and Statesmen, John Adams and Thomas Jefferson* (Hartford, 1826), 6-7. For an indication of the currency of similar sentiments, see Green, "Listen to the Eagle Scream," *N. C. Hist. Rev.,* XXXI, 303, 305, 548.

4. Laura A. White, *Robert Barnwell Rhett, Father of Secession* (New York, 1931), 50-52; Merle Curti, *The Roots of American Loyalty* (New York, 1946), 137-38, 153-54.

5. Curti, *American Loyalty,* 68, 154; R. M. T. Hunter, *An Address Delivered before the Society of Alumnia of the University of Virginia . . . on the 4th of July, 1839* (Charlottesville, 1839), 4.

6. Curti, *American Loyalty,* 41, 43, 61, 72, 102-3, 152; Horace Montgomery, *Cracker Parties* (Baton Rouge, 1950), 3.

7. Green, "Listen to the Eagle Scream," *N. C. Hist. Rev.,* XXXI, 314, 319-20, 534-36.

8. Daniel R. Goodloe, *The Southern Platform: or, Manual of Southern Sentiment on the Subject of Slavery* (Boston, 1858), 91.

9. William S. Jenkins, *Pro-Slavery Thought in the Old South* (Chapel Hill, 1935), 37-38.

10. Goodloe, *Southern Platform,* 94.

11. *Ibid.,* 3-5.

12. Hinton Rowan Helper, *The Impending Crisis of the South: How to Meet It* (New York, 1860), 197.

13. *Register of Debates,* 24th Cong., 2nd Sess., 719-23.

14. Russel B. Nye, *Fettered Freedom: Civil Liberties and the Slavery Controversy, 1830-1860* (East Lansing, Mich., 1949), 72.

15. Lillian A. Kibler, *Benjamin F. Perry, South Carolina Unionist* (Durham, 1946), 31; Pulaski *Tennessee Beacon and Farmers Advocate,* June 16, 1832.

16. W. G. Bean, "Anti-Jeffersonianism in the Ante-Bellum South," *North Carolina Historical Review,* XII (April, 1935), 111.

17. John Hope Franklin, *The Militant South, 1800-1861* (Cambridge, 1956), 222.

18. Goodloe, *Southern Platform,* 49.

19. E. Mitchell to John C. Calhoun, February 5, 1849, John C. Calhoun Papers (Clemson College Library).

20. Goodloe, *Southern Platform,* 49; Helper, *Impending Crisis,* 195, 208-9; John J. Flournoy, *An Essay on the Origin, Habits, &c. of the African Race . . .* (New York, 1835), 25; Kenneth M. Stampp, *The Peculiar Institution: Slavery in the Ante-Bellum South* (New York, 1956), 356.

21. Joseph C. Robert, *The Road from Monticello: A Study of the Virginia Slavery Debate of 1832* (Durham, 1941), 17-18, and *passim.*

22. Charles H. Ambler, *The Life and Diary of John Floyd* (Richmond, 1918), 172; Jenkins, *Pro-Slavery Thought,* 88n.

23. Nashville *Republican,* October 22, 1825.

24. Washington *United States Telegraph,* December 5, 1835.

25. Walter B. Posey, "The Slavery Question in the Presbyterian Church in the Old Southwest," *Journal of Southern History,* XV (August, 1943), 319; Betty Fladeland, *James Gillespie Birney: Slaveholder to Abolitionist* (Ithaca, 1955), 83.

26. Kenneth M. Stampp, "The Fate of the Southern Antislavery Movement," *Journal of Negro History,* XXVIII (January, 1943), 20, 22, and *passim.*

27. Stampp, *Peculiar Institution,* 422-23; Washington *United States Telegraph,* December 5, 1835.

28. Stampp, *Peculiar Institution,* 234, 423.

29. Clement Eaton, *Freedom of Thought in the Old South* (2nd edn., New York, 1951), xii-xiii; J. Merton England, "The Free Negro in Ante-Bellum Tennessee," *Journal of Southern History,* IX (February, 1943), 44-45. Cf. Stampp, *Peculiar Institution,* 234-35.

30. Eaton, *Freedom of Thought*, 18-19; Stampp, *Peculiar Institution*, 235-36; England, "Free Negro," *Jour. Southern Hist.*, IX, 43-44.

31. Jenkins, *Pro-Slavery Thought*, 236; Stampp, *Peculiar Institution*, 383.

32. Stampp, *Peculiar Institution*, 424; Eaton, *Freedom of Thought*, 19; Frank W. Klingberg, *The Southern Claims Commission* (Berkeley and Los Angeles, 1955), 11, 108; J. W. De Forest, "Chivalrous and Semi-Chivalrous Southrons," *Harper's New Monthly Magazine*, XXVIII (January, February, 1869), 200.

33. *Register of Debates*, 19th Cong., 1st Sess., 1649.

34. Wilbert E. Moore, "Slavery, Abolition, and the Ethical Valuation of the Individual: A Study of the Relations between Ideas and Institutions" (Ph.D. dissertation, Harvard University, 1940), 193-212.

35. Wilbert E. Moore, "Slave Law and the Social Structure," *Journal of Negro History*, XXVI (April, 1941), 171-202.

36. Stampp, *Peculiar Institution*, 217; Helper, *Impending Crisis*, 223-24.

37. Moore, "Slavery and Ethical Valuation," Ph.D. Dissertation (Harvard), 187-88.

38. Stampp, *Peculiar Institution*, 193; D. R. Hundley, *Social Relations in Our Southern States* (New York, 1860), 193.

39. Moore, "Slavery and Ethical Valuation," 233-35; Wilbert E. Moore and Robin M. Williams, "Stratification in the Ante-Bellum South," *American Sociological Review*, VII (June, 1942), 348-51; Robert, *Road from Monticello*, 103.

40. Stampp, *Peculiar Institution*, 89-90, 141, 191.

41. Moore, "Slavery and Ethical Valuation," 194-95; Moore and Williams, "Stratification," 345-46.

42. Stampp, *Peculiar Institution*, 423; Herbert Aptheker, *American Negro Slave Revolts* (New York, 1943), 59-60.

43. Jenkins, *Pro-Slavery Thought*, 214-18.

44. Jay B. Hubbell, "Literary Nationalism in the Old South," in David K. Jackson, ed., *American Studies in Honor of William Kenneth Boyd* (Durham, 1940), 183n.; David Outlaw to Mrs. David Outlaw, July [28], 1848, David Outlaw Papers (Southern Historical Collection, University of North Carolina); Robert W. Barnwell to Robert Barnwell Rhett, November 1, 1844, Robert Barnwell Rhett Papers (Southern Historical Collection, University of North Carolina).

45. Louis Hartz, *The Liberal Tradition in America: An Interpretation of American Political Thought since the Revolution* (New York, 1955), 145-200.

46. Jenkins, *Pro-Slavery Thought*, 239-40.

47. Ollinger Crenshaw, *The Slave States in the Presidential Election of 1860* (Baltimore, 1945), 253.

48. *Congressional Globe*, 33rd Cong., 1st Sess., Appendix, 230.

49. Goodloe, *Southern Platform*, 93.

50. Jenkins, *Pro-Slavery Thought*, 281; Harvey Wish, *George Fitzhugh: Propagandist of the Old South* (Baton Rouge, 1943), 111.

51. Wish, *Fitzhugh*, 111.

52. Harold S. Schultz, *Nationalism and Sectionalism in South Carolina, 1852-1860: A Study of the Movement for Southern Independence* (Durham, 1950), 182.

53. Stampp, *Peculiar Institution*, 278; Schultz, *Nationalism and Sectionalism*, 158-59.

54. Dwight L. Dumond, ed., *Southern Editorials on Secession* (New York, 1931), 315-16.

55. Crenshaw, *Slave States*, 100, 103, 106; Laura A. White, "The South in

the 1850's as Seen by British Consuls," *Journal of Southern History*, I (February, 1935), 44.

56. Crenshaw, *Slave States*, 111; Robert C. Gunderson, "William C. Rives and the 'Old Gentlemen's Convention,' " *Journal of Southern History*, XXII (November, 1956), 460.

57. Crenshaw, *Slave States*, 111n., 237; Klingberg, *Southern Claims Commission*, 13. Cf. Cantril, *Psychology of Social Movements*, 61.

58. White, *Rhett*, 177n.

59. Klingberg, *Southern Claims Commission*, 138.

60. *Report of the Joint Committee on Reconstruction, at the First Session, Thirty-Ninth Congress* (Washington, 1866), 133.

CHAPTER FOUR

1. Samuel A. Stouffer and others, *The American Soldier: Adjustment during Army Life* (Princeton, 1949), I, *passim*, especially 102, 432.

2. Arthur J. L. Fremantle, *Three Months in the Southern States: April, June, 1863* (Mobile, 1864), 293.

3. *Ibid.*, 123.

4. George Cary Eggleston, *A Rebel's Recollections* (New York, 1889), 29.

5. *The War of the Rebellion: A Compilation of the Official Records of the Union and Confederate Armies* (Washington, 1880-1901), series 1, XLII, part 2, 1276-77. Hereafter cited as *Official Records*.

6. Frank Lawrence Owsley, *Plain Folk of the Old South* (Baton Rouge, 1949), *passim*.

7. W. J. Cash, *The Mind of the South* (New York, 1941), 4 ff.

8. Fletcher M. Green, "Democracy in the Old South," *Journal of Southern History*, XII (February, 1946), 3-23; Allan Nevins, *Ordeal of the Union* (New York, 1947), I, 419.

9. Bell Irvin Wiley, *The Life of Johnny Reb: The Common Soldier of the Confederacy* (Indianapolis, 1943), 27.

10. Edmund Cody Burnett, ed., "Letters of Three Lightfoot Brothers, 1861-1864," *Georgia Historical Quarterly*, XXV (December, 1941), 389.

11. Stouffer, *et al.*, *The American Soldier*, I, 396.

12. Eggleston, *A Rebel's Recollections*, 32.

13. Wiley, *Johnny Reb*, 27.

14. Fremantle, *Three Months*, 247.

15. Douglas Southall Freeman, *Lee's Lieutenants: A Study in Command* (New York, 1942), I, 367.

16. Fremantle, *Three Months*, 226, 123.

17. Stouffer et al., *The American Soldier*, I, 55.

18. Wiley, *Johnny Reb*, 236, 140.

19. Stouffer et al., *The American Soldier*, I, 372.

20. Wiley, *Johnny Reb*, 49, 242.

21. John Q. Anderson, ed., *Brokenburn: The Journal of Kate Stone, 1861-1868* (Baton Rouge, 1955), 162-63.

22. Eggleston, *A Rebel's Recollections*, 34.

23. Emory Upton, *The Military Policy of the United States* (Washington, 1917), 460-61.

24. Susan Leigh Blackford, ed., *Letters from Lee's Army: Or Memoirs of Life in and out of the Army in Virginia. . .* (New York, 1947), 81.

25. Freeman, *Lee's Lieutenants*, I, 173.

26. Wiley, *Johnny Reb*, 20.

27. William Pitt Chambers, "My Journal: The Story of a Soldier's Life. . . ," *Mississippi Historical Society Publications: Centenary Series* (1925), V, 234.

28. T. R. R. Cobb, "Extracts from Letters to His Wife, February 3, 1861-December 10, 1862," *Southern Historical Society Papers*, XXVIII (1900), 292.

29. E. P. Alexander, "Sketch of Longstreet's Division," *ibid.*, X (1882), 37.

30. *Official Records*, series 1, X, part 1, 779, and XI, part 3, 503.

31. Chambers, "My Journal," 248. (See N. 27 above for complete citation.)

32. Joseph T. Durkin, ed., *John Dooley: Confederate Soldier, His War Journal* (Georgetown, 1948), 89.

33. Frank E. Vandiver, ed., "Letters from the Confederate Medical Service in Texas, 1863-65," *Southwestern Historical Quarterly*, LV (January, 1952), 390.

34. *Official Records*, series 4, II, 948, 1001.

35. E. Merton Coulter, *The Confederate States of America, 1861-1865* (Wendell H. Stephenson and E. Merton Coulter, eds., *A History of the South*, VIII, Baton Rouge, 1950), 329.

36. Dunbar Rowland, ed., *Jefferson Davis, Constitutionalist: His Letters, Papers and Speeches* (Jackson, 1923), IX, 543.

37. *Ibid.*, VII, 410.

38. *Official Records*, series 1, XLII, part 3, 1213.

39. Eggleston, *A Rebel's Recollections*, 34-35.

40. For the power and prestige still retained by the planter aristocracy, see Nevins, *Ordeal of the Union*, I, 416-19; Clement Eaton, *A History of the Old South* (New York, 1949), 444-54; and Roger W. Shugg, *Origins of Class Struggle in Louisiana. . .* (University, La., 1939), *passim*.

41. Richard Taylor, *Destruction and Reconstruction: Personal Experiences of the Late War* (New York, 1879), 63.

42. Eggleston, *A Rebel's Recollections*, 36-37.

43. Robert Stiles, *Four Years under Marse Robert* (New York, 1903), 46.

44. Wiley, *Johnny Reb*, 344.

45. *Official Records*, series 4, III, 709.

46. Bessie Martin, *Desertion of Alabama Troops from the Confederate Army: A Study in Sectionalism* (New York, 1932), 122.

47. *Official Records*, series 4, II, 949.

48. Burton J. Hendrick, *Statesmen of the Lost Cause: Jefferson Davis and His Cabinet* (Boston, 1939), 9.

49. Charles C. Jones, Jr., "A Roster of General Officers, Heads of Departments, Senators, Representatives, Military Organizations, &c., &c., in Confederate Service during the War between the States," *Southern Historical Society Papers*, I (June, 1876), 467 ff.

50. For biographical data about these commanders I have relied chiefly upon Allen Johnson and Dumas Malone, eds., *Dictionary of American Biography* (New York, 1928-1944, 21 vols.); *National Cyclopaedia of American Biography* (New York, 1892-1954, 39 vols.); and Francis B. Heitman, *Historical Register and Dictionary of the United States Army. . .* (Washington, 1903, 2 vols.). To prevent duplication, I have counted each general only once in my statistic, listing him under the date of his highest-ranking appointment.

51. Thomas M. Spaulding in *Dictionary of American Biography*, VI, 533.

52. Wiley, *Johnny Reb*, 338.

53. Blackford, *Letters from Lee's Army*, 9.

54. Taylor, *Destruction and Reconstruction*, 38.

55. Blackford, *Letters from Lee's Army*, 12.

56. Stiles, *Four Years under Marse Robert*, 110.

57. Wiley, *Johnny Reb*, 243.

58. I have developed this theme in more detail in my *Lincoln Reconsidered: Essays on the Civil War Era* (New York, 1956), 82-102.

CHAPTER FIVE

1. John W. Burgess, *Reconstruction and the Constitution, 1866-1876* (New York, 1902), 296-97, 263-64. Some additional examples of this view of Reconstruction are: William A. Dunning, *Reconstruction, Political and Economic, 1865-1877* (New York, 1907); James Ford Rhodes, *History of the United States from the Compromise of 1850 . . .* (7 vols., New York, 1906), V-VII; Walter L. Fleming, *The Sequel of Appomattox* (New Haven, 1921); Claude G. Bowers, *The Tragic Era* (Boston, 1929); and E. Merton Coulter, *The South during Reconstruction, 1865-1877* (Baton Rouge, 1947).

2. See such important revisionist writing as: Francis B. Simkins and Robert H. Woody, *South Carolina during Reconstruction* (Chapel Hill, 1932); W. E. Burghart Du Bois, *Black Reconstruction* (New York, 1938); C. Vann Woodward, *Tom Watson, Agrarian Rebel* (New York, 1938); Alrutheus A. Taylor, "Historians of Reconstruction," *Journal of Negro History*, XXIII (January, 1938), 16-34; Horace Mann Bond, *Negro Education in Alabama* (Washington, 1939); Roger W. Shugg, *Origins of Class Struggle in Louisiana* (Baton Rouge, 1939); Francis B. Simkins, "New Viewpoints of Southern Reconstruction," *Journal of Southern History*, V (February, 1939), 49-61; Howard K. Beale, "On Rewriting Reconstruction History," *American Historical Review*, XLV (July, 1940), 807-27; T. Harry Williams, "An Analysis of Some Reconstruction Attitudes," *Journal of Southern History*, XII (November, 1946), 469-86; Vernon Lane Wharton, *The Negro in Mississippi, 1865-1890* (Chapel Hill, 1947); Thomas B. Alexander, *Political Reconstruction in Tennessee* (Nashville, 1950); and C. Vann Woodward, *Reunion and Reaction* (New York, 1951).

3. Charles S. Sydnor, *The Development of Southern Sectionalism, 1819-1848* (Baton Rouge, 1948), 14.

4. Fletcher M. Green, "Democracy in the Old South," *Journal of Southern History*, XII (February, 1946), 3-23; Frank Lawrence Owsley, *Plain Folk of the Old South* (Baton Rouge, 1949), 133-49.

5. See Bell Irvin Wiley, *The Life of Billy Yank: The Common Soldier of the Union* (Indianapolis, 1952), 109.

6. James C. Bonner, "Plantation Architecture of the Lower South on the Eve of the Civil War," *Journal of Southern History*, XI (August, 1945), 370-81.

7. Braxton Bragg to Edward G. W. Butler, December 27, 1859, Edward George Washington Butler Papers, Duke University Library.

8. Bragg to Mrs. Bragg, April 8, 1862, William K. Bixby Collection of Braxton Bragg Papers, Missouri Historical Society, St. Louis.

9. Douglas Southall Freeman, *R. E. Lee: A Biography* (4 vols., New York, 1935), IV, 220-21.

10. J. G. Randall, *The Civil War and Reconstruction* (Boston, 1937), 694-95.

11. P. L. Rainwater, ed., "Letters of James Lusk Alcorn," *Journal of Southern History*, III (May, 1937), 209.

12. William B. Hesseltine, *Confederate Leaders in the New South* (Baton Rouge, 1950), 16.

13. David H. Donald, "The Scalawag in Mississippi Reconstruction," *Journal of Southern History*, X (November, 1944), 447-60; Thomas B. Alexander, "Whiggery and Reconstruction in Tennessee," *ibid.*, XVI (August, 1950), 291-305.

14. R. H. Woody, ed., "Behind the Scenes in the Reconstruction Legislature of South Carolina: Diary of Josephus Woodruff," *Journal of Southern History*, II (February and August, 1936), 91, 235n.

15. Braxton Bragg to William Preston Johnston, July 3, 1873, Mrs. Mason Barret Collection of Albert Sidney and William Preston Johnston Papers, Tulane University Library.

16. Merton L. Dillon, "The Failure of the American Abolitionists," *Journal of Southern History*, XXV (May, 1959), 176.

17. William B. Hesseltine, "Economic Factors in the Abandonment of Reconstruction," *Mississippi Valley Historical Review*, XXII (September, 1935), 209.

18. Helen J. and Harry Williams, "Wisconsin Republicans and Reconstruction, 1865-70," *Wisconsin Magazine of History*, XXIII (September, 1939), 22.

19. Hesseltine, "Economic Factors in the Abandonment of Reconstruction," 192.

20. Thomas D. Clark, "The Country Newspaper: A Factor in Southern Opinion, 1865-1930," *Journal of Southern History*, XIV (February, 1948), 8.

21. Horace Mann Bond, "Social and Economic Forces in Alabama Reconstruction," *Journal of Negro History*, XXIII (July, 1938), 290-348.

22. Nelson Morehouse Blake, *William Mahone of Virginia: Soldier and Political Insurgent* (Richmond, 1935), 70-195.

23. C. Vann Woodward, *Origins of the New South, 1877-1913* (Baton Rouge, 1951), 1-22.

24. Henry W. Grady, "The New South," *The Literature of the South* (ed. by Richard Croom Beatty *et al.*, Chicago, 1952), 492.

25. Booker T. Washington, "Speech at the Atlanta Exposition," *The Negro Caravan* (ed. by Sterling A. Brown *et al.*, New York, 1941), 674.

CHAPTER SIX

1. Ulrich Bonnell Phillips, "The Central Theme of Southern History," *American Historical Review*, XXXIV (October, 1928), 30-43, reprinted in E. Merton Coulter, ed., *The Course of the South to Secession* (New York, 1939), 151-65. Quotations are taken from the latter source, 152.

2. James Weldon Johnson, *The Autobiography of an Ex-Coloured Man* (Pelican Mentor Edition, New York, 1948), 55.

3. Gunnar Myrdal, *An American Dilemma: The Negro Problem and Modern Democracy* (New York, 1944), 4.

4. Howard W. Odum, *The Way of the South Toward the Regional Balance of America* (New York, 1947), 49-54; and *Race and Rumors of Race: Challenge to American Crisis* (Chapel Hill, 1943), 17-21.

5. Comer Vann Woodward, *The Strange Career of Jim Crow* (New York, 1955), 26-47.

6. The relative newness of racial segregation is one of the main points of emphasis in Woodward's *Strange Career of Jim Crow*.

7. Guion Griffis Johnson, "The Ideology of White Supremacy, 1876-1910," in Fletcher Melvin Green, ed., *Essays in Southern History* (Chapel Hill, 1949), 139. Mrs. Johnson's essay provides an excellent survey of a long neglected area of southern history.

8. A contemporary example of this argument may be found in a pamphlet by Carey Daniel, *God the Original Segregationist* (Dallas, 1955). The quotation is from Acts 17:26.

9. Ex-Governor Hugh Smith Thompson of South Carolina, quoted in Charleston *News and Courier*, January 23, 1890.

10. Governor Luther Hodges of North Carolina, quoted in *New South*, X (September, 1955), 7.

11. William Sumner Jenkins, *Pro-Slavery Thought in the Old South* (Chapel Hill, 1935), 254-84; Buckner H. Payne, *The Negro: What is His Ethnological Status?* (Cincinnati, 1872); Charles Carroll, *"The Negro a Beast"; or "In the Image of God"* (St. Louis, 1900); and *The Tempter of Eve . . .* (St. Louis, 1902). See also William P. Calhoun, *The Caucasian and the Negro in the United States* (Columbia, 1902); William B. Smith, *The Color Line: A Brief in Behalf of the*

Unborn (New York, 1905); Robert W. Shufeldt, *The Negro, A Menace to American Civilization* (Boston, 1907). For examples of less extreme attitudes, see Alfred Holt Stone, *Studies in the American Race Problem* (New York, 1908); Edgar Gardner Murphy, *Problems of the Present South* (New York, 1904) and *The Basis of Ascendancy* (New York, 1909); and G. G. Johnson, "Ideology of White Supremacy," in Green, *Essays in Southern History.*

12. Phillips, "The Central Theme," *Course of the South,* 152.
13. Stone, *Studies in the American Race Problem,* 64.
14. Franklin Henry Giddings, *The Principles of Sociology* (New York, 1896); William Graham Sumner, *Folkways* (Boston, 1906).
15. Stone, *Studies in the American Race Problem,* 9.
16. Woodward, *Strange Career of Jim Crow,* 108-24.
17. Wilbur J. Cash, *The Mind of the South* (New York, 1941), 88.
18. Myrdal, *American Dilemma,* 800.
19. Eric Voegelin, "The Growth of the Race Idea," *The Review of Politics,* II (July, 1940), 312. Voegelin was writing about Europe and not the United States.
20. Myrdal, *American Dilemma,* 1029.
21. Virginius Dabney, *Below the Potomac: A Book about the New South* (New York, 1942), 206, gives the results of the Gallup poll.
22. Francis Butler Simkins, *A History of the South* (New York, 1953), 425.
23. Jefferson, *Notes on the State of Virginia,* 163; John Q. Anderson, ed., *Brokenburn: The Journal of Kate Stone* (Baton Rouge, 1955), 8; Atticus G. Haygood, *Our Brother in Black: His Freedom and His Future* (Nashville, 1881), 237.
24. Howard W. Odum, *Southern Regions of the United States* (Chapel Hill, 1936), 527.
25. Ruth Landes, "A Northerner Views the South," in Howard W. Odum and Katherine Jocher, eds., *In Search of the Regional Balance of America* (Chapel Hill, 1945), 134, 137.
26. Quoted in Rupert B. Vance, "Aycock of North Carolina," *Southwest Review,* XVIII (Spring, 1933), 306.
27. *A Practical Approach to the Race Problem,* pamphlet issued by the Commission on Interracial Cooperation (1939), cited in Myrdal, *American Dilemma,* 845.
28. William Edmund Burghardt Du Bois, *The Souls of Black Folk* (Chicago, 1903), 186.
29. James Louis Petigru to William Carson, Charleston, March 2, 1861. James Louis Petigru Papers, Manuscripts Division, Library of Congress.
30. Woodward, *Strange Career of Jim Crow,* 11.
31. See, for example, John T. Westbrook, "Twilight of Southern Regionalism," *Southwest Review,* XLII (Summer, 1957), 231-34, and Harry Ashmore, *Epitaph for Dixie.*
32. Cash, *Mind of the South,* 49-50.
33. Samuel W. Williams, "The People's Progressive Party of Georgia," *Phylon,* X (3rd quarter, 1949), 229.
34. Katherine DuPre Lumpkin, *The Making of a Southerner* (New York, 1947), 235-37.

CHAPTER SEVEN

1. "Paths to Desegregation," *New Republic,* CXXXVII (Oct. 21, 1957), 15.
2. From my *Crusader Without Violence: A Biography of Martin Luther King, Jr.* (New York, 1959), 90-91.

3. From Carter G. Woodson, *The Mind of the Negro as Reflected in Letters Written During the Crisis 1800-1860* (Washington, 1926), 205.

4. Bell I. Wiley, *Southern Negroes, 1861-65* (New Haven, 1938), and W. E. B. Du Bois, *Black Reconstruction* (New York, 1935), *passim*.

5. 18 *Stat. L.* 335 (1875).

6. Dumas Malone (ed), *Dictionary of American Biography* (New York, 1936), XIX, 65-66.

7. For general accounts of events mentioned in this essay, see John Hope Franklin, *From Slavery to Freedom* (New York, 1956), and for supporting documents, see Herbert Aptheker, *A Documentary History of the Negro People in the United States* (New York, 1951).

8. *The Negro In American Life and Thought: The Nadir, 1877-1901* (New York, 1954).

9. "My View of Segregation Laws," *New Republic*, V (December 4, 1915), 113-114.

10. See Martin Luther King, *Stride Toward Freedom: the Montgomery Story* (New York, 1958), and my *Crusader Without Violence*.

CHAPTER EIGHT

1. Page to Edwin Mims, April 6, 1911, in Walter Hines Page Papers, Houghton Library, Harvard University.

2. *The Liberal Tradition in America: An Interpretation of American Political Thought Since the Revolution* (New York, 1955), 172-73.

3. Especially in *Tom Watson: Agrarian Rebel* (New York, 1938), and *Origins of the New South, 1877-1913* (Baton Rouge, 1951).

4. Shugg points out that except in individual cases it was not so much the "rise of the poor whites" as it was the "uprising of poor white people against intolerable economic and social conditions." *Origins of Class Struggle in Louisiana, A Social History of White Farmers and Laborers during Slavery and After, 1840-1875* (Baton Rouge, 1939), 275.

5. Charleston *News and Courier*, quoted in Virginius Dabney, *Below the Potomac* (New York, 1942), 62.

6. William Alexander Percy, *Lanterns on the Levee, Recollections of a Planter's Son* (New York, 1941), 153.

7. Wiley Rufus Huddleston, "The Senatorial Campaign and Career of James Kimble Vardaman, Mississippi's White Chief" (Unpublished M. A. thesis, Louisiana State University, 1935), 42.

8. *The Mind of the South* (New York, 1941), 247-48.

9. V. O. Key, Jr., *Southern Politics in State and Nation* (New York, 1949), 160.

10. *Stars Fell on Alabama* (New York, 1934), 67.

11. James W. Lee to Walter Hines Page, June 22, 1908, Page Papers.

12. *The Growing South*, 16.

13. Aubrey Lee Brooks, *A Southern Lawyer, Fifty Years at the Bar* (Chapel Hill, 1950), 61.

14. "Freedom of Speech in the South," *Nation*, LXXXIV (April 25, 1907), 383.

15. Quoted in James Aubrey Tinsley, "The Progressive Movement in Texas" (Unpublished Ph.D. dissertation, University of Wisconsin, 1953), 60.

16. Aubrey Lee Brooks and Hugh Talmage Lefler (eds.), *The Papers of Walter Clark, 1857-1924*, 2 vols. (Chapel Hill, 1948-1950), II, 324, 328.

17. For a good discussion of this point with respect to Texas progressives, see Tinsley, "The Progressive Movement in Texas," 320.

18. Allan P. Sindler, "Bifactional Rivalry as an Alternative to Two-Party Competition in Louisiana," *American Political Science Review,* XLIX (September, 1955), 641-62. Professor Sindler concludes that about fifty of Louisiana's sixty-four parishes were usually pro-or-anti-Long in their voting behavior during the period 1928-1952.

19. Page to Edwin Mims, April 6, 1911, Page Papers.

20. Benjamin F. Long to Walter Hines Page, March 15, 1913, *ibid.*

21. Arthur S. Link, "The South and the 'New Freedom': An Interpretation," *American Scholar,* XX (Summer, 1951), 314-24; John W. Davidson, "The Response of the South to Woodrow Wilson's New Freedom, 1912-1914" (Unpublished Ph.D. dissertation, Yale University, 1953), 136, 145-46, 151-60, 178, 230.

22. *The Attack on Leviathan: Regionalism and Nationalism in the United States* (Chapel Hill, 1938), 141-42.

23. Marian D. Irish, "The Proletarian South," *Journal of Politics,* II (August, 1940), 231-58.

24. "On Fear: The South in Labor," *Harper's Magazine,* CCXII (June, 1956), 31.

25. Wayne S. Cole, "America First and the South, 1940-1941," *Journal of Southern History,* XXII (February, 1956), 36-47.

26. For a provocative discussion of the persistence of southern sectionalism, see Fletcher M. Green, "Resurgent Southern Sectionalism, 1933-1955," *North Carolina Historical Review,* XXXIII (April, 1956), 222-40.

27. "The Southern Governors' Conference as a Pressure Group," *Journal of Politics,* VI (August, 1944), 345.

28. Walter Prescott Webb, "The South and the Golden Slippers," *Texas Quarterly,* I (Spring, 1958), 4-9.

29. Cortez A. M. Ewing and James E. Titus, "Urbanism and Southern Politics," in Rupert B. Vance and Nicholas J. Demerath (eds.), *The Urban South* (Chapel Hill, 1954), 231, 242, 251.

30. Alexander Heard, *A Two-Party South?* (Chapel Hill, 1952), 155-56, 247.

31. Donald S. Strong, "The Presidential Election in the South, 1952," *Journal of Politics,* XVII (August, 1955), 343-89; Samuel Lubell, *Revolt of the Moderates* (New York, 1956), 179-87.

32. These figures were compiled from Richard M. Scammon (comp. and ed.), *America Votes: A Handbook of Contemporary American Election Statistics,* 2 vols. (New York, 1956-1958).

33. James W. Prothro, Ernest Q. Campbell, and Charles M. Grigg, "Two-Party Voting in the South: Class Vs. Party Identification," *American Political Science Review,* LII (March, 1958), 131-39.

34. Herbert J. Doherty, Jr., "Liberal and Conservative Voting Patterns in Florida," *Journal of Politics,* XIV (August, 1952), 403-17.

35. For evidence of the effective use of violence and discriminatory registration practices in the Deep South, see John H. Fenton, "The Negro Voter in Louisiana," *Journal of Negro Education,* XXVI (Summer, 1957), 319-22, 328, and Earl M. Lewis, "The Negro Voter in Mississippi," *ibid.,* 333-45.

36. Margaret Price, *The Negro Voter in the South* (Special Report of the Southern Regional Council, 1957), 1, 5; Clarence A. Bacote, "The Negro Voter in Georgia Politics Today," *Journal of Negro Education,* XXVI (Summer, 1957), 306-8.

37. Fenton, "The Negro Voter in Louisiana," 327.

38. Quoted in Francis L. Broderick, "W. E. B. Du Bois: The Trail of His Ideas" (Unpublished Ph.D. dissertation, Harvard University, 1955), 164.

39. Samuel Lubell, *The Future of American Politics* (Doubleday Anchor Edition, New York, 1956), 108-14, 128.

40. *Politics in America* (New York, 1954), 118.

41. Henry Lee Moon, "The Negro Vote in the Presidential Election of 1956," *Journal of Negro Education,* XXVI (Summer, 1957), 219-22.

42. Dabney, *Below the Potomac,* 57.

43. Lubell, *The Future of American Politics,* 120.

44. Quoted in "How Big Is the North-South Split?" 814.

45. Frank E. Smith, "The Changing South," *Virginia Quarterly Review,* XXXI (Spring, 1955), 285.

46. V. O. Key, Jr., "The Erosion of Sectionalism," *ibid.,* 161-79.

47. James McBride Dabbs, "Southern Challenge," *South Atlantic Quarterly,* LV (January, 1956), 34.

48. H. C. Nixon to the editor, February 1, 1956, New York *Times,* February 12, 1956. See also Nixon, "Politics of the Hills," *Journal of Politics,* VIII (May, 1946), 123-33.

49. For an able discussion of these problems, see V. O. Key, Jr., *American State Politics: An Introduction* (New York, 1956).

CHAPTER NINE

1. Robert Penn Warren, *Segregation: The Inner Conflict of the South* (New York, 1957), 15; see also Virginia Rock, "Agrarianism as the Theme in Southern Literature: The Period Since 1925," *Georgia Review,* XI (Summer, 1957), 154-60.

2. "The Southern Revival: A Land and Its Interpreters," (London) *Times Literary Supplement,* September 17, 1954, xvi.

3. See Cleanth Brooks, *Modern Poetry and the Tradition* (Chapel Hill, 1939).

4. See Allen Tate, "Tension in Poetry," *The Man of Letters in the Modern World* (New York, 1955), 64-77.

5. Cotton Mather, *Bonifacius, An Essay Upon the Good, that is to be Devised and Designed* (Boston, 1710); a work popularly known as *The Essays to Do Good.*

6. Richard Beale Davis, *George Sandys* (New York, 1955), 198-226.

7. C. Hugh Holman, "European Influences on Southern American Literature: A Preliminary Survey," *Comparative Literature: Proceedings of the Second Congress of the International Comparative Literature Association,* ed. W. P. Friederich (Chapel Hill, 1959), I, 444-55.

8. *Southern Quarterly Review,* XXIX (1856), 205.

9. See, for example, Henry Wadsworth Longfellow's *Kavanagh: A Tale,* Chapter XX.

10. See John Stafford, *The Literary Criticism of "Young America"* (Berkeley, Calif., 1952), and Perry Miller, *The Raven and the Whale* (New York, 1956), for detailed accounts of this literary war and the participation of Poe and Simms in it.

11. Robert Frost, "The Gift Outright," *A Witness Tree* (New York, 1942), 41. Copyright, 1942, by Robert Frost. Quoted with the permission of the publishers, Henry Holt and Company, Inc., and of the author.

12. M. C. S. Oliphant, A. T. Odell, and T. C. D. Eaves (eds.), *The Letters of William Gilmore Simms* (Columbia, S. C., 1952-1956), II, 90.

13. *Letters of Simms,* I, 264.

14. See Jay B. Hubbell, "Literary Nationalism in the Old South," *American Studies in Honor of William Kenneth Boyd,* ed. D. K. Jackson (Durham, N. C., 1940), 175-220.

15. W. G. Simms, "The Writings of James Fenimore Cooper," *Views and Reviews in American Literature, History, and Fiction,* First Series (New York, 1845), 216-18.

16. W. G. Simms, "Dedication," *The Damsel of Darien* (2 vols.; Philadelphia, 1839), I, 9.

17. W. G. Simms, "Literary Statistics of New York," *Southern and Western Monthly Magazine,* II (September, 1845), 205-7; Simms, "The National Volume," *ibid.,* I (June, 1845), 435-36.

18. W. G. Simms, *The Wigwam and the Cabin* (New York, 1856), 4-5.

19. Allen Tate, "The New Provincialism," *The Man of Letters in the Modern World,* 322, 330.

20. Thomas Wolfe, *Of Time and the River* (New York, 1935), 898-99.

21. Thomas Wolfe, *You Can't Go Home Again* (New York, 1941), 741.

22. See W. K. Wimsatt, Jr., and Cleanth Brooks, *Literary Criticism: A Short History* (New York, 1957), 3-76.

23. See Robert D. Jacobs, "Poe and the Agrarian Critics," *Southern Renascence: The Literature of the Modern South,* ed. L. D. Rubin, Jr., and R. D. Jacobs (Baltimore, 1953), 35-46.

24. W. G. Simms, "Modern Prose Fiction," *Southern Quarterly Review,* XV (April, 1849), 41-83.

25. Bernard Smith, *Forces in American Criticism* (New York, 1939), 128.

26. Allen Tate, "The New Provincialism," *The Man of Letters in the Modern World,* 328.

27. William P. Trent, *William Gilmore Simms* (Boston, 1892).

28. *Letters of Simms,* I, 256, 259. The letter originally appeared in the *Magnolia,* III (August, 1841), 376-80.

29. C. Vann Woodward, "The Irony of Southern History," *Southern Renascence,* 65.

30. Alexis de Tocqueville, *Democracy in America,* trans. Henry Reeve, rev. Francis Bowen (New York, 1957), II, 78.

31. W. G. Simms, *The Cassique of Kiawah* (New York, 1859), 207.

32. W. G. Simms, *Charlemont* (New York, 1856), 292.

33. Ellen Glasgow, *The Woman Within* (New York, 1954), 42.

34. Ellen Glasgow, *A Certain Measure* (New York, 1943), 144.

35. *Ibid.,* 155.

36. *Ibid.,* 175.

37. *Ibid.,* 250.

38. William Faulkner, *Go Down, Moses* (New York, 1942), 345.

39. Walt Whitman, *Democratic Vistas,* in *The Poetry and Prose of Walt Whitman* (New York, 1949), 816n.

40. Nathaniel Hawthorne, *The Scarlet Letter,* ed. Newton Arvin (New York, 1950), 274. It is worthy of note that Hawthorne is the American writer to whom Faulkner has most often been compared; see Randall Stewart, "Hawthorne and Faulkner," *College English,* XVII (February, 1956), 258-262.

41. John P. Kennedy, *Swallow Barn* (1832), Ch. XLVI. This entire chapter is worthy of close attention for the student interested in the attitude of ante-bellum southern writers on the slavery issue.

42. William Faulkner, *Light in August* (New York, 1932), 239.

43. Robert Penn Warren, "Original Sin: A Short Story," *Selected Poems 1923-1943* (New York, 1944), 23.

44. Allen Tate, "The Wolves," *Poems—1922-1947* (New York, 1948), 110-11.

45. Ellen Glasgow, *A Certain Measure,* 188.